# MANAGING FICTION IN LIBRARIES

# MANAGING FICTION IN LIBRARIES

*Edited by*

Margaret Kinnell

Senior Lecturer, Department of Library and Information
Studies, Loughborough University

LIBRARY ASSOCIATION PUBLISHING
LONDON
A CLIVE BINGLEY BOOK

Published by
Library Association Publishing Ltd
7 Ridgmount Street
London WC1E 7AE

First published 1991


British Library Cataloguing in Publication Data

Managing fiction in libraries.
  I. Kinnell, Margaret
  025.17

  ISBN 0-85157-470-X

Typeset in 10/11pt Palacio by Library Association Publishing Ltd
Printed and made in Great Britain by Billing and Sons Ltd, Worcester

# Contents

# Editor's acknowledgements

Each of the contributors has acknowledged the help and cooperation of individuals and organizations at the appropriate point in their chapter. However, there are additional debts I owe as an editor. Peter Mann and Lionel Durbidge of Loughborough University and John Boyd of Nottinghamshire County Libraries have been generous in sharing their experience and wide knowledge of this field, and Margaret Drabble responded with alacrity to a request for a foreword. Jennifer MacDougall helped with research and Cynthia Robinson and Carol Booles provided much-appreciated typing support. To them, and the innumerable other colleagues who have helped shape a belief in the power of fiction that underlies this book, thank you.

Margaret Kinnell
Loughborough University

# Foreword

The value of a good choice of fiction in a public library seems to me to be self-evident. But clearly it is not, or we would not see it under threat. Over the past few years, various crazy proposals, such as the charging for borrowings of newly published novels, have been sounded out in Green Papers. Some authorities have already ceased to buy new fiction and children's books as a matter of policy, and cuts in public spending have reduced provision even in those regions committed to buying fiction. So, in the present climate, it is timely to reaffirm a faith in the importance of fiction, from childhood to old age.

Novels are not, as all who read and write them know, a frivolity, a luxury, an indulgence. They are a means of comprehending and experiencing and extending our world and our vision. They can exercise the imagination, they can widen our sympathies, they can issue dire and necessary warnings, they can suggest solutions to social problems, they are the raw material of the historians of tomorrow. And I am not speaking only of so-called 'classic' fiction here: we all recognize the impact of George Orwell's *Nineteen eighty-four* or Aldous Huxley's *Brave new world*, but the yearly output of science fiction contains many brilliant and stimulating hypotheses which may capture the attention of readers and change the way we perceive our future. Similarly, the subtle shifts in the social role of heroines in what may seem to be light romances can help to redefine the way we see ourselves and our possibilities. Fiction can be a mirror to nature, but it can also project for us images of what is to come.

On a practical level, the public library offers both reader and writer the space to experiment, to try new things, to attempt new discoveries. Only a tiny dedicated percentage of us spend money on buying first novels in hardback, or on buying books by untested writers whose work we do not know. Many, many more of us are willing to meet a new author in the public library. We discover by browsing at random along the shelves, or by picking up a faintly familiar title. The new author is supported by library purchases, and the established author, through Public Lending Right, may receive comforting and rewarding evidence of a popularity not always reflected in sales. If the libraries do not support fiction, the publishers will inevitably move more and more towards the best-selling title, the safe and tested favourite. A good supply of fiction in libraries offers real choice to the consumer, and encourages a greater diversity of writing from authors.

Fiction, I repeat, is not an indulgence, though it may be a comfort. I would like to stress that writing novels is hard labour, and, for most of us, an entirely serious enterprise. There is a widely perceived view that 'non-fiction' and in particular 'information' or anything to do with 'information technology' is somehow more hard, more serious than fiction. This is not so. I spent five years editing a reference book, *The Oxford companion to English literature*, and it was a very challenging task which taught me a great deal. But it was nothing like as difficult as writing a novel. Compiling a reference book is like undertaking a long, arduous, carefully paced and at times exhausting march across terrain which varies from the difficult to the pleasant. It is a long haul to the end, but you know you can get there, and that your support team will help out over the worst stretches. Writing a novel is solitary, dangerous, and occasionally fatal. You can find yourself clinging to an unexpected cliff face, or lost in an endless plain. There are no markers. No one has been here before. This is the thrill of fiction, and it communicates itself to the reader. The fiction shelves of the public library contain peril, adventure, failure, triumph, and sometimes in very unexpected places. Let us keep them well stocked.

Margaret Drabble

# Contributors

**Deborah Goodall** worked as a research assistant in the Library and Information Statistics Unit (LISU) at Loughborough University after graduating, where she published papers on browsing in public libraries and performance measurement. Following her job as a librarian with Coventry City Libraries dealing chiefly with the fiction service and research for the mobile library service, she has joined Loughborough University Department of Library and Information Studies as a lecturer.

**Michael Greenhalgh** is Course Director of the Library and Information Studies' Master's Degree and Postgraduate Diploma Courses at Ealing College of Higher Education, where he has taught since 1976. In 1988 he had published *Lawrence's uncollected stories 1907–1913: a critical commentary* and his current research is concerned with the indexing and analysis of short stories.

**Stuart Hannabuss** lectures in management, statistics and communication studies at Robert Gordon's Institute of Technology School of Librarianship and Information Studies. Recent monographs include *Knowledge management* (1987), *Negotiating meaning* (1988) and *Managing children's literature* (1989). His current research is on cognitive styles in management and the uses of metaphor in children's fiction. He has also had a number of short stories broadcast on BBC Radio 3.

**Karen Nelson Hoyle** is Professor and Curator of the Children's Literature Research Collections at the University of Minnesota Libraries and teaches the history of children's literature at the University of Minnesota. In addition, she lectures and writes about immigrant contributors to American children's literature and international exchange of children's books and has served on many professional committees. Published articles and monographs based on research in special collections of children's literature include essays in the *Journal of youth services and libraries* and reference books, *Danish children's books published in English* (1983) and *The Kerlan collection of manuscripts and illustrations* (1985).

**Margaret Kinnell** lectures in management, marketing and children's literature at Loughborough University Department of Library and Information Studies and has also taught courses in fiction librarianship. Recent books include *Planned public relations* (1989); and she has also had numerous articles and reports published in both the management and children's literature fields. She is managing editor of *The international review of children's literature and librarianship* and current research interests are management strategies for public libraries, marketing in public libraries, and comparative children's literature.

**Peter Labdon** was Director of Arts and Libraries for Suffolk County Council for 13 years, until March 1990. He was also the first Chair of the National Acquisitions Group from 1985 to 1989.

**Helen Lewins** was until recently a lecturer in Loughborough University's Department of Library and Information Studies, and her specialist interests have included school librarianship and public library work with children. She has published widely in both these fields, as well as co-editing *The international review of children's literature and librarianship.*

**Peter H. Mann** developed an interest in books and readers in 1967 and wrote two books, *Books and readers* and *Books, buyers and borrowers*, on his early researches. He later wrote *Students and books* and *From author to reader, a social study of books*. He was at Loughborough University from 1983 to 1990, initially as Director of the Centre for Library and Information Management and subsequently as Director of the Library and Information Statistics Unit. He is now retired.

**Lyn Sear and Barbara Jennings** both work for Kent Arts and Libraries Department, and collaborated on the research projects described in the chapter. Lyn Sear is Group Librarian, Chatham, and at the time of the research into fiction services was the Systems and Development Librarian. Barbara Jennings is Senior Librarian at the Central Lending Library, Maidstone, with special responsibility for literature.

**James H. Sweetland** is Associate Professor in Library and Information Science at the University of Wisconsin–Milwaukee. With a background in reference services in academic and special libraries, he has spent a total of 12 years in collection management, most of this in large research libraries, including Tulane

University and the State Historical Society of Wisconsin. Active in state and national professional organizations, he is currently President of ALA's Reference and Adult Services Division. His current research interests centre around the management of library collections, especially the role of reviews in selection decisions; and computerized information retrieval, especially in the social and behavioural sciences.

# Introduction

*Margaret Kinnell*

Fiction matters. At a time when, as Richard Hoggart remarked recently in his autobiography, 'some politicians, even some members of governments, do not see very well the justification for a free library service and certainly would not set up one if we did not have one already', it is vital to affirm the importance of fiction provision by public libraries. The possibility of roaming the shelves, 'like a jackdaw'[1] still holds the promise of a fulfilment – for adults and youngsters alike – quite distinct from any other they will experience, despite the enticements of television and the video cassette. One of the most pertinent statements in the Scottish Arts Council's *Readership report* was that 'the reading of literature, and quite possibly the reading habit generally, is in some danger of being eroded by other, omnipresent forms of entertainment and that something must be done to ensure that the unique experience offered by a good book is recognized and sought after'.[2] Fiction reading remains the surest means to challenging the ubiquity of audiovisual media.

The purpose of this book therefore is to look afresh at the support to continuing readership offered by fiction provision in public libraries, and to consider how best librarians can manage their resources given the dwindling of public funding and political support. The reading habit requires nurturing, and public libraries are still, despite the retrenchment of recent years, an unrivalled resource in this process. The means by which fiction is being offered to the public also, however, requires nurturing, to develop the expertise and skills in service provision for meeting new needs and expectations.

Thankfully, the perception of the public library is still of somewhere providing entertainment, erudition and enlightenment through the novels it lends; fiction is what most readers and intending readers want from libraries. However, there are now enhanced expectations of public service, from a public that is more discriminating than ever before. Every other service provider, from banks and building societies to MacDonalds, pays attention to the detail of delivering services, through the design of the service itself, the organization and look of service outlets, the projection of a corporate image, to the smiles on the faces of employees. In providing fiction services for a discerning public, libraries must therefore be equally concerned with the overall quality of their service delivery. Information services and the varied media now available from libraries are of course also important; they comprise an increasingly significant part of what libraries can offer their communities. Community use of libraries means providing for *all* needs. However, a good selection of every kind of fiction – all genres, all formats, every conceivable point of world and personal view – is the hallmark of all that is best and most truly community oriented in a free public library service. Thackeray described novels as 'sweets', but added that 'all people with healthy literary appetites love them'. Librarians then have a responsibility to cultivate this appetite in the public and to tempt and educate the palate with fiction collections for all tastes, and to do it professionally.

To achieve all this, it is becoming more important than ever to manage resources in such a way that libraries compete with all the other calls on people's attention for leisure pursuits. Fiction collections should win readers back into libraries. Buying enough fiction, of the variety to cope with all needs, organizing it for ease of access and promoting it sufficiently well to stand comparison with the techniques of other service providers, and of booksellers and other media, places tremendous demands on the library manager. Managing the fiction service effectively is the most visible sign to a critical public of the success of a library. The contributors to this book have therefore offered a broadly based perspective on fiction in public libraries that considers the whole range of these issues that have relevance to the provision of a thoroughly professional, user-oriented fiction service, a service for the consumer-conscious 1990s.

Before beginning the process of selecting fiction, librarians need to understand their readership: what people want to read, the patterns of reading at present and the likely trends in future fiction reading. In Chapter 1 therefore, Peter Mann surveys the place of book reading in the UK at present, assesses the problem of illiteracy, and considers readership patterns from childhood through into adulthood. Understanding the complexities of the fiction industry and the context within which books are published and then bought by libraries and booksellers is similarly fundamental to librarians. Stuart Hannabuss highlights the main characteristics of this context in Chapter 2, and draws on a wide range of data spanning both the UK and US situations.

In Chapter 3 Peter Labdon describes how fiction is acquired using computerized systems, within the complex environment of the book trade and the management problems faced by librarians. He highlights the general lack of concern for selecting adult novels, compared with the care over selecting for children, a point which Helen Lewins develops in Chapter 4. Fiction for children in libraries has always been seen as a vital support to developing the reading habit, and the selection systems she describes are evidence of the care with which many library authorities develop their fiction collections for children. Nevertheless, much remains to be done to keep collections fresh for each succeeding generation, and as Karen Hoyle highlights in Chapter 5 with her consideration of young adults' needs, there is a need to integrate library services with appropriate selection procedures.

In Chapter 6 James Sweetland compares the management of adult fiction collections in the US with UK practice. There is an attempt throughout the book to consider fiction services in both countries; however, as this chapter makes clear, there are considerable differences in approach between US and UK public libraries. For example, the influence of book-store design on public libraries' selection and organization of fiction has been very marked in the US, and while methods of organizing fiction in the UK have also begun to be influenced by ideas on 'customer behaviour' there is still some way to go before these techniques are fully developed. Lyn Sear and Barbara Jennings describe their research into this at Kent County Libraries in Chapter 7, and consider the implications for the traditional 'cat and class' approach of the past.

Without a clear view of the range of fiction information sources that a fiction service should offer its readers, the librarian cannot, however, begin to develop a professional service. In Chapter 8, Michael Greenhalgh offers a critical overview of the sources that any public library system should provide and compares the UK and US literature. He also introduces the idea of direct user involvement in the fiction service, through panels of local reviewers. This kind of consumer orientation is now well established as the most significant philosophy underpinning public library service development today, and in Chapter 9 Deborah Goodall describes how the judicious marketing of fiction services can enhance service delivery. Finally, in Chapter 10, the implications for initial education and in-service training are considered. Fiction services are of major importance and their effect on standards of literacy and the development of a reading habit should not be underestimated, either by educators or politicians.

It is hoped that this book will add to the debate on the value of public library fiction provision, and enhance perspectives on the development of fiction services. For in furthering this development, librarians are engaged in the highly professional and worthwhile activity of supporting and enhancing a literate society.

## References

1  Hoggart, R., *Local habitation 1918 – 1940*, London, Chatto and Windus, 1988, 173.
2  Working Party of the Literature Committee of the Scottish Arts Council, *Readership report*, Edinburgh, Scottish Arts Council, 1989, 36.

# 1 Fiction readers: what people want to read

*Peter H. Mann*

## Introduction

Before considering what fiction people want to read it is wise to look first at the place of book reading in general in the UK at the present time. Although many people who work with books may find it hard to think of a life in which books play little or even no part, it is essential to recognize from the very beginning of any discussion of reading habits that there are people who cannot read, there are people who do not read (even though it may be supposed that they can) and there are people who do read. Even those people who can read and do read may not necessarily be avid readers of books. The reading of newspapers and magazines is more widespread than the reading of books. Even when we consider book reading there are problems of defining what is meant by 'a book' and there are problems of deciding what is meant by the concept of 'reading'.

Fortunately, there has been considerable growth of interest in research into book reading in recent years and there are national surveys available which give a much clearer picture of people's reading habits than was available ten years ago. Nevertheless there are still many gaps in our knowledge of people's book-reading habits which need further research to be carried out, so there are no grounds for complacency in this area of knowledge.

To start from the bottom and then to work our way up in reading habits, it is useful to remind ourselves of the considerable numbers of people who either cannot read or do not read. This chapter will emphasize the positive as it develops but it is wise to take account initially of the problem areas which face anyone wanting to encourage people to read books and especially to read books for pleasure, which is what fiction is really all about.

## The problem of illiteracy

One might imagine that the UK, an advanced industrial society with compulsory education for all children between the ages of 5 and

16, is a literate nation. With 31% of children remaining at school or in full-time education until the age of 18 and then 14% of the age group going on to higher education in colleges, polytechnics or universities, these surely are indications of a prolonged period of education for many young children that would be expected to produce a fully literate population, apart from those people who suffer from physical or mental handicaps.

With adult literacy schemes having been run locally for over 30 years, over 160 library authorities in the country offering free loans of and reference to books and Britain being one of the largest book-publishing nations, there is clearly no shortage of reading material available. The opening of so many new bookshops in town centres in very recent years also testifies to the demand for books.

Nevertheless there is a continuing problem of those people who cannot read well enough to participate fully in the opportunities of modern living. The Adult Literacy and Basic Skills Unit (ALBUS) in London has carried out research on a group of 12,500 men and women born between 3 and 9 March 1958 and in a report published in 1983 (based on research when the people were aged 23) they estimated that approximately two million adults in Great Britain were 'functionally illiterate'.[1] By this they meant that these people's daily lives were affected by difficulties with reading, writing and spelling. Whilst it must be accepted that these assessments were largely subjective ones made by the people themselves, nevertheless they did indicate that the people with literacy problems had reading and writing difficulties which affected their ability to get work, filling in forms, writing letters, reading advertisements and getting places on training schemes. There were more men than women claiming to have literacy problems, though 1 in 10 men compared with 1 in 20 women had tried to improve their literacy skills by attending special classes.

In a further report published in 1987 it was estimated that only 7% of those people with literacy problems were completely unable to read or write and from this survey it was concluded that less than 1% of the total population was actually illiterate.[2] The great problem of literacy research is that there is a continuum from absolute illiteracy to full literacy, and it is at the various points on the continuum moving away from full illiteracy that measurements are difficult to make. It has been pointed out by critics that some people who rate themselves as very low on literacy nevertheless leave school with educational qualifications and are rated as functionally competent by their teachers. The relationship between subjective and objective assessment is a difficult one.

However, for the purposes of the present analysis of reading, it is important to note that a higher than average proportion of adults with reading difficulties have lived in overcrowded housing, in rented council (rather than owner-occupied) houses, received state benefits and experienced periods of unemployment. Adults who when children had received free school meals and who were the later-born children of large families were also over-represented amongst people with literacy problems. Many social surveys amongst lower social class families have shown that their culture of communication favours the spoken, rather than the written, word. Amongst such families there is a greater use of radio, television and speech than of books, magazines or 'serious' newspapers (as compared with the tabloid press). Nevertheless, as will be demonstrated later in this chapter, interest in reading is by no means absent amongst working-class people and it would be very misleading indeed to think of working-class people as non-readers.

But reading, especially book reading, must be seen in the total context of people's lives and especially that of their leisure hours. People who are functionally illiterate or not far from that stage can develop a lifestyle in which the written word plays a minimal part. For example, the daily news can be obtained through radio or television and any newspaper reading may be limited to cartoons, the captions to photographs and simple headlines. Entertainment can be derived (massively) from television, from evenings at public houses, attendance at sporting functions and so on. The learning of skills for hobbies can be done by face-to-face instruction rather than by way of manuals or specialist magazines. It is, therefore, necessary to acknowledge that for many people the lack of 'the reading habit' is not necessarily seen as a deprivation. People can lead what are to them perfectly happy lives with only a minimum of reading, and even that reading may virtually exclude the reading of books. The adult reader is the product of a childhood and adolescence in which the young person is gradually introduced to the book and may or may not encompass book reading for pleasure in his or her circle of activities. It is, therefore, to young people we will now turn to consider what books offer them.

## Young people and books
In her article published in 1986, Carter reviewed the research carried out in Britain into young people and reading (from pre-school to sixth form) from 1970 onwards.[3] She concluded from this survey of research that young people were likely to become voluntary readers; that is that they were likely to acquire the reading habit if they had certain attributes or experiences. For example, girls were more likely than boys to become book readers and girl readers were

likely to read more books than boy readers. Voluntary reading was seen in several surveys to decline between the ages of 10 and 16, during which time young people decided whether or not to become 'readers'. To some people's surprise voluntary readers were found to be active in other pursuits and to be 'doers' rather than 'watchers' and the stereotype of the young book reader as a rather reclusive person was shown to be quite misleading. To some extent the fact that young people were readers was linked to their having a wide range of interests, rather than simply having more time to read. In fact many young people who lead active lives are also very active readers. Not surprisingly, young readers tend to show a more positive attitude to school, where reading is an inescapable activity, and the greater the young person's reading ability the more they tend to read. Again, unsurprisingly, young readers tend more to be members of public libraries, with parents who are also library users. The home background of young readers is crucial in their development as readers and many studies testify to the importance of books in the home, young people's own book collections, being read to by a parent when a young child and all those factors which make books and reading an integral and perfectly normal part of home and family life.

By contrast it has to be recognized that school lessons almost always require children to be able to read and for those children whose reading skills are low certain subjects (and especially English) will give them little pleasure, or hope for success. Not surprisingly, then, the child who reads poorly at school will associate lack of success in reading with lack of success at school and is hardly likely to want to undertake more voluntary reading outside school in his or her leisure time. During these formative years at school young people can learn that reading can be a means towards self-improvement but it can also be a straightforward personal pleasure and these two functions can link and intertwine.

Boys tend to read more for information than do girls, who tend to read more fiction than boys. Boys also tend to watch television rather more than do girls and it is boys who fall away more from book reading than do girls in the early teens. There is now quite a lot of evidence to show that, whilst younger children still enjoy fairy stories and, later, animal and family stories and ghost stories, older children can rapidly progress to adult books of varying types.[4] Girls in their early teens read romantic fiction written for adults and occult/horror stories are popular with both sexes – sometimes as if in defiance of teachers and parents. Books written specially by adults for teenagers meet with mixed receptions and young people are very quick to spot those books that are written especially for them and which they feel condescend to them. The modern teenage novel is quite likely to deal with problems of rising sexuality, perhaps even abortions, the troubles in Northern Ireland and inner city deprivation. This is a far cry from the girls' school stories of Angela Brazil or the boys' adventure stories from the time of G. A. Henty right through to the later works of Percy F. Westerman into the 1940s. Such books treated young people as young people and young adults as examples to emulate. All that is left today of this genre is the spoof play *Daisy pulls it off*, which guys the codes of behaviour of those bygone days.

The movement from reading as a child to reading as an adult has always, to some extent, been a difficult one and a transitional period over which many parents, wanting to do their best for their children, have agonized. Book lists from such bodies as the (now) Children's Book Foundation, ex-National Book League, have been of great help to the few, but for the ordinary parent and the ordinary child help has been limited. Librarians themselves do not agree about 'teenage fiction' collections. In schools 'recommended reading' lists quickly move into the world of adult fiction and the reasonably intelligent and literate teenager will certainly be able to cope with a Jeffrey Archer or a Catherine Cookson if he or she is being expected to read Hardy or Orwell for school. Young people's favourite television programmes are very often adult programmes and, whilst young people may not wish yet to accept all the responsibilities of adult life, they at the same time hate to be treated as children.

Adolescence has, from time immemorial, been a time of painful adjustment for young people, with physical and psychological development frequently out of step with each other, and young people themselves, as a group, are probably more self-conscious of themselves as a 'target group' for the media and for marketing policies than ever before. Ever since market researchers discovered 'the teenage consumer' in the early 1950s there has been pressure on young people to conform in their nonconformity and to see themselves as a distinct group between childhood and adulthood. Their social behaviour is particularly manifested in their leisure time, when the voluntary reading of fiction may be expected to take place, and so it is useful now to look at what is known about the major aspects of people's leisure activities, so as to see what book reading has to compete with at the present time.

## Leisure activities and reading

All recent research on the use of people's time for their leisure activities indicates the overwhelming part that television plays in that time. The most recent General Household Survey published by the government Social Survey Division of the Office of Population Censuses and Surveys, based on 1987 data, shows that 99% of the population aged 16 and over had watched some television in the previous four weeks. This led visiting/entertaining friends or relations at 95%, listening to radio at 88%, listening to records/tapes at 73% and reading books at 60%.[5]

From data published by the BBC Broadcasting Research Department for 1988 it was estimated that for all the population from the age of four the average time each week spent on television viewing that year was 25 hours and 21 minutes for everyone, with women averaging 27 hours and 28 minutes per week and men averaging 22 hours and 56 minutes per week.[6] As Table 1.1 shows, children viewed less than adults and the 16–24 age group viewed much less than older adults, whilst the age group of 65 and over did by far the most viewing. Social class was also linked to viewing hours and the DE (lowest social grade) group with 31 hours and 44 minutes were by far the most avid viewers.

**Table 1.1　Television viewing in 1988**

|  | Hours:minutes per week |
| --- | --- |
| Population age 4 + | 25:21 |
| Male | 22:56 |
| Female | 27:28 |
| Age |  |
| 4 – 7 | 17:20 |
| 8 – 11 | 18:12 |
| 12 – 15 | 20:08 |
| All children | 18:44 |
| 16 – 24 | 17:06 |
| 25 – 34 | 24:07 |
| 35 – 44 | 21:56 |
| 45 – 54 | 26:44 |
| 55 – 64 | 33:07 |
| 65 + | 37:25 |
| Social grade |  |
| AB | 17:42 |
| $C_1$ | 22:46 |
| $C_2$ | 25:25 |
| DE | 31:44 |

Source: BARB/AGB.

The most popular programmes shown on the four channels are monitored every week by BARB (Broadcasters' Audience Research Board Ltd), with monthly cumulations, and the regular pattern is that each week the ten programmes with the biggest audiences are episodes of *Coronation Street*, *Neighbours* and *Eastenders*, with these three soap operas filling the top 40 places each month. In 1990, for example, the Wednesday 7 February and repeat on Saturday 10 February of Granada's *Coronation Street* had an estimated 21,730,000 audience and was in top place. The Tuesday 6 February and repeat on Sunday 11 February episode of *Eastenders* was in 40th place with an audience of 17,650,000.[7] In strong contrast to these figures the most viewed programmes on BBC2 and Channel 4 for the week ending 25 March, for example, were *French and Saunders* on BBC, with 5,890,000 viewers, and *Brookside* on Channel 4, with 5,030,000 viewers.[8]

For the week ending 25 March 1990 the average week's viewing per head of the population aged four and over was 24 hours and 57 minutes, of which 11 hours 57 minutes was with the BBC and 13 hours with any of the ITV stations. It was estimated that 80% of the population watched some television each day and 95.3% had viewed at some time during the week. Whilst daily viewing patterns will obviously vary, especially during work-free times at the weekend, a daily average of about 3 hours and 34 minutes must take up a considerable amount of available leisure time.

It is also estimated that people spend, on average, nine hours a week listening to the radio, though with some young people it must be difficult to define what is actually meant by 'listening', as many parents are acutely aware. But in addition to 'live' television and radio there are also hours spent on watching videos and listening to records or cassettes. The rapid growth in very recent years of video cassettes should be carefully noted as it is estimated that over half of British households now have video cassette recorders, nearly two-thirds of the population watch videos each week and between four and five hours per week are spent on such viewing. Recently published trade figures show that between 1987 and 1989 the total video market rose from £517 million to £856 million, with rentals increasing from £421 million to £556 million but actual sales more than trebling, from £96 million to £300 million.[9] The total rentals and sales figure of £856 million is more than ten times the total expenditure on books by 155 library authorities in the UK, who in 1988 – 9 spent just over £84 million, and is 60% more than the total library expenditure for the country.

Whilst it is true, as the book trade argue, that television can stimulate interest in books (and the book of the series *Around the world in 80 days* by Michael Palin rapidly became a bestseller in late 1989) the fact remains that it is virtually impossible to watch a television set and read a book at the same time. So, with perhaps upwards of 30 hours a week spent on live television, videos and radio, the book has very serious competition for people's leisure time. The table of viewing statistics does show that young adults, the 16–24 age group, have the lowest viewing hours per week of all adults, but this age group also form the most important part of the current cinema audience and are also the market for pubs and discos that cater particularly for young people seeking entertainment outside the home.

From the above analysis of leisure activities, and particularly those which attract young people, it can be seen that there is great competition for people's leisure time and the 'leisure market' is a very important one today. At this stage of the analysis it might almost be wondered at that people do have any time left for leisure reading after all their other activities. Two-thirds of the population read a national daily newspaper and three-quarters read a Sunday paper, so there is plenty of reading done each day.[10] *The Sun* is the most popular daily paper, with a readership in 1988 of 11.3 million people, and on Sunday *The News of the World* is the most popular paper, with a readership of 13.2 million. In addition to newspapers there is a wide range of magazines published in Britain, with (*TV times* and *Radio times* excepted) *Readers' digest* the most popular general magazine with 6.4 million readers, and *Woman's own* the most popular women's magazine, with 4.6 million readers and read by 17% of all women. All these publications too compete for time with books, so it is now appropriate to see how book reading fares as an activity with so many competitors.

## Reading of books

Information about adult book reading can at times seem confusing because of the different questions that are asked of respondents in reading surveys. For example, the General Household Survey carried out by the government's own social survey organization in 1987 asked people if they had participated in selected leisure activities in the four weeks before the interview and 60% of respondents said they had participated in book reading.[11] This showed a slight increase from a figure of 54% in 1977, which indicates that book reading had competed well over those ten years with the other forms of leisure. As Table 1.2 shows, women were greater readers than men, the 30–44-year-old age group were the greatest readers and middle-class people read more than did working-class people.

**Table 1.2  Reading books in past four weeks, 1987**

|  | % |
|---|---|
| All (age 16+) | 60 |
| Males | 54 |
| Females | 65 |
| Age |  |
|   16–19 | 59 |
|   20–24 | 56 |
|   25–29 | 60 |
|   30–44 | 64 |
|   45–59 | 60 |
|   60–69 | 62 |
|   70+ | 55 |
| Social grade |  |
|   Professional | 80 |
|   Employers and managers | 68 |
|   Intermediate and junior |  |
|     non-manual | 71 |
|   Skilled manual | 47 |
|   Semi-skilled manual | 52 |
|   Unskilled manual | 47 |

Source: General Household Survey 1987.

Two national sample surveys carried out by the market research firm MORI in 1987 and 1988 asked respondents if 'you have read a book for yourself' in the past year. In 1987 17% and in 1988 20% of all respondents (all aged 18 and over) said they had not read any books in the past year. In contrast, 56% in 1987 and 53% in 1988 said they had read books 'more than ten times'.[12]

The most regular national survey of book reading is the Euromonitor Book Readership Survey, for which the most recent data are from October 1988.[13] This survey covers all the population aged 16 and over, with a sample of 2,000 people, and has results going back to the 1960s. The question put to respondents is 'are you currently reading a book, either hardback or paperback, but *not* a magazine?' The answer 'yes' has been given by 45% of respondents four out of seven times between 1981 and 1988 (there were no surveys in 1985 and 1987). In 1988 45% of all respondents were currently reading a book and, as is regularly found in reading surveys, women were greater readers than men, age was not a highly discriminating factor and middle-class people read more than working-class, as Table 1.3 shows.

*Managing fiction in libraries*

**Table 1.3  Currently reading a book, 1988**

| Penetration | % |
|---|---|
| All (age 16+) | 45 |
| Males | 40 |
| Females | 50 |
| Age | |
| 16–34 | 43 |
| 35–44 | 44 |
| 45–54 | 45 |
| 55+ | 49 |
| Social grade | |
| AB | 65 |
| $C_1$ | 53 |
| $C_2$ | 37 |
| DE | 36 |

| Social grade reader profile | | Social grade population profile |
|---|---|---|
| AB | 23 | 16 |
| $C_1$ | 29 | 25 |
| $C_2$ | 23 | 27 |
| DE | 25 | 32 |
| | 100 | 100 |

Source: Euromonitor, 1988.

However, it should be noted with care that the percentages for various subgroups, such as 65% of the AB social grade, are figures for the 'penetration' of book reading within that group. These percentages cannot be added to each other to make 100%. The addable percentages are those for the 'profile' of all readers in Table 1.3, and here the subgroups do add up to 100%. So, for example, whilst 65% of ABs are reading books now they form only 23% of the total 100% of current readers. Thus of all the readers, as analysed by social grade, 52% are middle class ($ABC_1$) and 48% are working class ($C_2DE$) – virtually a 50:50 split. This helps us to understand that whilst middle-class people do read more than working-class people the total (profile) readership is made up almost equally of the two classes and this is because, as the column for 'national sample' shows, there are only 41% middle-class to 59% working-class people in the total population. These figures illustrate the point that was made previously that book reading is not just a middle-class habit and that working-class readers are a very important subgroup of the total readers.

## What books people read

The total book market in Britain encompasses a wide range of educational, technical, scientific and professional books amongst the 50,000 and more titles published each year. In 1988 there were 56,514 titles published in all, of which 13,326 were reprints or new editions, 1,355 were translations and 72 were limited editions. Amongst the total there were 5,063 children's books, 4,307 books on political science, 3,423 on medicine, 2,047 on religion and 2,007 school textbooks.[14] However, fiction alone accounted for 6,496 titles, of which 3,076 were reprints. Avid readers of fiction could have a choice of roughly eight new novels to choose from every day of the week. Fiction published in paperback covers accounts for a very large amount of all adult reading and fiction itself dominates all the analyses of what people read for pleasure.

The Euromonitor surveys include analyses of the subjects of the books being read by respondents and fiction always accounts for two-thirds or more of the books being read; in 1988 the fiction figure was 69%, as Table 1.4 shows. For men, though, the figure was 59% and for women it was 76%, and these surveys always show women to be greater readers of fiction than men. Of the 11 fiction categories used for analysis, 'romance' consistently comes out as the most popular subject of reading, accounting for 17% of all readers, only 2% of men but an absolute runaway 29% of all women readers in 1988. Crime/thriller fiction is popular with both sexes and produces a more level 14% of all readers, 16% of men and 13% of all women. The Euromonitor survey does not have a category labelled 'literary' fiction but it does have one called 'modern novel' and this is the third category in overall popularity, with 10% of all readers, 6% of all men and 13% of all women. No other fiction categories attain a 10% penetration of readers and the most popular non-fiction category is that of biography, with 7% of all readers, 6% of men and 7% of women.

It is worthwhile considering how people obtain the books they read, since this throws some light on the type of book being read. In 1988 38% of the books currently being read had been bought (including purchases through book clubs), 33% had been borrowed from libraries and 17% had been borrowed from friends or relatives. The rest were gifts or books already in the home. Whilst half of the books being read had been borrowed, the 37% that had been

**Table 1.4  Main type of book being read, 1988**

|  | Male (%) | Female (%) | All (%) |
|---|---|---|---|
| *Fiction* |  |  |  |
| Romance | 2 | 29 | 17 |
| Crime/thriller | 16 | 13 | 14 |
| Modern novel | 6 | 13 | 10 |
| Historical | 5 | 7 | 7 |
| War/adventure | 8 | 2 | 4 |
| Classic | 2 | 3 | 3 |
| Science fiction | 4 | 1 | 3 |
| (All fiction) | 59 | 76 | 69 |
|  |  |  |  |
| *Non-fiction* |  |  |  |
| Biography | 6 | 7 | 7 |
| History | 7 | 4 | 6 |
| Educational | 5 | 2 | 3 |
| Religion | 3 | 3 | 3 |
| (All non-fiction) | 36 | 22 | 28 |
| Don't know/other replies | 3 | 2 | 3 |

Note: Percentages below 3% are omitted above.
Source: Euromonitor, 1988.

bought is an appreciable proportion. Buying amongst men readers (40%) was higher than amongst women (35%), and people aged 55 or over were the lowest buyers (26%), but buying amongst the AB, $C_1$ and $C_2$ social groups hardly differed (41%, 39% and 40%) and only the DE group (29%) were low purchasers of books. Borrowing from a library was not significantly different between men and women, but increased with age to 48% amongst the 55 and over age group and was highest amongst the DE social group, at 40%.

The above figures are for penetration, and if we look at the population *profiles* for buyers and borrowers (Table 1.5) we can see that amongst all those people currently reading a book women are particularly noteworthy as borrowers from friends or relatives (65%). The age distribution shows that the youngest age groups, the 16 – 34 readers, are 43% of all the borrowers from friends and relatives and only 23% of the library borrowers. The 55 and over readers account for 52% of all the library borrowers and form only 25% of the book buyers. Borrowing books from friends or relatives is not as prevalent amongst the AB social group as it is amongst the others but it should

**Table 1.5  Profiles of buyers and borrowers**

|  |  | Buyers | Library borrowers | Friend/ relative borrowers | Current readers |
|---|---|---|---|---|---|
| Sex | Male | 46 | 42 | 35 | 42 |
|  | Female | 54 | 58 | 65 | 58 |
|  |  | 100 | 100 | 100 | 100 |
| Age | 16–34 | 39 | 23 | 43 | 35 |
|  | 35–44 | 21 | 12 | 17 | 16 |
|  | 45–54 | 15 | 13 | 12 | 14 |
|  | 55+ | 25 | 52 | 28 | 36 |
|  |  | 100 | 100 | 100 | 100 |
| Social grade | AB | 26 | 23 | 16 | 23 |
|  | $C_1$ | 30 | 27 | 34 | 29 |
|  | $C_2$ | 24 | 18 | 24 | 23 |
|  | DE | 20 | 31 | 26 | 25 |
|  |  | 100 | 100 | 100 | 100 |

Source: Euromonitor, 1988.

be noted that the $C_2DE$ social groups account for 44% of all the book buyers. This group is also 49% of all the library borrowers and 50% of borrowers from friends and relatives, so the working-class readers account for an appreciable proportion of all buyers and borrowers in the population.

Each year in early January *The Guardian* newspaper publishes an analysis of those 100 paperback books that have sold the most copies over the previous 12 months.[15] The top book of the year has usually sold about a million copies over the year, home and export, and the names of the leading authors are indicative of the type of books that sell the most copies. In 1989 the four best-selling authors were Jeffrey Archer, Barbara Taylor Bradford, Rosemary Conley and Jackie Collins. In 1988 they were Wilbur Smith, Catherine Cookson, Sidney Sheldon and Shirley Conran. Other authors near the top are writers such as Dick Francis, Len Deighton, Virginia Andrews, Robert Ludlum, Judith Krantz – authors who are invariably described, and rightly so, by their publishers as 'bestselling' authors. Non-fiction only occurs occasionally in the annual bestseller list but health and diet books can be very successful, and Rosemary Conley's *Complete hip and thigh diet* was in third place in 1989. Successful literary fiction, in paperback format, can be placed in the top 100, but even Penelope

Lively's *Moon tiger*, which won the Booker prize for the best novel of 1987, only achieved 55th place.

Public libraries in the UK are provided by 167 different local authorities and all loans are free, though charges are usually made for reserving books or books overdue for return. In 1988–9 155 public libraries spent over £84 million on books and 149 of them held a total bookstock of over 126 million books, which averaged out at about 2½ volumes per head of population. Loans made during the year by 148 authorities came to over 540 million, averaging more than ten issues per head of population over the year.[16] There are no official statistics for the proportion of the UK population who use public libraries (and not all users necessarily borrow books) but the MORI poll in December 1988 reported 43% of adults (aged 18 and over) saying that they had not borrowed a book from a public library at all in 1988, whereas 33% of the sample claimed to have borrowed from a library over ten times. This survey, incidentally, came to the conclusion that about 10% of the adult population had no contact at all with books in that they had not read a book or been into a bookshop or library in the previous 12 months.

Public library statistics consistently show that, for England and Wales, the proportion of books available for loan are roughly 43% adult non-fiction, 37% adult fiction and 20% children's books. However, analyses of books borrowed each year show that adult fiction accounts for about 60% of all loans, the rest being roughly divided between adult non-fiction and children's books. Thus, taking the adult books separately from the children's, fiction accounts for about 44% of stock, but about 75% of issues.

The government-funded Public Lending Right, introduced in 1982, pays a royalty to British (and some other) authors for the loans of their books from public libraries. The system is based on a changing sample of 20 public libraries which have computerized issue systems and no author is permitted to earn more than £6,000 each year from the overall fund, which was £3.5 million for 1988–9. The PLR office maintains a certain degree of confidentiality about its individual payments, but statistical analyses in 1987–8 showed that of 523 authors earning over £1,000 367 wrote adult fiction, 46 adult non-fiction, 101 children's books and 9 were translators, illustrators, etc. A special analysis of PLR estimates of the 100 books most issued during the year 1988–9 gave 32 written by Catherine Cookson, 9 by Dick Francis and 7 by Danielle Steel. The popularity of Catherine Cookson is quite phenomenal and booksellers and librarians are in agreement that no other author has both the output and the readership that she has achieved and maintained.

Whilst the readership of literary fiction has increased in recent years, stimulated by the publicity cleverly associated with the Booker prize and helped by more and more library campaigns to increase people's reading interests, all library research shows that people looking for books in the public libraries tend to browse a great deal and few people are systematic searchers for books or have a wide range of authors for whom they search. Even those people who are avid readers are not easily categorized, since people who read a great deal will enjoy 'popular', 'literary' and 'classic' fiction according to their feelings at any given time. For example, one survey showed that fiction readers could happily read one novel for absolute relaxation and another for intellectual stimulation and challenge.[18] A retired teacher enjoyed books by Alice Walker, Colleen McCullough, Penelope Lively, Norah Lofts and Dorothy L. Sayers. Another woman's favourite novelists were Margaret Drabble, Anita Brookner and Barbara Taylor Bradford. Keen fiction readers are often very catholic in their tastes and the limitations that many library borrowers demonstrate in their choice of fiction arise mainly from their lack of knowledge of alternative authors whom they might enjoy.

It is therefore very important indeed that librarians should do all they can to introduce borrowers to authors who are new to them. The great advantage of the library is the wide range of novels available for choosing and the fact that failure – choosing a novel that the reader does not enjoy – costs nothing. The book trade itself, not surprisingly, is always pushing its new product before the eyes of possible buyers – institutional or personal. But for the few new novelists who succeed there are many who fail to establish themselves with the public. The great advantage for the librarian is in having in stock the back titles of so many novelists who have achieved success and whose books can be offered to readers who have not yet 'discovered' these authors. There is as much joy in discovering Trollope at the age of 40 as there is in discovering Margaret Drabble at the age of 20 and, as Samuel Butler said, 'The oldest books are still only just out to those who have not read them'. Only the novel that is unread is the novel that is dead. The joy of fiction is that the reader can constantly find new books that are over a hundred years old. And librarians can participate in that joy by introducing the readers to those 'new' authors.

## References

1    Adult Literacy and Basic Skills Unit, *Literacy and numeracy: evidence from the national child development unit*, London, ALBSU, 1983.

2    Adult Literacy and Basic Skills Unit, *Literacy, numeracy and adults*, London, ALBSU, 1987.

3    Carter, C., 'Young people and books: a review of research into young people's reading habits', *Journal of librarianship*, 18 January 1986, 1–22.

4    See Heather, P., *Young people's reading: a study of the leisure reading of 13–15 year-olds*, Sheffield, Centre for Research in User Studies, 1981.

5    Office of Population Censuses and Surveys, Social Survey Division, *General household survey 1987*, London, HMSO, 1989.

6    BBC Broadcasting Research Department, *Annual review of BBC broadcasting research findings, No. 15*, London, BBC, 1989.

7    BARB, *The month's viewing in summary, four weeks ending 25th February 1990*, London, BARB, 1990.

8    BARB, *The week's viewing in summary, week ending 25th March 1990*, London, BARB, 1990.

9    'UK double act has Hollywood taped', *The Independent on Sunday*, Business News Section, 18 March 1990, 6.

10   Central Statistical Office, *Social trends 20*, London, HMSO, 1990, 157.

11   Office of Population Censuses and Surveys, Social Survey Division, *General household survey, 1987*, 56.

12   MORI (Market and Opinion Research International), 'Books and libraries 1988', research conducted for the *Sunday Times*, London, 1989. Data kindly supplied to the author by MORI.

13   Euromonitor, *The book report 1989*, section 9, the Euromonitor book readership survey 1988, London, Euromonitor, 1989.

14   *The Bookseller*, 3 February 1989, 375.

15   Hamilton, A., 'Mole triumphant over Archer', *The Guardian*, 11 January 1990, 24.

16   See *CIPFA public library actuals, 1988–89* for the full details of all statistics.

17   Sumsion, J., *PLR in practice: a report to the advisory committee*, Stockton-on-Tees, Registrar of the Public Lending Right, 1988 and PLR press release *PLR estimates of public library borrowing, July 1988–June 1989*, January 1990.

18   Turner, S., 'A survey of borrowers' reactions to literary fiction in Beeston Library, Nottinghamshire, unpublished MA dissertation, Department of Library and Information Studies, Loughborough University 1987.

## 2 The fiction industry

*Stuart Hannabuss*

The management of fiction in libraries takes place in the context of the complex structure of the book trade. This chapter aims to highlight the main characteristics of this context, emphasizing output and prices, marketing and distribution. It suggests how fiction in hardback and paperback finds its place there, the extent to which the notion of 'a fiction industry' helps to explain how and why fiction appears, and how far it implies exploitation of cultural values. It also reviews the phenomenon of the bestseller, and explores how genre and list analysis can help librarians familiarize themselves with trends in this ever-changing setting. Specific data are fleeting, and so a secondary aim has been to point to the historiographic and methodological structure of source materials.

### Publishing output and book prices

There is no doubt about the scale of publishing activity. In 1987 400,000 titles were currently listed in print. Looking at the UK book market for 1988, the Publishers Association (PA) suggested that it was worth £2.3 billion* at retail prices. Another reliable source, the Euromonitor Book Report (for 1989), gives the figure of £1.6 billion (the difference arises because the PA figure includes £200 million of imported books). On an average discount of 40%, this gives £1.4 billion at publishers' prices.[1] About 40% of sales are paperback sales. Total sales of books in the UK at end-user prices were about £1.7 billion.[2] Comparing the US, a market 4.5 times larger, 1988 figures are £10.5 billion, with consumer books earning £6.5 billion of that total. Turning to book titles, their numbers show continual growth: in 1988 56,514 titles were issued, of which 43,188 were new books and 13,326 new editions including paperbacks. This was a 3.2% increase on 1987, itself a 4.1% increase on 1986.[3] The value of British book exports in 1987 was over £107 million to the US, over £60 million to Australia, and over £22 million to the Federal Republic of Germany, the largest importer of British popular paperbacks (Department of Trade and Industry (DTI) figures).[4,5]

American book production over the last three years shows a slight decline: in 1987 hard and paper totals were 56,027, in 1988 55,483, and in 1989 45,718.[6] Based on the Bowker Weekly Record/American Book Publishing Record database, *Publishers weekly* analyses for 1987 – 9 reveal that 'fiction' stayed at over 5,000, and 'biography' around 2,000 (hard and paper). Mass-market paperbacks showed 2,243 separate titles in 1989.[6] The American Association of Publishers estimates for 1989[7] indicate the following percentage changes upwards from 1988: adult hardbound 21.8, adult paperbound 14.6, juvenile hardbound 19.1, and juvenile paperbound 22.6, an average percentage change of 19.3. Monthly and year-to-date analyses are also found in *Publishers weekly*. In 1988 99 million units of mass-market paperbacks were exported from the USA.[8]

Book trade statistics are complicated. The Department of Trade and Industry data are based on the quarterly returns of 125 booksellers and define volume not as units sold but as value of sales adjusted for inflation.[9] The Publishers Association Statistics Collection Scheme (PASCS) data are based on value turnover in pounds sterling and unit turnover (i.e. total number of books sold): 'if value turnover increases more than unit turnover then obviously average prices will increase, but great care must be taken in interpreting what this particular average means'.[10] A major area is that of book prices, of special interest in a price-sensitive and competitive world like the book trade. Data on book prices, in sources like the *Library Association record, The Bookseller* and *Publishers weekly*, are useful for a full understanding of activity. Of importance is the behaviour of book prices in relation to the retail price index (RPI) (general prices), representing inflation. An analysis of the decade 1978 – 9 to 1988 – 9,[11] taking 1978 – 9 as the base year 100, shows 1987 – 8 at 201, and suggests a 6% increase in 1988 – 9 on 1987 – 8. Care should be taken in using this index since it was re-referenced to 13 January 1987.[12]

Two major reports have both suggested that book prices have been increasing faster than this index. The Peat Marwick study of UK book prices undertaken for the British Library (BNB Research Fund), the Library Association and Somerset Libraries[13] argues that between 1980 and 1987 the average prices of books bought by libraries increased by 131% against a retail price index increase of just under 72%.[14] They conclude that prices for books have risen substantially above those for other products generally, and such rises 'are almost wholly accounted for by mass market paperbacks increasing in price by more than other products'. Inflationary effects on British book prices of US imports were also noted.[15]

The other report was the Fishwick Report on the economic

implications of the Net Book Agreement, which concluded[16] that book prices between 1962 and 1987 had risen by a factor of 14.36, while general retail prices rose by 7.59, 'a relative rise in the price of books of nearly 90%'. Arguing the other way, Clive Bradley, Chief Executive of the Publishers Association,[17] asserts that 'consumer books' ('the main staple of public libraries'), by changing by −2.1 in 1981 and by −2.5 in 1987, against an adjusted RPI, have not even kept pace with general inflation. Even within 1988−9, it is claimed that general prices have now outstripped book prices; books at 5.8% are one percentage point less than the all-items index.[18] In hard terms average book prices were £15.81 in early 1986 and £17.02 in late 1989.[19]

In the UK, average prices of fiction new books in 1988 are listed as £7.62 for all bindings, £3.64 for paperback, and £11.00 for other bindings.[20] Paperback new books average £8.46, and non-fiction new books, all bindings, £14.61. In the USA mass market paperbacks in 1989 averaged $4.38, compared with trade paperbacks at $16.60, and show 'a hike in fiction against a downtrend in nonfiction'.[21] The pricing of books is influenced by many factors, from trade discounts and manufacturing costs to marketing and authors' royalties,[22] and the Europe-wide debate about VAT threatens complications.[23] The 'golden hello' has been blamed for accelerating price increases: such advances to authors as £30,000 for *A brief history of time* and Chatto's £625,000 to Michael Holroyd for his biography of Shaw inflate frighteningly.[24]

Rising prices form a major concern for libraries: public libraries in England and Wales spent £73 million in 1988−9 on books and pamphlets, and lent 29 million adult fiction works,[25] 36% of total lending (non-fiction was 43% and children's 21%). Gross additions to stock for these libraries included nearly 5 million adult fiction and 3 million children's books, working out at £81 (for books) per 1,000 population. This upward creep of prices stimulated Roger Stoakley of Somerset to get Peat Marwick McLintock to examine book prices.[26] The chairman of Bantam Doubleday[27] argues that higher prices do not necessarily deter sales, yet examination of *Public library statistics 1987−1988*[28] suggests that for public libraries in England and Wales adult fiction lending bookstock is down by 3.5% and adult fiction loans down by 2.8%. There is a 24.6% increase between 1983−4 and 1987−8 in total expenditure per 1,000 population in such libraries (a 30.7% increase in metropolitan districts). Noticeable trends include a proportional increase in children's stockholding at the expense of adult non-fiction, though it is not clear if this change is 'the result of deliberate acquisitions policy or a reaction to book prices'.[29] Recently, total library expenditure for 1988−9 was up by

5.99%, while the RPI annual rate of inflation outstripped it at 8% by mid-year.[30] Peter Mann's regular series of analyses on library expenditure in *The Bookseller* are invaluable. Developments in other sectors, like changes in school bookselling and direct purchasing organizations,[31] are relevant.

Yet there is a further dimension, equally important: what people buy and borrow. The survey 'Books and the consumer' commissioned by the Book Marketing Council of the Publishers Association has thrown up findings from its first year (of three) to the effect that four in five adults in Britain buy at least one book a year, and that heavy book buyers (more than 16 purchases a year) are more likely to have library tickets. Of these heavy buyers, the age group 25–34 predominate (80% of the adults who buy books); 40% of books purchased were gifts, and 41% were purchases for children.[32] US book trade data tell that consumer book spending has increased primarily from price increases rather than from higher unit sales, and that the average price of a consumer book in 1988 was $6.72 compared with $4.63 in 1983.[33] Frank Fishwick's survey of the market for books in the Republic of Ireland[34] reports that total expenditure on books per head there was £14.60 in 1984, which, with the demographic profile biased to the young (39% under 20), reveals an emphasis on school buying. A *Sunday Times* MORI survey in 1989 shows that figures for people not borrowing or buying books is increasing,[35] while other evidence from Euromonitor hints that there is a slight swing towards buying rather than borrowing,[36] possibly underlining the impact of diminished library purchasing power.

### Marketing and distribution

Pricing up is said to increase profits for publishers but it also enables them to spend a higher proportion of revenue on promoting new and backlist titles.[37] Book marketing, which includes distribution, market research and promotion, is probably the most widely known aspect of the fiction industry, not least of all through the hype of bestselling fiction. Yet fiction in general, books indeed, compete with other leisure attractions for the disposable income in people's pockets.[38] The marketing of books is made difficult because of the diversity of unique new products (some 50,000) each year, and there is little brand loyalty to imprint names.[39] Moreover, for many publishers a modest 2% of turnover is spent on advertising,[39] although this varies with the product.[40] Marketing works only if the distribution system allows it to do so. Traditional book trade structures have evolved in a Byzantine manner, and we will examine these briefly before looking at the promotional side of marketing.

Among British booksellers and stationers in 1988 turnover reached £2 billion, a 17% increase on 1987: sales have increased by 176% since 1980, an average annual rate of 13.5%.[41] In these and in CTNs (confectioners, tobacconists and newsagents), volume sales are both up.[42] However, channels of distribution are complex: from publishers, variously through retailers or wholesalers, book clubs, or by direct mail. Some 70% of all book sales in the UK, and 80% of sales to individuals, are through the retail shops,[43] while most of the rest are sold to consumers via book clubs and mail order. Most paperback sales go through bookshops, including mixed retail businesses like W. H. Smith or John Menzies, through which much fiction in magazine as well as book form is sold; about 5% through supermarkets and about 30% through CTNs and stores like Boots and Woolworths.[44] Most non-bookshop sales of paperbacks go through wholesalers and most bookshops use them for supply. A typical paperback publisher, therefore, might distribute books to individual booksellers (e.g. a Charter Group bookseller or a chain like Pentos/Dillons or Blackwells), to chains with their own branches like W. H. Smith and Hammicks (a John Menzies business with 28 outlets),[45] to wholesalers and library suppliers and organizations selling books to schools.[46]

Increases in book sales at the end of the 1980s contrast with decline in the early part of the decade – a decline attributed by management consultants Arthur Young to book prices rising ahead of the RPI,[47] endangering continued investment. Similar increases can be seen in US bookstores.[48] For the UK the use of Standard Book Numbering and tele-ordering (with 40% of UK order lines from nearly 1,000 shops, of which W. H. Smith is 8% because of its own warehouse) has been important in the turn-around, enabling booksellers to place orders with any UK publisher and search on the Whitaker database, a facility now available on CD-ROM.[49] Since 1986 W. H. Smith has invested £20 million in information technology and has installed EPOS (electronic point of sale) in 280 of their largest high street shops.[50]

In recent years chains such as Blackwells and Pentos have grown, increasing competition for supremacy, encouraging mergers and takeovers (Waterstones and Sherratt & Hughes by W. H. Smith), and threatening independents. This phenomenon can be seen elsewhere (e.g. Japan).[51] The wholesalers, with competitive delivery rates (the claim is 1.8 working days from bookseller order to receipt),[52] demonstrate success, particularly at seasonal highpoints like Christmas (e.g. for popular books like *'Allo 'allo: the war diaries of Rene Artois, A brief history of time,* and *The Guinness book of records*).[53] This swift response has assisted wholesalers in the distribution battle for the mega-seller market, and at the same time has given booksellers greater confidence in getting backlist titles overshadowed by books of the moment.[54]

Mergers and integration, horizontal and vertical, suggest a trend towards greater oligopoly in the book trade. There is a financial concentration of influence in popular fiction publishing (e.g. in the USA with firms like Simon & Schuster, Random House and Bantam Doubleday). The top eight world book publishers (including Reed and Time Inc. and Random House) have internationalized popular writers. Octopus bought Heinemann and Hamlyn, and then was bought by Reed. Multi-national and multi-media conglomerates are highly influential on what is published and distributed: e.g. Gulf & Western own Simon & Schuster, while Pearson own Penguin and Longman. As a major shareholder in British Satellite Broadcasting, Reed International may be said to have ready access to possible channels of distribution and advertising. Bertelsmann's plan to purchase W. H. Smith's 50% share in BCA (Book Club Associates) in 1988 would have given them access to book club sales of £64 million and nearly 2 million members if the Monopolies and Mergers Commission had not blocked it on grounds of public interest. Time Inc. own BOMC (Book of the Month Club) in the USA.

An economic survey of booksellers revealed that the median bookshop held a mere 3.6% net income after cost of goods, personnel expenses, premises and promotion were taken out.[54] The most recent results from UK Charter bookshops, with an average of 75% retail sales of new books, show a similar net (trading) profit of 3.4%.[55] Booksellers battle with publishers over discounts, and are faced with problems of stock turn, credit terms and shrinkage.[56] Book prices affect volume sales directly, and the role of popular fiction in this equation is central. Publishers Association research in 1988 pointed to declining paperback unit sales as unit prices have increased, threatening to fall below economic levels.[57] It was argued too that there was a greater output of popular hardbacks, using economies of scale to keep unit prices down and maintain demand.

Retail price maintenance in the form of the Net Book Agreement (NBA) lies at the heart of this. The Fishwick Report came out in favour of its retention:[58] its abolition would lead to higher gross margins and greater returns (i.e. titles sent back unsold to publishers), encourage shops to order and hold fewer titles, and publishers to publish fewer titles. The general arguments are well rehearsed, and most publishers and booksellers support its retention[59] (and in the USA its increasing adoption by publishers.)[60] Ron Pybus makes a spirited case for its effect on libraries,[61] and the Office of Fair Trading so far has decided not to review the NBA (at early 1990). Arthur Young gloomily prognosticates only three national bookselling multiples and the closure of over 200 independent retail outlets by 1995.

The general issues would be so much background if controversy had not arisen in 1989. It centred on the Pentos 'lower prices' campaign launched in November 1989. By discounting non-net books, the affair was regarded as a 'quality against hype' debate, reawakening perennial issues of quality and commercial reading which characterized studies of adult fiction like John Sutherland's *Fiction and the fiction industry*[62] and of children's fiction like Fred Inglis's *The promise of happiness*.[63] Of particular interest were the items promoted in the campaign: leading titles included *Hugh Johnson's pocket wine book 1990* and *Millers' antiques price guide*. Using their Dillons and Athena outlets, new 'popular' titles published by the Octopus group (mostly Hamlyn) were advertised with prices slashed by 20%. Children's bestsellers like *The jolly postman* and *Winnie the Pooh* were among 50 such titles. Increased sales, particularly over Christmas, were claimed. It was argued that such increased sales will encourage publishers to publish some fiction non-net, but few have come forward.

Countries with experience of having abolished RPM, like Australia, have discovered that prices, far from going down generally, have gone up punitively.[64] Some there claim that free market forces are not the best regulators of culture and that minority book reading interests are being ignored: 'you sell more books on cats and sex and fewer on literature'.[65] In Belgium, too, no market growth is alleged, with deep discounting and the pricing of bestsellers at cost plus, thus penalizing general fiction and the very bestsellers which the trade most hopes will underwrite profitability and high sales. Lost-leader selling in France and fewer bookshops led France to reintroduce RPM in 1982 after a decade of deregulation.

It has been said that marketing books is difficult because each one is different. Brand loyalty is erratic. Some books are known by brand name, like Ladybird,[66] but the promotional 'handle' (compare cosmetics) is elusive.[67] Not all popular book titles or authors are promotable on television or posters. The market itself has many segments, each with its own habits and valuation of reading. An analysis of the US publisher Harper[68] divided mass-market children's products into three classes: high demand (heavy advertising on TV, translated into books with licensed characters), low price (competing solely on price), and brand name (products like Barbie and GI Joe, and book series like Western Publishing's 'Golden Books'). Many publishers are building promotion into high discounts (as much as 50%) for non-returnable books, and link book promotion with toys and games. Recent figures on book tokens suggest that sales are up (over £15 million in 1989).[69]

A study of promotional budgets in the field of popular fiction suggests that they are either very generous or very sparse. One of the most famous UK examples was Penguin's Peter Mayer's promotion of M. M. Kaye's *The far pavilions*, described by Sutherland as 'unprecedented' in 1978.[70] Since then, many lavish promotional campaigns have taken place, with advertising on TV and all major national and Sunday newspapers, press features in the regional press, promotional mailings to libraries, display and merchandising materials for bookshops, and guest appearances on radio and in magazines. Rebecca Sydnor, author of bestselling *Making love happen* (Simon & Schuster, 1990) held author seminars in ten American 'tour cities'. There was a £10,000 national radio campaign from Sphere to promote Stephen King's *The drawing of the three* (second in his trilogy *The dark tower*).

Even bestselling authors like Frederick Forsyth, John le Carré and Wilbur Smith are said to gain from such expenditure: for Wilbur Smith in 1989 £250,000 sought to lift hardback sales, especially in non-book trade (like Asda Stores) and export markets. For Smith, print runs are correspondingly large: Heinemann printed 270,000 hardback copies of *Rage*, of which BCA took 12,000 copies and the UK trade 100,000, the rest going for export.[71] Book clubs like BCA are able to buy at a substantial discount from publishers and sell at a price below net price to members: e.g. hardback fiction £10.95, book club simultaneous edition £7.95, and book club reprint edition £5.95.[72] Their advertising budgets are often high: BCA's World Books, for example, spent £3.2 million in 1988, and the Literary Guild £1.4 million. In all, BCA spent £8.2 million on advertising in 1988, mainly on recruiting new members.

There are many times when chance factors work in favour of a bestseller. Hill & Wang (parent company Farrar, Straus and Giroux) produced John Allen Paulos' delightful *Innumeracy: mathematical illiteracy and its consequences* in 1989. Its off-putting title belied its witty and urbane presentation of a subject many people fear, and it fortuitously coincided with two major government reports on the poor state of number teaching in the US educational system. Six impressions were rushed from the publishers in as many months.[73] Less serendipitous was the attempt by Collins to enlist the support of the book trade to the tune of £2 million to finance a generic TV advertising campaign for books, based on the assumption that collaboration made financial sense, and symptomatic of the trade's flirting with the idea of a levy-sustained Book Promotions House. Would it, critics argue, benefit those who do not contribute to its costs?[74]

There is disagreement about the effect of the media on book sales. Some, citing the growing influence of media tie-ins, claim that particular genres gain at the expense of others; for example, Victorian family sagas, war stories, and the supernatural have all gained in the last two years at the expense of Westerns, romance and science fiction. The serialization of Len Deighton's *Game, set and match* trilogy stimulated sales throughout the UK, and radio helped in the large sales of Ray Moore's *Tomorrow is too late*.[75] Promotion is never cheap, reputed to be £11,000 to promote one hardback in all the major Christmas bookshop catalogues.[76]

Research suggests that 64% of booksellers believe that publishers could help them market and sell better to their customers through mechanisms like more stands and display shelves, support through in-store promotions, and acceptable margins and selling prices. A Pentos programme gives publishers the chance to buy space to mount window and in-store displays (e.g. £750 plus VAT for a window in any large bookstore). There is scepticism about publisher-bookseller marketing,[77] though many are working well, like that between the AA, Ordnance Survey, Yellow Pages Guides, Fodor's Guides, the Consumer Association, and Berlitz Guides in the field of travel books.[78] Houghton Mifflin, through its interactive news-sheet 'Network', shows how successful this strategy can be.[79]

Marketing can take other forms: in the southeast USA the tabloids *Book page* and *Book talk* are distributed as inserts in local papers;[80] there are national book weeks; there are the book prizes, notably the Booker which adds to sales from the long- and short-list; and finally there is reformatting, recently shown when Agatha Christie's novels were given revamped jackets and increased sales by 40%, reversing a trend away from her to newer authors in the genre, in particular by younger readers, and away from the genre of crime fiction into horror and science fiction.[81] It will be interesting to observe the effect of the Centre for the Book planned by the British Library to promote 'the significance of the book in all its forms', particularly in view of the alleged parallel development to curtail the legal deposit acquisition of popular fiction.

## Bestsellers and genre popularity
High sales of authors as diverse as Ted Allbeury and Anita Brookner, Jack Higgins and Primo Levi, Salman Rushdie and Stephen King, demonstrate the variety of quality and appeal of popular fiction. With a product so varied, it is difficult to generalize. Nevertheless, particular forms of analysis can be used to characterize major patterns. The approach in this final section will be to examine bestsellers and popular hardback and paperback fiction and non-

fiction, using 'extrinsic' methods like list analysis; and then to consider genre sales and appeal, and consider the implications for the practitioner and researcher, in library work and more broadly in the field of the sociology of literature.

The fiction industry has probably been described in terms of, and occasionally patronized for, its emphasis on popularity at the expense of quality. This relationship takes on an acerbic edge in highbrow criticism and in the selection of children's books. Examining bestsellers shows this clearly. Assumption: that a bestseller is a trivial ephemeral work hyped to a gullible marketplace. Finding: right and wrong. *The Amityville horror* sold more than six million copies, but then so did *All quiet on the Western Front*. All-time bestsellers include Dr Spock's *Baby and child care*, *The hobbit*, *The thorn birds*, *Animal farm* and *Love story*. All these in paperback, except Dr Spock, have been outranked by sales of the *Merriam Webster dictionary*.[82]

Information of this kind can be arranged in many ways: by sales figures, country, language, time period, format, readership. For example, in the 1980s, top-sellers in hardback non-fiction included Lee Iacocca's autobiography and Bill Cosby's *Fatherhood*. Of 25 works cited in January 1990[83] for the USA, the breakdown includes management (6), diet (5), family (4), and biography (4), a fair snapshot of the preoccupations of the decade. Moving on to bestselling children's books, drawing on Bowker data,[84] *Peter Rabbit*, *The cat in the hat*, *Green eggs and ham*, Richard Scarry and *Winnie the Pooh* top the hardcovers (Dr Seuss cited seven times in the first 20), and Judy Blume, E. B. White, Laura Ingalls Wilder, and S. E. Hinton top the paperbacks (Judy Blume cited six times in the first 20). Sales for works like this are two million and above.

It is possible to examine bestsellers in terms of the seasonal book trade, where Christmas is the Everest of high sales. In 1988 Deighton and Douglas Adams vied with Larkin and Lord Carrington,[85] while the Booker winner Kazuo Ishiguro's *The remains of the day* and Eco's *Foucault's pendulum* contended with John le Carré's *The Russia house* and P. D. James's *Devices and desires* over Christmas in 1989.[86] Other works sell well by type, like cookbooks and film and TV tie-ins (like tales of EastEnders, *Yes, Prime Minister*, Colin Dexter's Inspector Morse series, spin-offs from *Casualty*, Corgi's version of the film *Born on the fourth of July* and Coronet's tie-in with the screen adaptation of Fay Weldon's *The life and loves of a she devil*). Regular updates are provided in *The Bookseller*. More specific scrutiny can be given to regional bestsellers: e.g. in Scotland consistent sellers include *A Scots Quair* and the photographic works of Colin Baxter. Gatwick Airport best reads included Jackie Collins and Jeffrey

Archer, Danielle Steel and James Herbert in late 1987, perhaps hinting that glitz, passion and the bizarre adequately suppress any fear of flying. Moving into specialized fields like religious bestsellers changes the ground rules, where the popularity of both fundamentalist and iconoclastic works suggests a yearning for certainty in a world of entirely one Church or none at all.

Some of these works are as transient as Pooh-sticks. An analysis of *Publishers weekly* hardcover bestseller lists from May 1989 to April 1990 confirms this: looking at the weeks that titles have been on the list allows us to identify three titles as *the* works of the year in the USA – Stephen Hawking's *A brief history of time* (Bantam), Robert Kowalski's *The 8-week cholesterol cure* (Harper), and Robert Fulghum's *All I really need to know I learned in kindergarten* (Villard). Eighty-three per cent of titles cited (including repeats) were cited for 20 weeks and below, and only two titles remained there for more than 100 weeks, confirming the 'high peak-long tail' phenomenon of bestsellerdom. But others live on and on, and it is worth picking these out. We might well ask if there is life after Adrian Mole,[87] Rubik cubes and the F-Plan.

Writers like Catherine Cookson, Alistair MacLean and Dick Francis never fail to appear in annual lists of bestsellers. It has been estimated that the top seven UK popular fiction authors sell 14% of all titles in the lists, excluding earlier titles.[87] This may indicate a conservatism of taste in the fiction readership, or alternatively that authors and publishers have identified perennial tastes and satisfy them. Yet this would not explain the recent popularity of Stephen Hawking or John Allen Paulos. Public Lending Right data can confirm the existence of a core of highly paid bestselling authors. Cookson dominates the list of 100 most borrowed adult books with 32 titles, followed by Dick Francis (9) and Danielle Steel (7). In the children's lists feature Roald Dahl, Goscinny and Uderzo, Eric Hill's Spot series, Shirley Hughes, Val Biro, Allan Ahlberg and Judy Blume.[88]

Comparisons between hardback and paperback sales and popularity, and sales in the UK and USA and elsewhere can be made. Looking at hardback titles in the UK and USA for 1988, similarities (e.g. Hawking) are less striking than differences: in the UK with the *Guinness book of records, Moonwalk* and *'Allo, 'allo*, and works by Ray Moore, John Harvey-Jones, John Stalker and Norman Tebbit (i.e. hardback emphasis on non-fiction), while in the USA non-fiction like Kowalski and Donald Trump and Tom Peters (management gurus), and fiction like Tom Wolfe and Donald Ludlum, James Michener and Tom Clancy. In 1989 Hawking and Forsyth, and the cause célèbre *The satanic verses* are common, but again differences are more noticeable: in the UK Adrian Mole, Michael Palin and the Prince of Wales, while in the USA Stephen King, Robert Fulghum and Roseanne Barr (of TV series fame). The popularity of Danielle Steel in the US lists is intriguingly matched by her loans in UK PLR data: buying and borrowing patterns, clearly related through availability and cost, may be investigated further. Clearly, too, the publication of titles in hardback or/and paperback is important: for example, hardback for library sales, hardback as market testers for larger paperback print-runs, and those genres like romance which exist in one format rather than both.

Other forms of analysis can identify relationships between publishers, authors, genres and formats. A full-scale bibliometric profile of a publisher[89] may not be necessary, but it is valuable to know which publishers are most involved and successful. Trade information suggests that for 1989 Transworld did well with 19 bestsellers, then Pan and Grafton and Arrow with 12 each, followed by Fontana, Penguin and Hodder.[90] Publisher-author links, like Viking (Salman Rushdie, Garrison Keillor, Stephen King), Bantam (Frederick Forsyth, Stephen Hawking, Shirley MacLaine), Random House (E. L. Doctorow, James Michener, Martin Cruz Smith, Nancy Reagan), can be pursued in both home and international markets, notably with co-publication and cross-border marketing campaigns in mind, and, more textually, with an eye to the actual topics and characterizations in the stories themselves. The extent to which story-telling and fact and fiction have been internationalized has still properly to be researched.

Formal list analysis can be carried out:

1  Decide on the sampling frame (e.g. all paperbacks reviewed in 'Paperback preview' in *The Bookseller* during 1989).
2  Design a list of major categories (these may derive classically from subject analysis, from stock headings in libraries or from trade classes), such as 'top sellers', 'thrillers and crime', 'SF fantasy and horror', 'historical'.
3  Then record items, price bands and publishers.

From such analysis, such findings as these emerge. For 'contemporary sagas, glitz and romance', 54 titles, 76% priced £3 to £3.99, major publishers Headline and Pan (each 7), Futura (6), and Grafton and Arrow (5 each). For 'SF fantasy and horror', 60 titles, 73% priced £3 to £3.99, major publishers Legend (12), Grafton (7) and Sphere (6). For 'thrillers and crime', 104 titles, 77% priced £3 to £3.99, major publishers Grafton (12), Fontana (11), Sphere (8), Arrow and Mandarin and Corgi (7 each). High, medium and low categories can be compared (e.g. in 1989 high included 'contemporary sagas and romance', 'SF fantasy and horror' and 'thrillers and crime'; medium included biography and history and food; and low animal, ecology, humour, short stories and war). Contrasts between years, countries and formats could be attempted, and seasonal patterns evaluated.

There has always been a tendency for fiction to be classified, not merely in interest categories or genres, but in terms of highbrow and lowbrow culture and value systems. Ken Worpole[91] reminds us of the snobbery attached to some of these distinctions. Genres have patterns, rules governing plot and characters. Readers get hooked on particular genres and authors. Such reading is, paradoxically, ephemeral and eternal. The probability is that popular fiction, as well as the 'entertainers' like Graham Greene and the forays of other 'quality' writers into popular forms like thrillers, tap deep archetypes in the human mind, dreams of heroism or villainy, rescues and romance, as well as orchestrating emotions and psychological scripts. It is important, therefore, to understand not just what materials exist[92] but why they have become mobilized within the last 200 years within popular culture. Writers like Cawelti, Radford, Mandel, Griffiths, Stafford and Hannabuss have tried to highlight some of these causes and effects.[93-98] Without these roots in the sociological and psychological make-up of both producers and consumers, phenomena like bestsellers, the marketing hype, and the tenacious hold of popular and quality fiction on buyers and borrowers throughout the world would simply not exist.

## Acknowledgement
The author would like to thank Mary Allard MA DipLib ALA for assistance with the list analysis.

## References
1  *The Bookseller*, 28 July 1989, 281.
2  *The book report 1989*, London, Euromonitor, 1989.
3  *The Bookseller*, 3 February 1989, 374.
4  *The Bookseller*, 9 September 1988, 989.
5  *Library and information news*, April 1990, 7.
6  *Publishers weekly*, 9 March 1990, 32–5 and 29 September 1989, 24–7.
7  *Publishers weekly*, 9 March 1990, 16.
8  *Publishers weekly*, 2 June 1989, 42–5.
9  Woodhead, M., 'Unit sales: have they passed their peak?', *The Bookseller*, 5 May 1989, 1553–5.
10  Mann, P. H., 'What price indexes?', *The Bookseller*, 6 October 1989, 1146–7.

11 Cope, C. and Mann, P. H., *Public library statistics 1978–1988: a trend analysis*, Loughborough, LISU, 1989 (report no. 3).

12 Dennis, G. (ed.), *Annual abstract of statistics no. 126*, London, HMSO, 1990, 323.

13 *The Bookseller*, 6 January 1989, 8.

14 *The Bookseller*, 9 September 1988, 983.

15 *The Bookseller*, 31 March 1989, 1138.

16 Fishwick, F., 'The economic implications of the Net Book Agreement', summarized in *The Bookseller*, 28 April 1989, 1470–89.

17 *The Bookseller*, 26 May 1989, 1794.

18 'Booksellers and stationers', (22–5) and 'CTNs', (16–21) of EIU *Retail business quarterly trade review*, no. 10, June 1989.

19 *The Bookseller*, 2 August 1986, 539; 6 February 1987, 509; 21 August 1987, 801; 19 February 1988, 626; 26 August 1988, 814; 3 March 1989, 761; 8 September 1989, 789.

20 *The Bookseller*, 17 March 1989, 943.

21 *Publishers weekly*, 9 March 1990, 32–5.

22 Hutchinson, T. H., 'The mathematics of book publishing', *The Bookseller*, 11 November 1988, 1923–6.

23 *The Bookseller*, 22 September 1989. See also the 'Don't Tax Reading' Campaign.

24 Clee, N., 'The rising cost of the golden hello', *The Bookseller*, 29 September 1989, 1056–60; Nixon, W., 'Agents and advances', *Publishers weekly*, 2 February 1990, 15–21; Greenfield, G., 'A tale of two novels', *The Bookseller*, 3 March 1989, 727–30.

25 CIPFA Statistical Information Service, *Public library statistics 1988–89 actuals*, London, CIPFA, 1990.

26 Stoakley, R., 'Publishers' pricing: the public librarian's dilemma', *The Bookseller*, 25 August 1989, 580–3.

27 Vitale, A., 'Returns: how explosive growth marks a growing crisis', *The Bookseller*, 4 August 1989, 391–4.

28 Cope, C. and Mann, P. H., *op. cit.*

29 Cope, C. and Mann, P. H., *op. cit.*, 36.

30 *The Bookseller*, 22 and 29 December 1989, 1997.

31 *The Bookseller*, 22 April 1988, 1605.

32 *Publishers weekly*, 13 April 1990, 19.

33 *Publishers weekly*, 30 June 1989, 24.

34 Fishwick, F., *The market for books in the Republic of Ireland*, Dublin, Book House Ireland, 1987.

35 Woodhead, M.

36 *The book report 1989*, London, Euromonitor, 1989.

37 Ross, N., 'Getting the price right', *The Bookseller*, 16 September 1988, 1096–8.

38 Rath, B., 'Books in the leisure time squeeze', *The Bookseller*, 1 December 1989, 1760 – 2.

39 Tongue, C., 'Opportunities to see: publishers' advertising in flux', *The Bookseller*, 6 January 1989, 20 – 4.

40 Dessauer, J. P., *Book publishing: what it is, what it does* (2nd edn), New York, Bowker, 1981, 155 – 99.

41 EIU, *Retail business quarterly trade review*, 10, June 1989, 22 – 5.

42 ibid., 16 – 21.

43 EIU, *Retail business*, 377, July 1989, 48 – 53.

44 EIU, *Retail business*, 290, April 1987, 24 – 30.

45 See ref. 41.

46 Scherer, P., 'Paperbacks', in Owen, P. (ed.), *Publishing: the future*, London, Peter Owen, 1988, 63 – 73.

47 Arthur Young, *Book retailing in the 1990s: the Arthur Young Report*, London, Publishers Association, 1989. (This was commissioned in 1986.)

48 *Publishers weekly*, 12 January 1990, 16.

49 Dove, R., 'Teleordering and EDI in the book trade', *The Bookseller*, 30 March 1990, 1074 – 8.

50 Sarchet, R., 'Epos at WHS: not so many black holes', *The Bookseller*, 18 August 1989, 487 – 90.

51 *Publishers weekly*, 12 January 1990, insert on Japan's book trade.

52 Davies, S., 'The hare and the tortoise', *The Bookseller*, 2 February 1990, 363 – 71.

53 *The Bookseller*, 8 December 1989, 1827.

54 'International Booksellers Federation Economic Survey 1986', *The Bookseller*, 3 July 1987, 29 – 30.

55 *The Bookseller*, 24 March 1989, 1048.

56 *The Bookseller*, 25 September 1987, 1275 – 6.

57 *The Bookseller*, 6 May 1988, 1815 – 16.

58 'The Fishwick Report', *The Bookseller*, 28 April 1989, 1470 – 8.

59 *The Bookseller*, 25 November 1988, 2081.

60 *Publishers weekly*, 9 June 1989, 36 – 9.

61 Pybus, R., 'The library case for the Net Book Agreement', *The Bookseller*, 26 February 1988, 744 – 50.

62 Sutherland, J., *Fiction and the fiction industry*, London, University of London Press, 1978.

63 Inglis, F., *The promise of happiness: value and meaning in children's fiction*, Cambridge, Cambridge University Press, 1981.

64 *The Bookseller*, 15 July 1988, 203.

65 Zifcak, M., 'The NBA debate: a view from Australia', *The Bookseller*, 24 June 1988, 2459 – 60.

66 *The Bookseller*, 10 March 1989, 832.

67  Levin, M. P., 'The marketing of books: a national priority for the eighties', *Library trends*, 33, Fall 1984, 185 – 214.

68  Burroughs, R., 'Selling children's books in the mass market', *Publishers weekly*, 19 January 1990, 66 – 70.

69  *The Bookseller*, 12 January 1990, 106; 23 March 1990, 961 – 5.

70  Sutherland, J., *Bestsellers: popular fiction of the 1970s*, London, Routledge and Kegan Paul, 1981.

71  Geare, M., 'Bestsellerdom without hype', *The Bookseller*, 18 and 25 December 1987, 2372 – 3.

72  EIU, *Retail business*, 377, July 1989, 48 – 53.

73  Goodrich, C., 'Big numbers for innumeracy', *Publishers weekly*, 2 June 1989, 46 – 7.

74  *The Bookseller*, 23 June 1989, 2093.

75  *The Bookseller*, 13 January 1989, 96.

76  *The Bookseller*, 29 July 1988, 384.

77  Reavell, C., 'Joint promotions or burnt fingers?', *The Bookseller*, 23 February 1990, 560 – 1.

78  Birn, R., 'Effective togetherness in mapping a market', *The Bookseller*, 26 January 1990, 258 – 9.

79  Burroughs, R., 'Targeting the hard-sell', *Publishers weekly*, 19 May 1989, 52 – 4.

80  *Publishers weekly*, 18 August 1989, 27 – 8.

81  Williams, S., 'Agatha Christie and the mystery of the declining sales', *The Bookseller*, 24 March 1989, 1070 – 4.

82  Data from *Publishers weekly*, 26 May 1989.

83  *Publishers weekly*, 5 January 1990, 26.

84  *Publishers weekly*, 27 October 1989, 28 – 9.

85  *The Bookseller*, 28 October 1988, 1712 – 16.

86  *The Bookseller*, 27 October 1989, 1388 – 92.

87  England, L., 'Is there life after Adrian Mole?', *The Bookseller*, 13 March 1987, 977.

88  *The Bookseller*, 12 January 1990; Hasted, A., et al., *PLR loans: a statistical exploration*, Stockton-on-Tees, Registrar of Public Lending Right, 1988.

89  De Glas, F., 'Fiction and bibliometrics: analyzing a publishing house's stocklist', *Libri*, **36** (1), 1986, 40 – 64.

90  *The Bookseller*, 19 January 1990, 165.

91  Worpole, K., *Reading by numbers: contemporary publishing and popular fiction*, London, Comedia, 1984, 15 – 30.

92  Dixon, J., 'Types of fiction material', in Dixon, J. (ed.), *Fiction in libraries*, London, Library Association, 1986, 21 – 111.

93  Cawelti, J. G., *Adventure, mystery, and romance: formula stories as art and popular culture*, Chicago, University of Chicago Press, 1976.

94  Radford, J. (ed.), *The progress of romance: the politics of popular romance*, London, Routledge and Kegan Paul, 1986.

95  Mandel, E., *Delightful murder: a social history of the crime story*, London, Pluto Press, 1984.

96  Griffiths, J., *Three tomorrows: American, British and Soviet science fiction*, London, Macmillan, 1980.

97  Stafford, D., *The silent game: the real world of imaginary spies*, Toronto, Lester and Orpen Dennys, 1988.

98  Hannabuss, S., *Managing children's literature* (Library Management Monograph 10 (1)), Bradford, MCB University Press, 1989.

---

\* Note: One billion is one million million.

# 3 Acquiring adult fiction

*Peter Labdon*

According to *Public library statistics (1988–89 actuals),*[1] in that year the public libraries of the UK and Northern Ireland added 4.29 million adult fiction books to their collections, contributing to a total 35.5 million copies of this type of book in stock on 31 March 1989. This vast collection generated 254 million loans, a stock turn of just over 7 : 1 – hardly a tribute to the efficient use of resources. After a discussion of the general context, this chapter describes the means by which one public library system, Suffolk County Information and Library Service (SCILS), acquired its share of the 1988–9 additions to stock.

## The general context

### The acquisitions context

Suffolk bought 35,000 adult fiction books in that year. In a 'normal' year the additions would have been around 40,000 – about 1% of the national total – but Suffolk's budget was skewed in favour of computerization from 1987 to 1989, and it did not regain its proper proportions until 1990–1. For practical purposes the discrepancy is not important – the methods used in 1990–1 are those developed during the late 1980s – but the context is significant. It is important to realize what a small exemplar even a large public library system represents, and 1% is a graphic indication of this principle. So much for the acquisitions context.

### The supply context

Over-production has become a book trade cliché; that is to say, it is largely common ground (except among would-be authors) that UK publishers produce too many books for the domestic market. Granted that the annual figure is inflated by the practice of counting by ISBN, so that one title can contribute more than once to the total statistic, and granted again that the English language is omnivorous as to markets outside the UK; even so, to produce some 55,000 new titles and editions in a year – over 1,000 a week – argues a degree of gluttony on the part of publishers that would certainly qualify them for the Third Circle of Hell, were it not an established fact that by virtue of the book, if not through any of their own, they all go to Heaven.

## The demand context

And the demand context? Well, local government never has enough to spend, it says: but this is a perennial problem. However, it has been a particular feature of public service in the last decade that local authorities have been pressured by central government to reduce their share of public funding both relative to inflation and absolutely. During that time, both sides have been more interested in the promulgation of political propaganda than objective information. Statistics have been used as weapons to obscure rather than enlighten the debate, as any Prime Minister's Question Time will demonstrate.

Furthermore, money is a means, not an end. The end is the service offered, and the consumer's reaction to it, and to see demand in that context we might take the information offered by UK public librarians to the Chartered Institute of Public Finance and Accountancy (CIPFA) in 1978–9 and 1988–9 (see Table 3.1).[2]

**Table 3.1**

|                                           | 1978–9       | 1988–9       |
|-------------------------------------------|--------------|--------------|
| (a) Books and pamphlets expenditure       | £43,127,686  | £73,126,516  |
| (b) Price base                            | 100          | 169          |
| (c) Total lending bookstock               | 92,436,000   | 96,988,000   |
| (d) Total issues                          | 482,879,000  | 432,629,000  |
| (e) Stock turn: (d) divided by (c)        | 5.22         | 4.46         |

Note that Table 3.1 includes *all* lending library books and loans, not just adult fiction. Bookstock and issues figures have been rounded to the nearest 1,000.

It is apparent that public librarians have used their 69% cash increase in bookfunds to increase their stockholding by nearly 5%, while the use of their product (measured by issues) has fallen by a little over 11% in the same period. It might have been better to concentrate resources on a smaller, better-quality bookstock, in the circumstances.

Adult fiction comprised 36.6% of the total public library lending bookstock in 1988–9, and contributed 58% of the loans. It follows that efficient selection and acquisition policies and procedures for this category have a proportionately larger impact on the effectiveness of the stock as a whole, measured in terms of loans. Each adult novel generated 1½ loans to every loan from the whole stock. This is hardly a revelation. All public librarians know that their bread and butter comes from the mass lending of novels; even the government knows it, in terms of the political damage it would suffer by imposing charges for borrowing them relative to the income to be derived. So it must be true.

Yet fiction is the category of stock which, on the whole, receives less managerial consideration than any other. More time is spent on acquiring adult non-fiction (admittedly there is more of it to choose from) and more still, proportionately, on children's books, than on adult fiction. The care and attention lavished on the development of children's reading skills and taste is dissipated by the loan fodder placed before the adult borrower. There is a reason for this, of course: public librarians have never felt able to act in relation to an adult borrower as they readily do to a child, by excluding that which they judge to be qualitatively inadequate. That would have blunted demand still further. 'If the punters will borrow it, buy it', has been the motto. And who is to say they are wrong, especially in a political climate which has encouraged quantity more than quality?

As a specialism, the art of selecting novels for adults is virtually dead in public libraries, though it flourishes in the field of children's fiction. Acquisitions processes, consequently, have evolved to maximize the speed and accuracy of supply, in that order, of large quantities of new and replacement stock. Library suppliers have naturally responded in kind. Indeed, they have gone further. Realizing that librarians would be likely to buy what was offered, rather than needed, they have geared themselves to provide a highly efficient approval service, pre-buying new and replacement titles and editions in bulk and distributing these to their customers as collections from which specific orders can be placed. Coupled with the warehousing of novels for selection from the shelves and the publication of comprehensive stock catalogues, the average public librarian can order in bulk at his or her convenience from a wide range of pre-selected, high-impact titles. The selection of adult fiction, as it has been practised recently, has relied more on the judgement of the supplier than of the local librarian.

This culture has been further encouraged by the increasing use of the paperback format in public libraries. The paperback has two inherent practical advantages over the hardback book, one general and one specific to adult fiction. The general one is that it is preferred by users; that is to say, presented with a choice of formats, the paperback is likely to be borrowed before the hardback, other things being equal. The specific advantage is that the paperback format, with a shelf-life of about three years on average, more accurately represents the effective life of an ephemeral novel than a hardback, with a minimum shelf-life of seven years. To put it another way, it is more economic to buy a paperback novel if, (a) there is a choice, and (b) if the title is not likely to become a classic or standard item in use. This is a difficult concept to put into practice, however, because first publication in paperback is still the exception and the trade in paperback rights assumes that what is reissued in that format will tap a new market. In fact, publishers rely to some extent on public libraries to buy first-publication hardbacks (especially novels) to establish such a market. The public librarian, consequently, tends to over-buy in hardback because he or she cannot assume the subsequent appearance of the title in paperback, and compounds that by buying the paperback edition as well, when it appears. The motive for this sequence of decisions is not necessarily to multiply a particular title, so much as a primary failure to accept the logic of William Hazlitt's observation that, 'Any book is new to me, until I have read it'.

The impulse to provide books, especially adult fiction, immediately on first publication is strong in public librarians. In part, librarians have made themselves the victims of Lionel McColvin's dictum, 'The right book to the right reader at the right time', which has been corrupted into a simple 'Give 'em what they want when they want it'. This philosophy, promoted by effective reviewing and marketing aimed at stimulating immediate sales demand on publication, has created a spurious urgency in public libraries' request services and the supply process which supports them – spurious in the Hazlittian sense that nothing essential would be lost to the reader by waiting for a paperback to appear. If the paperback never appeared, its absence would conclusively demonstrate the lack of demand for the original publication and the need to buy it would be avoided; but that is perhaps pushing the argument too far, even in today's congested publishing environment.

In greater part, the urge to buy quickly is a result of the changes in publishing practice. The inflationary spiral of the 1970s, coupled with the following recession, forced publishers into a new commercial strategy – 'small profit, quick return' – in marked contrast to the more leisurely marketing practice, relying for profit on stockholding a comparatively large number of established titles, which had prevailed for much of the century previously. Librarians, consequently, were faced with a most difficult conundrum – a falling level of resources, in real terms, with which to absorb a greater variety of product, within drastically shorter print-runs and, hence, availability. The pressure to spread resources more thinly, and buy more quickly, before titles went out of print, became intolerable, with the result that considered selection based on objective criteria became rarer, if not extinct.

The borrowing public, knowing nothing of the resources/supply context, reacted as it had been trained to do; it continued to demand books immediately on publication, and across the full range of material available. Whatever titles achieved publicity would be requested, and these requests (emanating from no more than 5% or 6% of borrowers at any given time) fuelled the acquisitions engine. Librarians were, in fact, led to treat *all* their purchases as urgent, in order to satisfy the demands of a small proportion of their borrowers. They could do no other; without the means to anticipate demand for a particular title, they had to assume that any would be required immediately on publication, lest they could not be acquired at all.

The book trade supply chain is simple and traditional:

author ⟶ publisher ⟶ printer ⟶ bookseller ⟶ customer

Intermediaries intrude, of course: authors have agents; publishers have editors, publicists and rights negotiators; booksellers have wholesalers, book clubs and Book Tokens Ltd; customers have mothers and fathers, aunts, uncles and friends desperate for Christmas presents. Librarians are both customers and inter-mediaries in their own right; as customers they have suppliers and as intermediaries they have borrowers – thousands of them. Over all, the product: 450,000 books in print, each different from the other and capable of being demanded at any time, in any place under the sun dominated by that most permanent legacy of Empire, the English language.

These factors convert a simple supply chain into a complex mechanism, further complicated by factors outside the direct control of the trade. Of these the internationalization of the market (or at least its Europeanization) and the Net Book Agreement are the most obvious. The irony of the latter, invented originally to bring order out of chaos, and now honoured as much in the breach as in the observance, should not be overlooked. To cope with this complexity, retail bookselling developed a substructure to deal specifically with the institutional market, of which the local authority sector is much the larger part.

Library supply companies are part wholesale, part retail, part service enterprises. Generally (but not in every case) they buy and stock titles in multiples sufficient to meet the anticipated demand from their customers, by subscription in advance of the publication of new titles; otherwise according to their judgement of the demand for replacement copies of standard books. They also accept and order single copies of unstocked items. Their on-approval services have been noted already, but their willingness to prepare books for the shelves of the library to which they are to be delivered, according to that library's specification, constitutes their *raison d'être* and the basis for competition between them within (or approximate to) the terms of the Net Book Agreement.

This facility is highly valued by their customers, who would otherwise have to fit protective covers and labels to their purchases, and document them, at their own, greater expense. Library suppliers do the work more economically (or at least more cheaply), so that receiving libraries are not cluttered up with unserviced material and are enabled to make effective use of the limited space at their disposal. This is a contracted-out service, in effect, almost universally practised by librarians and their suppliers long before it became a political shibboleth.

The relationship between a library supplier and a local authority customer is nothing more than a convention, unprotected by the ordinary constraints of audit or contract processes. Because the Net Book Agreement does not permit competition based on the price of the book, and only to a limited extent on the price of services, librarians have avoided the normal obligation to invite tenders for book supply, against a written specification as the basis of a formal contract. Consequently, a public librarian's business relationship with a supplier is highly sensitive to accusations of partiality, corruption or plain inefficiency, the latter because the allocation of business is underpinned by little objective information about the performance of one supplier against another. That librarians have been able to maintain such an arrangement in the face of the rigid financial protocols which affect every other aspect of local government expenditure is a tribute to the relative probity with which both sides conduct themselves, and a rather sad comment on the incidental status of public library services within local government.

In fact, any order for a book is subject to contract law; in practice, this is overlooked by both sides, to the extent that librarians are able to cancel orders or switch suppliers at will. Library suppliers comply with this arbitrary power because of its universality – every order or customer lost is liable to be replaced by another on an equally arbitrary basis. Consequently, there is an ebb and flow of business within the relationship, having little to do with objectivity, efficiency or timescales. There has been a recent move towards the use of a form of call-off contract; that is to say, some library authorities have issued formal specifications for services to be provided within stated periods of time, subject only to cancellation on failure to meet agreed service targets. These 'contracts' do not invite tenders based on price; they are more concerned to establish parameters for computer-based services leading to the automation of the order-supply chain, and it is in the use of such a contract that the Suffolk experience is of interest.

## The Suffolk County Information and Library Service (SCILS) experience

Computerization was Suffolk's solution to the problem of unification set by local government reorganization in 1974. Until 1979 the newly created county library service struggled to absorb the different methods pursued for decades previously by its five constituent authorities. Some of these were bizarre; one had used the token issue system so indiscriminately as practically to give its books away. Another had a request service so rudimentary as to stultify demand. A third had spent so little on its libraries overall as to require a subsidy from the rest for many years thereafter.

By 1978–9, financial losses through the assorted issue systems amounted to about 30% of the annual bookfund and it was this factor which weighed most heavily in the decision to buy the (then) Plessey offline computer system and apply it to all of Suffolk's libraries, irrespective of size, except mobiles. Soon, early in the 1980s, unification was signalled by the adoption of a title and acronym by which the service has been known ever since: Suffolk County Information and Library Service – SCILS.

Limited in application though the Plessey batch-processing system was ten years ago, it served its purpose. It provided a single, uniformly applied, issue/discharge and request system, standard retrieval practices, and a rudimentary management information database. The latter allowed library managers to see clearly, by 1983, that the lending library service was vastly overstocked with redundant items. The bookfund could not support the large stock effectively and it was judged impossible, politically, to obtain sufficient resources to do so in the foreseeable future. So began the locally notorious process known as the Bookstock Efficiency Exercise (BEE) – a determined attempt to reduce local library bookstocks to effective proportions and to set achievable targets for use. Pursued over the remainder of the decade, BEE shed a substantial amount of stock. SCILS's bookstock in 1988–9 was just 1.2 items per head of population, while its comparators were still at 2 per head or thereabouts. Borrowing declined as well, but not out of proportion to the general reduction experienced by most library services since 1984 – 5.

Meanwhile, Nemesis approached: the Plessey system became obsolescent in mid-decade and no financial provision for its replacement had been made. With its small, relatively effective lending library bookstock and the control offered by the turnkey systems under consideration, it was decided to finance the new computer by screwing yet more efficiency out of the long-suffering bookstock and its users, principally by shortening the loan period for the sections of stock in highest demand – mostly adult fiction. The calculation was that either overdue income would rise to the extent necessary to finance the system, or the stock turn would rise to the degree required to allow further reductions in stockholding to occur – i.e. to permit the bookfund to pay for the computer system until re-financing was possible. In practice, the second of these occurred and from 1987 to 1990 SCILS was treading a precarious line between an effective bookstock and a disaffected readership. These decisions were made and implemented before and during the acquisition of the Geac 9000 four-processor computer system, which was acquired in 1987 and applied to all 41 Suffolk libraries (except mobiles) within 18 months of start-up. It is fortunately unnecessary here to describe the traumas associated with this enterprise.

In this context, the efficiency of the selection – order – supply process assumed greater importance and it was decided to take the unusual step of searching for one principal supplier with whom the automated acquisition systems could be consistently developed. The 'principal supplier' would not be the sole supplier; SCILS had a long-standing policy to provide business for local booksellers if they wanted it, and there were other needs which could not be met from a single source; but to all intents and purposes, it was agreed that nearly all SCILS business should be placed in the hands of one company for a period of three years.

In taking this decision, library managers realized that they were relegating the usual criteria for efficient acquisitions to a secondary position. While it was possible that the selected supplier would be the fastest, most accurate and best-loved firm in the business, it would be chosen principally for its ability to match automated processes with SCILS, rather than for any other virtue. Accordingly, the specification appended to this chapter was issued and in due course, following detailed interviews and discussions with interested parties, John Menzies Library Suppliers of Nottingham (now known as JMLS) were appointed as principal providers of books to Suffolk.

Three years on, the specification is due for reissue and a fresh round of negotiations with interested suppliers, but developments have been slower of achievement than anticipated and it will be 1991 before any new relationship is contemplated, other things being equal.

Within the general aim to improve the efficiency of the acquisitions process, Suffolk wished to achieve four precise objectives:

1   To automate as many acquisitions processes as possible, particularly those at the beginning and end of the chain – the placement of orders, and the certification of invoices followed by automatic payments.
2   To free itself from the benevolent tyranny of approvals preselected and offered by its suppliers.
3   To obtain access, through staff and public terminals, to JMLS stock catalogues online.
4   For these purposes, to develop system links between the Geac computer and the JMLS stock database via LIBTEL.

These objectives were approached cohesively; that is to say, all four were to be attained, eventually if not at once.

### The process

As this chapter is being written (April 1990), the adult fiction acquisition process has evolved as follows:

1   JMLS post pre-publication information to SCILS book selectors, on slips supplemented by a tape, for all fiction titles entered on LIBTEL II. The information is derived from publishers' publicity and specifies hardback or paperback format in each case. The information is not confined to titles JMLS proposes to order for its own purposes; it includes everything notified by publishers.

2   Current practice is to feed the LIBTEL II tape into SCILSnet – the Suffolk name for its Geac system database – and then to call up the records required for 'dummy orders' which are printed off the database and posted to JMLS once the selection process is finished.

3   Eventually, the intention is that the 'dummy orders' will be created by JMLS, who will enter the ISBN for the item required into LIBTEL II from the slips, and download that information via Telecom Gold to SCILSnet.

4   In future, therefore, the confirmed 'dummy orders' will constitute a SCILS 'Preferred Requirement File' or PRF, and for JMLS a pre-publication on-approval order – or as near to that as publishing practice and SCILS efficiency will allow.

5   JMLS supply four sets of selected titles on approval, one for

each of the administrative areas into which Suffolk is divided, and a master set for the Central Bibliographic Unit (CBU) which coordinates the selection process.

6 At present, CBU staff assign levels, material types and categories to all selected stock and amend the records accordingly. Eventually CBU staff will deal only with the titles selected for acquisition, converting the record into a catalogue entry when the confirmed orders are delivered. (Note: 'levels' are necessary to SCILS's stock management and lending policies. There are three 'levels' which determine the location of an item and whether it should be lent initially for six weeks (level one), four weeks (levels two and three) or two weeks (level three). Most (but not all) adult fiction is assigned to level three. 'Material types' allow SCILSnet to recognize and count different formats for management information purposes – 'hardback', 'paperback', 'large print' and so on. 'Categories' are the definitions used by SCILS for shelf display instead of classification or, in the case of fiction, alphabetical order).

7 On-approval sets arrive weekly with a selection/order list provided by JMLS. Book selection is done weekly by the professional teams working in each library area. The list is marked up with the number of copies ordered and the location of each copy, and posted or faxed to the CBU.

8 CBU staff call up the order records from SCILSnet, collate the orders received, edit them (after consultation) if under- or over-ordering is perceived, specify the location and cost centre for each copy, and confirm levels, material types and categories.

9 The SCILSnet circulation database then records each title as 'on order' and will accept 'holds' (reservations) against it (as soon as the software can be got to work!).

10 The confirmed orders are printed from SCILSnet and posted first class to JMLS as principal supplier, or to a local bookseller according to a pre-determined allocation of business. Eventually JMLS orders will be transmitted to JMLS via Telecom Gold.

11 JMLS fill the order, processing each copy including the attachment of category labels, security triggers and codabars, for delivery to the CBU.

12 Invoices are certified in the CBU by 'wanding' the codabar in each book into the SCILSnet order file as confirmation of receipt. The stock database records the item as 'NEW'.

13 Each week JMLS transport collects from the CBU the receipted books destined for the three principal libraries at Ipswich, Bury St Edmunds and Lowestoft. These are distributed to these locations at the same time as the weekly PRF on-approval collections are

delivered. Books destined for other libraries are delivered by SCILS transport.

14 Local library staff wand in the items on receipt and the books are available for loan from the shelves or through the circulation database. (Note: there are, of course, exceptions to this process. Not all large-print fiction is notified or obtained through the on-approval process and some on-approval genre collections (romances and westerns usually) also bypass the on-approval order file. Furthermore, JMLS's pre-bound fiction will be shortly available outside the current process).

Finally, the development of the process envisages downloading invoices from JMLS to SCILSnet, with payments made through a further downloading from SCILSnet to the creditors' database in the County Treasurer's ICL mainframe computer.

No acquisition process is, or should be, wholly consistent within itself. The supply environment within which it must work is too diverse and unregulated to enable a routine acquisitions system to be developed. Expert intervention is required at many points within the process. But the administration of the acquisitions process can be reduced to a routine, and it is here that electronic intervention is required. The processes described are designed to reduce the administrative elements of the acquisitions process to an automated routine as far as possible.

### References
1 CIPFA Statistical Information Service, *Public library statistics (1988 – 89 actuals)*, London, CIPFA, 1990.
2 Ibid., and CIPFA Statistical Information Service, *Public library statistics (1978 – 79 actuals)*, London, CIPFA, 1980.

### Appendix: Suffolk County Information and Library Services Book Supply Specification (issued 1987)*

#### General
1 The library proposes to introduce a fully automated online stock control system in all its libraries in 1987/88/89. The system will include a bibliographic database and acquisitions package, together with automated issue/discharge and OPAC (online public access to the catalogue) subsystems.

---

* The author is grateful to the Director of Arts and Libraries, Suffolk County Information and Library Services, for permission to reproduce this specification.

2   The system offers an opportunity to design afresh book supply arrangements.

3   Future arrangements will be based, as far as possible, upon the following principles:

(a)   that one library supplier will provide the bulk of the library's book requirements, holding the status of Principal Book Suppliers (PBS);

(b)   that the PBS must be able to supply books in all the formats used by the library;

(c)   that the PBS must be able to provide access to its curent stock database, from any library in the county;

(d)   that automated ordering, invoicing and direct debit facilities will be available between the library and the PBS;

(e)   that the library will commit a proportion of bookfund to the PBS commensurate with the status of the PBS and the scale of the services specified below.

### Specification

4   The Principal Book Supplier must be able to supply current and retrospective orders on all formats of bookstock, viz.:

Adult fiction *paperback* and *hardback*

Adult non fiction *paperback* and *hardback*

Junior *paperback* and *hardback*

Reference and information stock including standing orders.

5   The PBS must keep a current shelf stock representative of all academic levels, including 'standard' English authors in print and significant publications of the past two-year period. 'Significant' here means both titles with recognized literary or subject merit as well as titles having demonstrable commercial success; from minority publishers as well as the well-known houses. The selection should cover all age ranges from pre-school to books for the elderly. English literary 'classics' should also be available in good editions, in hardback and paperback. The supplier must hold new titles in sufficient quantity so as to meet the anticipated requirements of the library with minimal delay.

6   *The supplier's database* must contain bibliographic records representing the total stock of the supplier (retrospective for a minimum of five years) plus records of the total current UK publishing output as represented by BBIP, UK MARC or both; together with details of a wide range of publishers' announcements, including minority UK publishers and major foreign (English language) publishers.

7 *Database records* must contain in MARC or similar structured format:

Principal author/composer (surname and forenames)
Secondary authors, composer, directors and performers
Title of work
Publisher
Edition
Format
Date of publication (or approx.)
Price
Dewey class
ISBN
Subject or title keywords
Descriptive note (annotation or 'blurb')

8 *Access to the database*: the PBS must ensure that his database can be accessed by an agreed number of terminals (which could exceed 40) by dedicated line or dial-up facilities on all library working days, including Saturdays. Exact hours of access to be agreed and changed only by mutual consent. The database must be hospitable to searches by the general public as well as by library staff. It must therefore be both user friendly and secure from unauthorized book ordering. The database must be searchable online by title, author/title composite, ISBN and subject keywords.

9 *Downloading from the database*: new bibliographic data (all records received by the supplier *or* a selection based on an agreed bibliographic requirement profile) must be downloaded to the library's database weekly, at no direct cost to the library.

10 *Approvals* collections to be provided by the supplier, enhanced by items selected by the library staff from a variety of sources, principally from the downloaded information (9 above). The approvals collection must include all formats and academic levels of stock as identified in paragraph 4, above. Three approval collections must be delivered weekly to three nominated libraries.

11 *Orders* for approval items and other stock to be accepted by the supplier by electronic mail, by computer terminal or in writing.

12 *Servicing* to be carried out in accordance with the instructions in force at any one time. (Currently: correct date label to be correctly fixed; bar code ditto; plastic jacket to be fitted at back of book (only); category codes to be added; ownership stamp, copy number and date of accession to be added). Dewey class mark to be provided from the supplier's database.

13 *Bibliographical support*: the PBS must endeavour to enhance his database and stock to meet the expressed interests of the library both for new publications and retrospective stock and must produce,

on demand, special subject lists from the database, indicating items in stock, for purpose of stock revision. The lists must be delivered *either* in the form of offline search reports in hard copy *or* as electronic mail, as required by the library. The supplier must have adequate means of verifying or tracing current literature emanating from the USA, the principal Commonwealth and European countries.

14 *Delivery*: orders for items shown on the database as being in stock should be delivered within three weeks of the order date. Part orders should be indicated as such. Delivery must be direct to the area or divisional library named on the order and at no cost to the library.

15 *Reports*: the PBS must be capable of both responding to online requests for reports on books currently on order; and of supplying regular (fortnightly) offline reports for all orders not supplied within eight weeks.

16 *Cancellation*: the PBS must offer a cancellation facility for any order for any book not supplied within eight weeks or any other period specified when the order is placed.

# 4 Fiction for children in libraries

*Helen Lewins*

> Book selection is one of the most vital aspects of librarianship, requiring a mixture of imagination, common sense, intelligence, firmness, organizing ability, professional skill, knowledge of children and books and awareness of the society within which the librarian operates.[1]

This chapter will examine the complex issue of book selection for children as it relates to public libraries and the provision of fiction published for this age group. In particular, the special considerations which have to be taken into account when selecting for children will be examined, together with how selection is undertaken. However, it is not only with new fiction titles that this chapter is concerned. Selection of newly published material cannot be undertaken without consideration also being given to overall collection management, taking into account the special needs of the children in the community served, and the appropriateness and adequacy of the existing titles held in stock. So, identifying children's reading needs, stock assessment and replacement, as well as stock promotion, will also be discussed. But first, why should the provision of fiction for children be seen as important?

Children are the adult readers of the future. If we accept that there is an 'apparent decline of the reading habit, particularly of the reading of literature' and we have a desire to counteract this social change so that 'in an increasingly materialistic society, values other than monetary ones must be upheld',[2] then the readers of the future need our special attention.

The Scottish Arts Council's *Readership report* points to smaller print-runs and the decline of bookshop sales in real terms since 1981 despite a national growth of outlets.[3] The report further draws upon the Young report, *Book retailing in the 1990s*,[4] which demonstrates that over the last seven years spending on books has declined in real terms, as has the number of purchasers. One can add to this that it has been found that just over 13% of 23-year-olds in Britain have some problem with reading, writing or basic arithmetic.[5]

Television, video and computer games are popular pastimes of the young, eating into the time which could be available for reading. These are also far less demanding than reading, especially when one is just beginning to acquire and practise reading skills, and can be seen as more entertaining than the readers' series still being used in many British schools to teach reading: 'TV is an easy alternative to reading books'; 'It is so tempting to watch TV instead of sitting down reading a book'; 'I don't like reading. I would rather watch videos.'[6] Television in particular absorbs a good deal of children's time, with the average child spending 19 hours viewing a week.[7]

A survey of pupils attending 22 secondary schools, including two independent schools, undertaken by the Scottish Arts Council, found that from 2,484 responses about 49% read books for pleasure more than one hour a week, while only 21% read for over three hours. Further, 17% of the pupils read books for pleasure less than one hour per week, while 28% did not read a book for this purpose during every week.[8]

In Britain more than half the population does not buy books, and library loans are, overall, declining,[9] whilst in the USA it is reported that 85% of adolescents cannot cope with a printed page unless their reading is accompanied by a background of electronic music.[10]

Children and adults should read fiction because it 'offers to the individual a unique, imaginative and pleasurable experience that cannot be obtained by other means':[11] 'I read more than I watch TV; I think because it is more like a little world of mine that I am "escaping" to in the book (it's more personal).'[12]

Indeed the reading of fiction can widen the child's world and bring the opportunity of experiencing both happenings and feelings which sometimes could be otherwise unobtainable. Fiction permits travel to other lands, including those in fantasy, and to other times. It enables the child to empathize with children from ages past, from other cultures and other social backgrounds. While non-fiction can describe and provide statistical data, fiction permits the reader to feel what it is or was like to experience through the books' characters emotions, beliefs and actions. Not only do such experiences create greater understanding, they can also provide an opportunity to experiment, to ask how one would respond to the same situation or circumstances.

However, it must also be remembered that reading fiction is an enjoyable means to developing reading skills – skills which are paramount if children are to be successful in education, in seeking employment, and in understanding and responding appropriately to the immense amount of written information whether on the printed page, billboard, tax form, TV screen and so forth. Reading fiction is also an aid to language development, in that it can help to extend skills required for expressing ideas and opinions, which have been formed through a wide experience of other people, times and cultures.

The benefits of reading are manifold: Spink demonstrates that it can assist physical, intellectual, language, emotional, social, moral, spiritual and personality development.[13] To extend his thesis it is interesting to note that he calls upon examples from fiction, but also demonstrates that not all fiction has the components or characteristics to assist such development to take place. Thus if children are to grow in understanding and skills the selectors of their books must be alert to these needs and identify materials which will meet them.

By introducing children to the delights which fiction holds we can develop an interest and satisfaction which they will wish to fulfil long into adulthood. Public libraries have an important role in not only providing this introduction but also in maintaining the interest once aroused. In the Scottish Arts Council's survey[14] of secondary pupils' pleasure reading it was found that public libraries were the most cited source for obtaining books, followed closely by school libraries. However, more than half of the respondents reported having difficulty in finding books that they like: 'I think the main reason for not reading more books is because you can hardly ever find one that you know you are going to like.' Two-thirds expressed a desire for help in selecting books: 'I think there should be more help in finding the right book to read, because I think it is hard to choose, especially in the public library.' A significant interest in owning fiction was also established, with 60% preferring to purchase fiction rather than non-fiction if given a book token: 'I prefer fiction books, mostly because they are usually set in places I have never been, or the people are doing things I have never done.'

Over the years many assumptions have been made concerning the influence books have on their readers, both of a positive and negative nature. There is empirical evidence that books may well transmit cultural norms, and writers themselves certainly believe in the power of books: 'It is just the literature we read ... for pleasure that may have the greatest, least suspected, earliest and most insidious influence upon us.'[15] 'The brain of a boy is flexible, still able to absorb. It can be twisted in any direction.'[16]

Of course fiction is not the only possible means of passing on social mores. Television, videos, parents, school friends and teachers all play a role to some greater or lesser degree. It is also argued that books are only markedly influential when they persistently reinforce one view, and that where there is diversity that one view does not take root.[17] Hence those selecting fiction for children must see their role as ensuring that the material children choose from their libraries reflects an honest, accurate and unbiased view of life. Further, these books should be so presented and promoted that they encourage children to read them and then add their own interpretation of the world, its people and happenings, so that they experience from other media, their family, teachers and peers.

Spink defines 'bad' books as including 'those that limit readers' expectations of themselves, and those that limit expectations of others, especially those of another ethnic background, religion, sex, or social class'.[18] He also defines the 'gloriously bad and the awfully bad', taking as examples 'collections of groan-producing puns and nonsensical jokes and riddles', and the 'mediocre' which 'does not offend, it is not controversial, and it does not challenge. It is respectable, comfortable, and bland'.[19] Whilst there are benefits to be derived from wide-ranging reading, which will include all qualities of reading – for how else can one determine one's preferences and develop skills of discrimination? – it is highly important that such wide reading includes the best and the very best. At a time when children, their parents and grandparents, have readily accessible to them, through the newsagent, supermarket and chain store, quantities of the poor and mediocre, it is of paramount importance that the school and public library also give them access to better-quality fiction: books which will appeal and reward, and to which the child reader will respond. Through providing a range of quality fiction the selector 'is helping to bring about discerning, entertained, and informed young readers: young people equipped and encouraged to evaluate and to question'.[20]

Librarians should be 'capable of critical well-informed and sophisticated criticism' of 'good' books.[21] But what is meant by a quality or good book? How do we know one when we see one? What are the ingredients which produce the desired response? Spink suggests that a good book provides information, it may help the reader to escape from daily concerns, it has to be meaningful and bring meaning to daily life, it should be essentially concerned with the truth, and by no means least it should be a good story.[22]

During this century, both in the USA and in Great Britain, librarians have sought to protect children from the harmful. The extent to which this has been reflected in the selection of fiction has mirrored public opinion of the time. Since the 1960s, renowned for their liberalism, publishers have produced materials which have attracted to them debate and controversy. Librarians have subsequently become involved in a debate as to their responsibility to reflect the real world as it exists, and yet at the same time meet the needs of adult society to protect children from certain kinds of knowledge.

Those employed in public libraries to select, maintain and promote children's fiction can only undertake these important functions adequately when they possess an accurate knowledge of their child communities and their reading interests and needs: 'The natural reading tastes of children are generally far removed from those of most reviewers of children's books. There is a vast difference between the glib, euphoric talk that is heard of the "new golden age of children's books" and the reality of the librarian faced with the infinite variety of children and the limitations of bookstock.'[23] So wrote Hill in 1973, and yet criticisms of adult reviewers recommending for children the books that appeal to them in the hope, sometimes misguided, that child readers share their interests and tastes are still heard today. However, it would be totally unfair to ignore the many librarians who not only select highly appropriate fiction for their child readers, but also play a part in encouraging publishers to produce more of the same.

Whatever the merits of the selection skills of many librarians, the debate concerning 'quality' literature (often an expression used for books that are 'dull, worthy, unattractive to children') has been an issue over a number of years on both sides of the Atlantic. It has been argued that it is not the role of the public library to supply 'rubbish' in order to provide popular appeal, but rather fiction which will develop children emotionally and intellectually. In Great Britain there has been a long-running controversy concerning the works of Enid Blyton, which despite their popularity with children have not only not been selected by some but also banned from other library authorities. This pro-quality movement has been criticized as being elitist, pandering to the needs of the intellectual child and at the same time deterring the poor and reluctant reader. Be this as it may, this debate has done little to promote the professional recognition of those librarians selecting for children. Whilst the 1980s have seen in many libraries a more liberal view of 'rubbish' and less attention drawn to the banning of books, the ill-feeling generated by the 'quality' issue has devalued the important and professional role of selecting fiction for children.

Even in the more liberal 1980s, however, an oft-posed question has been, what is the difference between selection and censorship? 'The problems of censorship and children's books have occupied hours of discussion at conferences and weekend schools or whenever children's librarians, authors and publishers get together. So why bring up the subject again?'[24] The problem here is marrying together the librarian's role in inculcating healthy social values and the rights to intellectual freedom. All librarians involved in the selection of fiction must decide on their selection aims and their rights to censor when appropriate. Librarians are in highly influential positions, not only by giving or restricting access to fiction but, due also to their purchasing power, they can influence what is published. The strength of this influence is further embodied in the formation of such groups as Librarians Against Racism and Fascism in Britain. Whether librarians should hold such influence has been questioned, particularly their right to interfere with publishers' editorial decisions and the freedom of authors. However, librarians see themselves as guardians of social values, unbiased by commercial concerns which are governed by market forces. But how can one guarantee that the values held by individual librarians are those which the community in general wishes to see promoted? The only safeguard is open policy and debate, especially concerning the more controversial matters.

The independence of librarians as public servants has produced further debate. It has been alleged that because local government has become more party political in Britain this is affecting the selection of materials in library services, which are responsible to their ruling political masters.[25] National government in Britain has become involved in the debate over the power of the librarian in promoting some materials and restricting access to others. Richard Luce, as the Minister with ultimate responsibility for libraries, criticized the equal opportunities lobby, saying that 'libraries must not become an ideological battleground' concerned with the banning of racist or sexist materials.[26] Kenneth Baker, when Secretary of State for Education, further opposed the Inner London Education Authority's book selection guidelines because he considered them as coming 'very close to imposing thought control in London schools'.[27] As well as opening up the debate concerning the power of librarians and their library committees in influencing what their communities – including children – read, these and other such statements have illustrated that opinion concerning the social values which should be promoted are diverse, thus complicating further the responsibilities of those librarians aiming to select fiction for the children of their communities.

Working in direct contact with children, observing their choice of books and talking to them about what they look for in a good read, are essential to building up a knowledge against which intelligent decisions concerning the selection of fiction can be made. Further knowledge is obtained from intimate acquaintance with the fiction stock of the library, monitoring its use and identifying gaps, as well as titles which have proved popular and those which sit on the shelves. In this way the librarian, like the retailer, identifies successful lines but can also begin to analyse what it is about the less popular material that does not appeal and to assess whether there is a need for targeted promotion to bring the book to the notice of its intended readership. However, it must always be remembered that as with adult readers we cannot expect all children's books, even those we have knowledgeably selected, to appeal to all children. For example, Tucker has discovered that the same book can have 'an almost electrifying effect' on some children whilst for others it has none at all.[28]

Despite Hill as long ago as 1973 stating that a 'clear-cut book selection policy is essential',[29] the report of the results of the Schools' and children's libraries survey 1987–8, concerned with school library support services and public libraries, shows that in answer to the question 'Is there a written policy for stock selection for children?' there were 17 affirmative and 18 negative replies from shire counties, 7 affirmative and 22 negative replies from the London boroughs, 12 affirmative and 21 negative replies from the metropolitan boroughs, and 1 affirmative and 11 negative replies from Wales.[30]

According to Spink,[31] in order for a library to promote and support children's reading it is essential for there to be a collection policy, which has been discussed, formulated and publicized. This policy should cover:

1 The aims and objectives of the collection, which provide an understanding of what is to be achieved by the collection in light of the community's reading needs, together with clarification as to the priorities of provision, so essential when budgets are limited.
2 The scope of the collection, for example the languages, formats and levels to be provided.
3 Decisions concerning controversial subjects such as sexual and ethnic stereotyping.
4 An impartial and fair statement concerning gifts and how these should be handled.
5 The selection procedure and criteria, in order to demonstrate that selection is carried out in a controlled, systematic and consistent way.
6 The procedure for maintaining the collection, to include 'weeding', replacement and binding.

Spink draws particular attention to the complexity of selection criteria and the difficulty of applying long lists of criteria to any single item. Further, he feels that many sets of criteria 'while they invest-

igate such details as . . . style, plot, and characterization, . . . fail
to ask the fundamental questions: What is the item attempting to
do? . . . Is what it is attempting to do relevant to the needs of our
particular group of young people? . . . Is there evidence that it is
likely to succeed in its aim?'[32]

The fact that fiction is read subjectively presents further evaluation
problems, according to Spink,[33] who recommends Larkin's personal
set of criteria produced when he was involved with the Booker
award in 1977:

- Could I read it?
- If I could read it, did I believe it?
- If I believed it, did I care about it?
- And if I cared about it, what was the quality of my caring, and
  would it last?[34]

As his final statement on collection building Spink suggests that
'most materials select themselves' and that 'Exciting books like
Anthony Browne's *Gorilla* . . . cry out for acquisition, while poor
and mediocre materials cause more shrugging of the selector's
shoulders'.[35] However there is the danger here that because a title
strongly recommends itself to the adult selector, the appeal that it
will have to children could be badly misconceived: 'Book selection
involves decision making. No one can opt out. Books on the shelves
of any library reveal something of the ideas or lack of ideas behind
the selection.'[36]

While a selection policy provides guidance, by the very nature
of its flexibility, it also does not take away the responsibility for
selection from the librarian. Decisions have still to be made, and
for positive selection to take place the selector must have a sound
knowledge of readership and its needs together with informed and
carefully considered views on the provision of children's fiction:
'Group discussion about books can be extremely valuable. In any
library system there are bound to be some staff with longer
experience than others, as well as some with a surer instinct for
selecting books; yet others will have been given a better groundwork
in book selection during their time at library school.'[37]

During 1989 case studies were undertaken in order to examine
in detail the nature of selection policies and the implementation of
selection in five English library authorities.[38] The case studies
involved a London borough (A), a Midlands metropolitan borough
covering a large city (B), a Northern city metropolitan borough (C),
a Midlands shire county (D), and a large county authority covering
an area from the Midlands towards the South West (E).

Three of the five library authorities have drawn up selection policy statements (A, B, D). These statements comprise two main sections, each with very different functions. The first section states the aims and principles of stock selection for the library service whilst the second deals with the practical procedures by which these are to be realized. The practical procedures in the documents for A and B concentrate entirely on book assessment criteria: case study authority D uses this second section to describe desirable collection management procedures as well as assessment procedures, including not only assessment criteria but also stock maintenance, performance measures and budget control.

It was found that although each library authority phrased its aims in a unique way, these aims are markedly similar, as Table 4.1 shows.

The library authority designated as case study C is divided into four areas which act independently of one another as far as stock selection is concerned, and no overall policy exists. However, at the time of the research, this authority had established a working party to compile a selection policy. Both case studies C and E considered that a policy would be a valuable asset, and it was noted by the researcher that selection procedures and collection management were far more haphazard and lacking in control than in the three authorities with formalized policies.

An examination of the selection criteria for the case study authorities with selection policies found that all stress that stereotypes should be avoided, and that characters, settings and illustrations should all be realistic. Accuracy, and reflecting the diversity of the multicultural society, would appear to be the primary aim of policies for case study authorities A and D. The policy for case study D particularly stressed that the story line should still be seen as paramount here, and that books should not be seen purely as vehicles for a specific point of view. However, positive attempts to deal with issues such as prejudice, rather than to evade them, are actively to be looked for according to the selection policy for case study A.

A problem can exist where selection criteria take the form of a checklist rather than an advisory document, such as in the case studies A and D. Here it is assumed that definitions and limitations have been established, and that the selectors can recognize both good and bad qualities in books. During the research this difficulty was highlighted when library authority C quoted a fiction title as a good example of a multi-cultural book which avoided stereotypes and portrayed black characters in a positive way; however, case study A cited the very same title as an appalling example of stereotyping. Despite both authorities striving to avoid racist stereotyping individual selectors were using different criteria and standards.

**Table 4.1 Comparison of aims of case study selection policies**

| Aims | Case study A | B | D |
|---|:---:|:---:|:---:|
| Encouraging the enjoyment of reading | * | * | * |
| Encouraging library use | | * | |
| Promoting intellectual development | * | * | * |
| Promoting emotional development | | | * |
| Helping children to grow into adult readers | | | * |
| Improve reading/language skills | | * | * |
| Help children acquire basic learning skills | | * | |
| Provide as full a range as possible to meet the needs of all age ranges and abilities | * | * | * |
| Fulfil information needs | * | | * |
| Fulfil recreation needs | * | | * |
| Fulfil educational needs | * | | * |
| Fulfil cultural needs | | | * |
| Serve the local community | * | * | * |
| Combat bias in books and the library collection | * | | |
| Offer a balanced view of society | * | * | * |
| Exclude books which offend against the law | * | | |
| Work with community publishers | * | | |
| Support useful but non-commercial titles | * | | |
| Update and assess the collection | * | | |

Note: the aims have not been quoted verbatim but the meaning of each has been extracted to make comparison possible.

This diversity of opinion is also evident in opinions concerning the *Asterix* series, which relies on cultural stereotyping for its humour. Case study authorities A, B and C excluded this series from their stocks because of these stereotypes; however, many other library authorities do select these for their shelves, as evidenced by the Public Lending Right figures for 1986–7, which contain 16 *Asterix* titles in the top 100 issued from the public libraries monitored.[39]

Selection policies, however adequate, cannot be fulfilled without appropriate selection procedures. The purpose of these procedures is to provide the opportunity to assess and order materials as efficiently and as effectively as possible. The following selection procedures are followed by the case study authorities.

### Case study A (Figure 4.1)

Collections of approval copies are received from a number of suppliers at either two- or four-weekly intervals. Pre-selection then takes place, with the young people's services librarian compiling details of the number of reprints and comparing new titles with those already stocked. The books are divided into two categories: those which merit further discussion and those about which a decision can be made immediately. Some of the titles requiring further assessment are sent for review, whilst other more questionable titles are first considered by those attending the selection meetings. These selection meetings comprise representative children's library specialists from each area of the library authority, and not only consider the titles which require further assessment, but also those which have been reviewed following pre-selection. Only certain categories of books are reviewed, for example, those dealing with controversial subjects, first novels, TV tie-ins. All titles agreed as meeting the selection criteria of the library authority are purchased and placed in a pool of stock from which area librarians can select. Where titles are assessed as possible purchases, these are only selected if an area has a particular need.

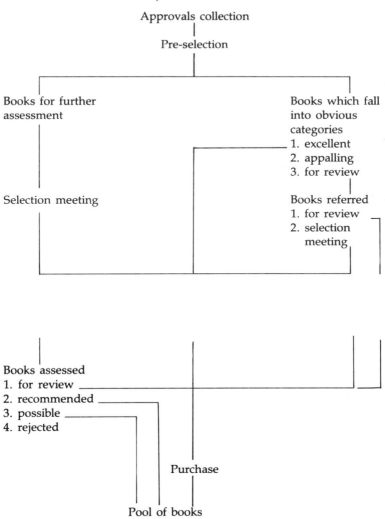

**Fig. 4.1 Case study A: selection procedure**

**Case study B** (Figure 4.2)

Books are received on approval and pre-selection is undertaken by a senior children's library service specialist. Following the rejection of certain titles, all of the remaining new books and reprints of books published before 1984 are sent for review. There are 100 reviewers, comprising professional and non-professional staff. Once a month the children's book panel meets. This panel consists of four members from each children's team of librarians, a representative from each of the four regions, the head of services for children and young people and her deputy. The reviews are checked at this meeting, controversial materials are discussed, and decisions made. A selection day is then held, during which branch librarians have complete freedom of choice, even from those titles rejected by the children's book panel, although such a decision has first to be discussed with the head of services for children and young people. Reprints of post-1984 titles are also available at this meeting. It is interesting to note that books specifically for ethnic minorities are selected quite autonomously from this procedure by the ethnic minorities librarian.

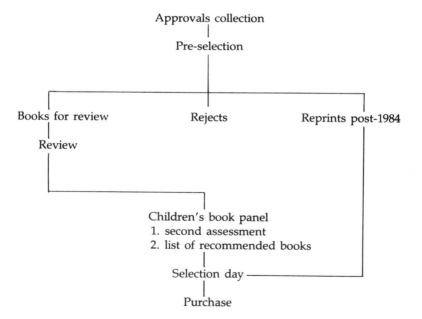

**Fig. 4.2  Case study B: selection procedure**

***Case study C*** (Figure 4.3)
Books are received on approval by each of this authority's four areas and presented at monthly selection meetings. These area meetings are attended by the librarians in the children's library services team, area team leaders and other interested parties, such as local teachers. The meetings usually comprise about 17 people. The books are divided into categories, for example 'board books', 'ten-plus', 'teens', 'easy readers', and each category is dealt with in turn. Each person is allocated a pile of books to examine, and assessment and discussion takes place. There is no reviewing system. Team librarians are able to place orders for those materials which are recommended.

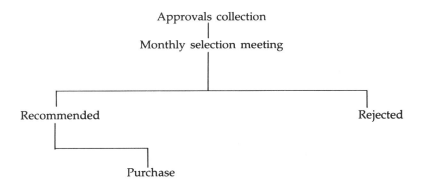

**Fig. 4.3  Case study C: selection procedure**

***Case study D*** (Figure 4.4)
Each division of this library authority receives a monthly approvals collection, which it is responsible for reviewing. A pre-selection meeting is held and approximately half of each division's children's team of librarians will attend. The books are inspected, reviews checked and tentative orders are placed. An inter-divisional coordination meeting follows at which senior staff check through the provisional orders, discuss controversial choices, check the range of titles each division has selected and place final orders.

Approvals collection
|
Reviews
|
Pre-selection meeting
|
Coordination meeting
|
Purchase

**Fig. 4.4  Case study D: selection procedure**

*Case study E* (Figure 4.5)
Books are received on approval and left on display for two weeks,
or from their time of arrival, up to the next selection meeting. This
meeting is held every two weeks and is attended by the staff of
the school library support service. A list of recommended books
is produced and circulated so that orders can be made.

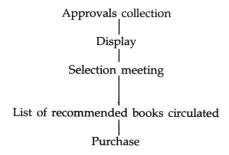

Approvals collection
|
Display
|
Selection meeting
|
List of recommended books circulated
|
Purchase

**Fig. 4.5  Case study E: selection procedure**

From these descriptions it can be seen that each library authority
has developed unique selection procedures; however, it can also
be seen that the different procedures can be placed into one of two
groups: either as a procedure involving reviewing of the books or
one that does not. A reviewing procedure should permit assessment
based upon a thorough knowledge of the text and against laid-down
criteria. Where forms are used, as in case study authorities B and

D, the reviews are standardized and the reviewers are steered towards producing comparable reviews. It can be said that the case study authorities not using reviewing as part of their selection procedure, C and E, do save a lot of staff time but in so doing have a far less thorough approach to selection. However, a complaint of case study authorities A and B, both using reviewing as part of their procedure, was that titles could be out of print by the time the selection process had been completed and orders placed. Further, the length of time it takes new titles to reach the shelves could be an irritation to library users, and case study authority B noted that the majority of requests was for books that were 'bogged down' in the selection process.

Case study authority E had tried to introduce a review procedure on two past occasions only to find that being a large library authority with isolated service points and an infrequent delivery service made it well nigh impossible to meet selection meeting deadlines.

Administering a review scheme is also time consuming, as well as costly, as books have to be allocated and distributed, and tardy reviewers chased up.

Those authorities in the case studies which operated a review scheme had attempted to overcome its in-built disadvantages. Authority A severely limited the number of books sent for review, and authority B used the pre-review selection stage to eliminate totally inadequate items. Authority D spread the load by sharing approvals and reviews between the divisions. Whilst authorities C and E saved a considerable amount of time and effort by eliminating the review stage, as already stated this was undoubtedly at the expense of thoroughness.

When examining selection procedures it is noticeable that they are concerned almost entirely with the selection of individual titles rather than with the building of a library collection. In the case studies the actual purchase of titles is left almost entirely to branch or area librarians, with only authority D examining the purchasing trends of each division at a further meeting. Yet it should be fundamental that the collection as a whole is properly planned, and coordination of stock purchasing should permit effective collection building at authority level: 'Anyone who is ever satisfied either with the methods of selection or the stock on the shelves must have limited goals. Book selection should always be a case of striving for perfection, but also knowing that it will never be achieved. Whatever the book selection policy there will be paradoxes which it is never possible to completely resolve.'[40]

Whilst a great deal of time and attention can go into the selection of new titles, it is equally important to ensure that existing stocks are revised. Stock revision should be a continuous exercise. As Hill has written: 'The bulk of replacements in a children's library require [sic] no more skill than that of the supermarket manager who ensures that certain brands of coffee and soup and a varied selection of cheeses are always available.'[41]

However, is it this straightforward? Although the librarian must consider that children are being born all of the time and new child readers can be entering the library each day, and that these children must be given the opportunity to read widely from the old as well as the new, 'The fact that a book has been previously in stock is never sufficient justification for buying again, but those books which are proven and good should be replaced in quantity.'[42] Here again we see the need for a knowledge of not only the use being made of existing stock, but also the nature of the community the library serves, its sociological changes and how these pertain to the child population. But wider issues must also be taken into account, such as those relating to social mores and ideological trends, which affect how acceptable a specific title is today, rather than how acceptable it was when first published. The selection of new books is not therefore all-important: careful consideration must also be given to stock appraisal and stock maintenance.

Replacements are essential in maintaining a children's fiction collection. Visits to bookshops and library suppliers provide librarians with the opportunity to replace worn out or lost copies of popular titles. Whilst such retrospective purchasing is a necessary part of the selection procedure, publishers are geared up to the publication of new titles and short print-runs, which bedevil even the selection of new titles and inevitably affect the effectiveness of replacing fiction previously stocked.

Referring again to the case studies undertaken by Blenkin[43] one can obtain some understanding of the practicalities of stock replacement. Case study authority A undertakes stock assessment in theory, but the high number of staff vacancies does not always make it possible. Efforts are made to obtain reports as to the effectiveness of stock from users such as playgroups, and the young people's service librarian visits a library in each area once a month and assesses the needs of a particular section of the stock. This assessment considers which titles to withdraw, replace or promote.

In case study authority B a sum of money is set aside each year for stock revision. Stock editing is undertaken by branch librarians, and the reassessment of individual titles is made centrally. Children's librarians in case study authority C plan a programme of retrospective stock maintenance sessions to be undertaken over 12 months. A day is allocated to each branch library and several librarians work together.

The selection policy for case study authority D contains sections about the maintenance of collections and stock revision. A core fiction list has also been drawn up to aid the checking of fiction provision. The teams of children's librarians are expected to organize stock assessment and to make time to examine each area of stock over the year. In addition the senior librarians make an annual visit to each library to undertake a stock edit, and to produce a stock plan which identifies priorities and indicates future developments. Stock revision is continuous at each branch library in the authority which formed case study E. Stock revision, like assessment, is monitored by the children's librarian in each group, but it is the branch librarians who actually organize stock revision, as these are seen to be those most in tune with community needs.

The purchase of both old and new titles should be dependent on overall stock control. Whilst stock revision can ensure the withdrawal or promotion of little-read material and the replacement of lost or worn fiction, it can also provide much of the knowledge required for the selection of new titles. Stock purchase should not be seen as purely based upon the assessment and selection of individual titles, but grounded in an understanding of community needs and the adequacy of the existing fiction collection.

Having ensured that there is appropriate collection management, incorporating a selection policy and new title and existing stock assessment, which will provide fiction to meet the reading needs of the children in the community, the librarian must then face the issue of seeing that this fiction is promoted to its young readership. Addressing the wider issue of promoting reading Spink recommends that: 'Before rushing into a range of activities, an expenditure of staff time and materials, and of children's energies and colleagues' toleration, it is necessary to have a strategy for the promotion of reading.'[44] Such a strategy he states requires clarification of what is meant by reading, what can be achieved both in the long and short term, and the range of possible means of achievement – bearing in mind cost, availability of materials, expertise, accommodation and equipment. A policy statement, based upon consultation with the community's young people and their carers, should form the basis of a plan of action.

The Schools' and Children's Libraries Survey of 1987–8[45] was concerned with school library support services and children's public libraries, but did not enquire as to whether such policies existed. There was, however, a question which asked whether regular activities or services are used to promote children's reading through public libraries, and the survey listed a number of book-orientated activities, which one assumes include fiction even if this is not specified. Those library services answering in the affirmative were as shown in Table 4.2.

**Table 4.2 Incidence of regular promotional activities/services**

|  | Shire counties (35) | London boroughs (29) | Metropolitan boroughs (33) | Wales (12) |
|---|---|---|---|---|
| Bookbuses | 11 | 4 | 8 | 11 |
| Storytelling | 32 | 29 | 32 | 9 |
| Children's bookweeks | 28 | 19 | 28 | 11 |
| Parents' meetings* | 16 | 8 | 13 | 3 |
| School holiday events | 34 | 29 | 32 | 11 |
| Reading lists | 30 | 22 | 25 | 7 |
| Book marks and publicity materials | 28 | 23 | 29 | 11 |

* It is assumed that these meetings are aimed at encouraging children to read and that fiction is included.

Hence it can be seen that whilst many types of promotion take place, and that many of these can be assumed to be partially if not wholly promoting fiction, there are many gaps in provision. The reasons for these could be many, but no doubt include the inadequacy of staff numbers, a problem which also limited selection procedures in the case studies referred to above. It is true to say that staffing has been badly affected by the attempts of local authorities in Britain to reduce public spending, in line with national government strategy. However, even when staffing is inadequately provided for, priority should be given to the young readers of today – the adult readers of tomorrow – who must be equipped to guide or be decision makers in matters concerning future society, in a knowing and caring way. As argued at the beginning of this chapter the reading of fiction has far-reaching influences upon the young, and its provision and promotion should therefore be seen as an important issue for all public librarians.

### References
1  Hill, J., *Children are people: the librarian in the community*, London, Hamish Hamilton, 1973, 103.
2  Keaney, D., Preface to: Working Party of the Literature Committee of the Scottish Arts Council, *Readership report*, Edinburgh, Scottish Arts Council, 1989, vii.

3 Working Party of the Literature Committee of the Scottish Arts Council, *Readership report*, Edinburgh, Scottish Arts Council, 1989, 4.
4 Young, A., *Book retailing in the 1990s*, London, Booksellers Association, 1987.
5 National Child Development Study reported in *The Times higher education supplement*, 897, 12 January 1990, 8.
6 Two quotations from secondary school pupils quoted in Working Party of the Literature Committee of the Scottish Arts Council, *Readership report*, 5.
7 Central Statistical Office, *Social trends 19*, London, HMSO, 1989.
8 Working Party of the Literature Committee of the Scottish Arts Council, *Readership report*, 12.
9 Ibid.
10 Steiner, G., 'The end of bookishness', *The Times literary supplement*, 8–14 July 1988.
11 Working Party of the Literature Committee of the Scottish Arts Council, *Readership report*, 6.
12 Secondary school pupil quoted in Working Party of the Literature Committee of the Scottish Arts Council, *Readership report*, 7.
13 Spink, J., *Children as readers: a study*, London, Clive Bingley, 1989, 29–43.
14 Working Party of the Literature Committee of the Scottish Arts Council, *Readership report*, 13–14, 18.
15 Eliot, G., quoted in Stanek, L. W., 'Real people, real books', in Lenz, M. and Mahood, R. (compilers), *Young adult literature: background and criticism*, Chicago, American Library Association, 1980, 50.
16 Johns, W. E., quoted in Milner, D., *Children and race, ten years on*, London, Ward Lock Educational, 1983, 84.
17 Tucker, N., *The child and the book: a psychological and literary exploration*, Cambridge, Cambridge University Press, 1981, 175.
18 Spink, J., 81.
19 Ibid., 81–2.
20 Ibid., 82.
21 Hill, J., 12.
22 Spink, J., 73–5.
23 Hill, J., 12.
24 Johnson, G., 'Silent pressures', *Library Association record*, **82** (10), 1980, 481.
25 Usherwood, B., 'The elected member and the library: learning from the literature', *Public library journal*, **2** (5), 1987, 72–4.
26 Luce, R., quoted in 'Balancing act', *Assistant librarian*, **79** (11), 1986, 149.
27 Baker, K., quoted in 'Balancing act', *Assistant librarian*, **79** (11), 1986, 149.
28 Tucker, N., 186.

29 Hill, J., 103.
30 Donoghue, M. (compiler), *Schools' and children's libraries in England and Wales*, Loughborough, AMDECL, SOCCEL, LISU, 1989, 12 – 13.
31 Spink, J., 99 – 101.
32 Ibid., 102.
33 Ibid., 103.
34 Larkin, P., *Required writing: miscellaneous pieces, 1955 – 1982*, London, Faber and Faber, 1983.
35 Spink, J., 103.
36 Hill, J., 103.
37 Ibid., 105 – 6.
38 Blenkin, S., 'Moulding the mind: book selection for children and young people', unpublished MA dissertation, Loughborough University, Department of Library and Information Studies, 1989.
39 Sumsion, J., *Public Lending Right in practice: a report to the advisory committee*, Stockton-on-Tees, Registrar of the Public Lending Right, 1988, 148.
40 Hill, J., 106 – 7.
41 Ibid., 108.
42 Ibid., 112.
43 Blenkin, S.
44 Spink, J., 97.
45 Donoghue, M.
46 Ibid., 16 – 17.

# 5 Serving young adults with fiction

*Karen Nelson Hoyle*

Serving young adults with fiction effectively necessitates integrating library services to young adults with the selection of appropriate fiction for their needs. During the last three decades specialization in library services and in the fiction published for young adults have both increased and gained in visibility.

In this chapter these two aspects of the development of library service for young adults will be considered. Much of the discussion will centre on the American situation; however, many of the examples of practice are of relevance on both sides of the Atlantic. Teen culture now spans both British and American societies and the needs of young adults are common to both.

## Definitions
In American society, the term 'young adult', has superseded the designations 'adolescent' or 'young people'. Perceived as bridging the years between childhood and adulthood, these 'young adults' and their literature do, however, frequently evoke dismay. First of all, experts disagree about the age-range of this group. Donelsen and Nilsen, the authors of *Literature for today's young adults*, consider they comprise junior and high school pupils, aged from 12 to 18, but they also extend the category to those 'still finding their way into adult reading'.[1] Moreover, they point out that the Educational Resources Information Clearinghouse (ERIC) defines them as being aged from 18 to 22, while the National Assessment of Educational Progress (NAEP) uses ages between 21 and 25.[2] Even within the American Library Association (ALA) there is contradiction. One youth division considers the parameter to be age 12, while another places it at age 13. There is, therefore, before beginning to look in any depth at library provision for young adults, a problem of definition. The concept of the young adult is not fixed and immutable.

**Professional organizations and education**
Historically, the ALA served older youth within its Division of
Libraries for Children and Young People. This organization con-
tained three sub units, namely Library Work with Children, the
Young People's Reading Round Table and the American Association
of School Libraries (AASL). The first schism was with school
librarians and the second with youth librarians. AASL created its
own organizational entity, becoming independent within the ALA
in 1957, while the Young Adult Services Division (YASD) became
an independent division within the ALA in 1957. In Britain there is
a similar division between the Youth Libraries and School Libraries
Groups of the Library Association, with the School Library
Association comprising a further, separate organization.

Currently, individual and organization members of the
Association for Library Service to Children division (ALSC) number
about 3,500, and the YASD numbers about 2,500. However, the
two divisions communicate and plan jointly on many projects and
together they publish the *Journal of youth services in libraries*.
Beginning with the Fall 1989 issue this became a refereed or 'juried'
journal, for at least the following three years.

The AASL division now numbers around 7,000 organization and
personal members and publishes its quarterly journal, *School library
media quarterly*. This division also sponsors and cooperates in many
arenas with one or two of the other youth divisions. Debate on
issues also occurs in journals such as *School librarian, School library
journal* (a Bowker publication edited by Lillian Gerhardt), *Emergency
librarian* and *Voice of youth advocates*, founded by Mary K. Chelton
and Dorothy M. Broderick, and now published by Scarecrow Press.
Professional interest in and support for work with young adults is
therefore lively and multifarious, despite the fragmentation into
these varied professional groups.

The training and certification of school and public librarians varies
between the sectors in the USA. Many school librarians attend
teacher-training institutions; they must be certified as teachers, and
they run 'school media programs'. In contrast, public librarians
attending an accredited library school must have a liberal arts
undergraduate degree. Moreover, in preparing librarians, adolescent
literature may be taught in several subject disciplines in colleges –
in Education, English or Library Science.

In some schools, the librarian for young adults supervises the
textbook room, audiovisual equipment and materials, and
computers. Textbooks and multiple copies of paperbacks enhance
the classroom opportunities for group reading and discussion.
Computers, computer literacy and software are now viewed as

extensions of the traditional book in the classroom and also therefore fall within the job description/purview of school librarians. This obviously has implications for the professional education of librarians working with youth in schools.

The best librarians in both the public and education sectors continue their professional education by reading and discussing the newest research findings in their fields as they are released. Ken Haycock has summarized the implications for professional practice resulting from research in teacher librarianship.[3] However, because there is a significant time-lag before the publication of research findings, librarians must participate in an 'invisible university' by communicating with people directly through correspondence and by attending conferences. Another activity undertaken by librarians is that of identifying areas for research and conveying these needs directly to academics in the field of library science.

**Young adult library users**
A survey published in 1988, *Services and resources for young adults and public libraries*, received widespread attention. The findings revealed that only half of the public libraries working with young adults cooperated in working with schools during 1986–7. In terms of staff, while a surprising 25% of the library patrons were aged between 12 and 18, only 11% of America's public libraries designated full-time staff for young adults: generalists (45%), adult librarians (22%), children's librarians (12%), or others, served the remaining population. (It should be added that this emphasis on public library generalism was also found by Helen Pain-Lewins in her survey of the education and training of public librarians working with children and teenagers in the UK.)[4] Moreover, while 84% of the reporting librarians had a designated youth collection, young adult patrons used the readers' advisory services for an equal balance of 'independent' and 'school-related' needs.[5] Chelton, who participated in the planning and report of the Fast Response Survey System, commented on this document in her essay, 'The first national survey of services and resources for young adults in public libraries'.[6] She concluded that despite librarians submitting the responses subjectively, the evidence nevertheless showed that while young adults form one-quarter of library users, they are being under-served – and by generalists rather than specialist librarians. Furthermore, there was a lack of inter-agency cooperation.

**Services to young adults**
Two agencies – school libraries and public libraries – serve the young adult in similar but distinct ways. Historically, school libraries

have supported the curriculum and responded to class assignments, while public libraries have responded to recreational reading needs; however, this distinction has become blurred. Nowadays a teacher may assign a choice of a work of fiction on a curriculum topic to enhance the knowledge of the student; or students may seek such books on their own. American teenagers can often enhance their school grades or get extra credit for an outside reading assignment related to the class assignment, and discussion. For example, a teacher might suggest reading 'a Russian novel' to support further a study unit on the USSR. According to the survey cited above, adolescents use both kinds of libraries for their information needs and for fiction reading.

School and public librarians assess their need for professional growth in developing services in guidelines and evaluation. Prepared jointly by the AASL and the Association for Educational Communications and Technology, *Information power: guidelines for school library media programs* is already in the process of being updated and evaluated.[7] In addition, *Competencies for young adult librarians* monitors and promotes quality control.[8]

Inter-agency cooperation becomes more imperative as resources dwindle and the duplication of collections becomes impossible. School and public librarians can become interdependent in their services and materials, so that when a teacher assigns a topic to students both school and public librarians will serve the clientele and each of the collections will be utilized. Networking may even extend out to the regions, to acquire adequate service and books.

**Promotion of reading**
School and public librarians promote fiction reading by providing access to the collections, by designating enticing locations and multiple formats, as well as involving teenagers, and by giving book talks and encouraging family reading.

Behind the scenes, librarians make a difference. They can aid fiction accessibility by assigning suitable subject headings, providing a card catalogue, or ensuring that an online system is easy to use, and locating the items in an inviting place within the library. These 'secret gifts' enable the young adult to gain access to the collection independently of the librarian. However, subject headings must be meaningful to the teenager; librarians can add relevant headings, while still conforming to current library practice. The provision of such subject headings and online access through computers facilitates a privacy which some students had previously lacked. An important point is that the equipment must be easy to use independently – a teenager can manipulate a computerized subject access far longer than a librarian can be patient. Also, the fiction books themselves need to be appropriately located, in a position attractive to the teens. Young adults resist the children's area, but may not yet feel welcome in the adult section, hence some public libraries inter-shelve young adult and adult fiction, while others create separate shelves.

Paperbacks attract some young adults, with their convenient pocket size and weight, and these extend the library budget. The Saint Paul (Minnesota) Public Library, for example, spends 70% of its young adult materials budget on paperbacks. The paperback revolution has made its impact on adolescent classroom reading assignments, for a whole class may read the same classic, like Mark Twain's *Adventures of Tom Sawyer*. Carousels of paperback books for young adults became a symbolic gesture of friendship from libraries.

One of the basic services from libraries is a first-hand knowledge of young adult literature. However, an occupational hazard for librarians who order, catalogue, recommend and handle books during their professional day is to neglect to read them. As we also read in Chapter 4, which considered the UK situation, selection procedures differ between library systems. Some libraries receive advance copies and designate a book selector, while other libraries favour committee discussion and selection. Unfortunately, some libraries order only on the basis of reviewing media, not from a first-hand examination of the books themselves.

Recommended booklists range from those produced by library organizations to lists by local systems, which prepare annual or occasional recommended booklists intended for youth. A YASD elected and appointed Best Books for Young Adults Committee, comprising 15 librarians, reads hundreds of books published during an assigned year. They correspond and then develop a list to discuss at the ALA midwinter meeting, and at this meeting select and annotate a list of adult and teenage 'Best books for young adults' from the previous year's publications. In 1988, 68 books appeared on the YASD list, which is published and then widely disseminated. YASD considers their 'Best books' selection so significant and powerful that yet another committee evaluates the policies and procedures governing the Committee. Furthermore, the YASD published *Nothin' but the best*, a selection of the best of the best books for young adults published between 1966 and 1986.

In the UK, the School Library Association published a similar listing, Jessica Yates' *Teenager to young adult: recent paperback fiction for 13 to 19 years*.[9] Annotations summarize the plot and provide a judgement on the quality of the books and their intended readership. In addition, Keith Barker selected books published in the USA and UK between 1954 and 1986 in his *Bridging the gap*[10] – books that ranged from Ray Bradbury's science fiction novel *Fahrenheit 451*[11] to Aidan Chambers' *Breaktime*.[12] As with the Book Trust's listing of *Children's books of the year* and the *Signal* guides, the emphasis in the UK is on individuals' choices, rather than selection by organizations.

In the USA, area groups and local libraries also publish booklists. The Association of Children's Librarians of Northern California includes young adult books among the reviews in *Bay views: a journal of book reviews and opinions with a Western perspective*.

Some librarians also invite young adults to participate in both the selection and marketing of books, thereby promoting reading. A young adult librarian in Connecticut provides a model for action. She focuses on two motivators: expanding the young adult paperback collection and founding a Youth Review Board. The seventh, eighth and ninth graders (approximate ages 12–18) read and evaluate books, place 'gold seals' on those they deem outstanding, and compile and annotate bibliographies for distribution to their peers. The public librarian not only organizes the group so that they can critically discuss books, she also interacts with the school librarian in all such events as a 'read-in'.[13]

Recent monographs and current journal articles highlight specific aspects of interactive service and selection techniques for the public librarian, such as book talks and family reading. Finding time to talk about a particular book to an individual young adult can be effective, but unfortunately this is a luxury. Book talks to an audience, such as a class, are a more efficient means of conveying information about the plot, characters, setting and mood, and eliciting the emotional reaction to a reading experience. A public librarian's appearance at a school reinforces the importance of reading and books. If possible, the books themselves should accompany the speaker, but book jackets or distributed booklists can be an acceptable compromise. One librarian describes her experience in 'Booktalking science fiction to young adults'.[14] Family reading experiences can continue into adulthood – a concept which librarians have nurtured for years. Jim Trelease extended the notion to a broader public with a book, travelling lectures and television appearances during the last decade. Television programmes based on young adult fiction increasingly move in a circuit including the UK, USA, Canada and Australia, but movies and television no longer threaten librarians, for the readership of a title increases following media exposure.

## Selection of fiction for young adults

A relatively recent development from the children's or adult literature field – the youth novel – is among the most exciting genres in current production. However, American publishers alone produce one thousand titles per year earmarked for the teen market. Selection of the appropriate books, choosing with both content and form in mind, must precede the service with books.

### Collection development and selection policy

Collection development and selection policies follow a pattern in the USA, with slight variations from library to library. Hennepin County Library (Minnesota), for example, developed a 'materials selection policy' which lacks differentiation between children's, young adult and adult materials. The Library Board reviews this at least semi-annually. As with most policies, a firm statement upholds the premise that the selection of materials does not constitute an endorsement of its contents; responsibility for use by children (and by implication, young adults) rests with parents or legal guardians. In order to avoid duplicating school and college collections, the library excludes textbooks and curriculum-related materials unless they are appropriate for the general public.[15]

Written selection policy and procedure statements endorsed by governing authorities prevent most of the potential censorship problems. A school administrator's view, expressed in *Censorship and selection: issues and answers for schools*,[16] is as appropriate for public as for school librarians. The author addresses the broad rights of intellectual freedom and specifically targets the issues of sex, language, secular humanism, witchcraft, internationalism, creationism and politics. On a practical level, the appendices include forms for complaints and samples of correspondence. A further helpful guide to the practical problems of dealing with sensitive issues in young adult books has been published by YASD; their *Hit list: frequently challenged young adult titles* (1989), describes 20 titles that have been frequently challenged.

Librarians should be aware of both the traditional selection tools, including standard texts, and the up-to-date journals and awards that indicate the trends in library taste. One standard text is Donelson and Nilsen's *Literature for today's young adults*, now in its third edition. This book follows 20 years on in the footsteps of Carlsen's landmark, *Books and the teenage reader*, which was sponsored by the National Book Committee and endorsed by three major professional organizations – the American Library Association, the International Reading Association and the National Council of Teachers of English.[17] Carlsen alerted teachers, librarians and parents to the wide range of reading for teenagers, including the adolescent novel, popular adult books, sub-literature and classics. Donelsen and Nilsen expand on these literary topics and add others, such as the 'literary aspects of young adult books', new realism, old romanticism, suspense including mysteries and Westerns, and fantasy. They also deal with aspects of evaluation, selection, relationships with the media, censorship, and provide a historic overview. A practical 'Appendix A' proposed an 'honor sampling' of outstanding books, charted with title, author, hardbound and paper publisher, genre, sex of protagonist, age, total pages, media (TV or movie), edition and ethnic group or unusual setting.[18]

Contemporary reviews of books appropriate for young adults appear in weekly, monthly and annual reviewing media, and librarians need to educate themselves on how each journal operates its reviewing selection. Some books are assigned to single reviewers, while other books are juried by a committee. Reviewing media in the USA include *The ALAN review, English journal, Horn book*, and the *Horn book guide to children's and young adult books, New York Times book review*, and journals mentioned elsewhere in this chapter and in the notes. In the UK reviews of young adult books appear in *The school librarian, Books for keeps, Growing point, Junior bookshelf* and *The Times educational supplement*, amongst a range of varied reviewing media.

After years of concern in the USA about the lack of an award for young adult literature, the first *School library journal*/YASD Young Adults Author Award was presented to S. E. Hinton in 1988. The award was established by YASD to honour an author writing for and about adolescence, and consists of a plaque, a cheque for $1,000 and a citation; it is presented every other year. The committees of the Newbery Award in the USA and the Carnegie Medal in the UK have also in recent years given their respective awards for distinguished writing to literature for older youth as often as to that for children, books that demand a higher reading level and more maturity from the reader. However, the parameters have extended in both directions, as Arnold Lobel's *Frog and toad together*, an easy-to-read book, received a 1973 Newbery Honor.

### Specialized groups

Specialized groups include multi-ethnic, multi-lingual and other targeted groups. Unfortunately, a dearth of multi-ethnic books still exists. During the 1960s there was a hopeful spurt of publication, but still only a few voices from the Asian, African and Latin American people find themselves in print. *Inter-racial books for children bulletin* and other publications from the Council on Inter-racial Books monitor the scene and criticize inappropriate books. However, authors productive two decades ago, such as Virginia Hamilton, Walter Dean Myers and Mildred Taylor, still dominate the Afro-American field; there are few newcomers.

Multi-lingual books in many libraries tend to be American books translated into Spanish, or perhaps French or German. Specialists occasionally review books in languages other than English for the ALA's publication *Booklist*, and other journals. Professor Isabel Schon at California State University in San Marcos, for example, offers her expertise in the area of Spanish language. After conducting a national survey on practices and attitudes in public libraries serving Spanish speakers she concluded that 'US librarians appear to be doing a conscientious job of serving the educational, informational and recreational needs of young Spanish-speaking readers'.[19] As well as this research, she reviews Spanish language books and has compiled *A Hispanic heritage, Series III: a guide to juvenile books about Hispanic people and cultures*.[20]

In addition to multi-ethnic and multi-lingual booklists, recommended reading lists exist for the college-bound and the reluctant reader, and YASD fosters discussion on both services to and selection for special groups. Committees select items for the 'Outstanding books for the college-bound lists', and 'Recommended books for the reluctant young adult reader', and the National Endowment for the Humanities produced 'Summertime favourites' in 1988, suggesting some books especially appropriate for grades nine to twelve. Further information sources are the Adolescent Literacy Center for Early Adolescence at the University of North Carolina at Chapel Hill, which recognizes that public libraries 'need collections of materials for older beginning readers and writers and the professionals and volunteers who work with them',[21] and the journal *Emergency librarian*, which occasionally publishes a column on 'Recommended books for the reluctant young adult reader'.

**Future directions**

The American Library Association Policy Manual includes a statement of mission that the 'ALA recognizes its broad social responsibilities', and that 'Guidelines, standards and codes are formulated and promoted to facilitate effective library service'.[22] AASL publishes a series, *Focus on issues and trends*, to aid in keeping up with the needs in the field, while the goals of the YASD are 'to advocate, promote, and strengthen service to young adults as part of the continuum of total library service'. Its purposes are further refined as follows. YASD:

1  Advocates the young adult's right to free and equal access to materials and services, and assists librarians in handling problems of such access;

2  Evaluates and promotes materials of interest to adolescents through special services, programs, and publications, except for those materials designed specifically for curriculum use.[23]

In order to expedite its goals, YASD is currently investigating research needs and will communicate these to academics in the field of library science who can conduct some of this research.[24] Research will continue to be conducted to ascertain what is possible, having determined the needs of young adults and evaluated the services to them.

Young adult librarians in both the public and school fields must acquire more 'techno-literacy', without sacrificing the current need for technical skills, human skills and conceptual skills. Consequently, training must be broad, encompassing these three areas. Future technology may overtake the current microcomputers, machine-readable formats, networking and databases; the education of professional librarians working with youth must also include a knowledge of adolescent psychology and communication skills. However, librarians should also not lose sight of their place in the greater scheme of the world, specifically how service to and literature for young adults interrelate with the larger scope of library, school, community, country and world.

**Summary**
Young adults, who form a bridge between childhood and adulthood, comprise a quarter of the public library clientele. School and public librarians continue specialization in both service to and literature for this age group. To remain vital, the two agencies of school and public libraries must define and heighten their distinct missions and also the areas for inter-agency cooperation, a message that holds good for both the American and British library environments. Promotion of reading can be enhanced in new ways as well as the traditional, involving young adults themselves in the selection and discussion of materials. Selection policy statements prevent potential censorship problems and it should be remembered that fiction for this age group is found in both the teen and adult arenas. Professionals therefore need to keep abreast of the traditional and new reviewing media to ensure adequate coverage. Moreover, they must continue to serve traditional and special groups, while remaining alert to the emerging groups demanding special attention, and research can aid in these goals.

**References**
1 Donelson, K. L. and Nilsen, A. P., *Literature for today's young adults*, Glenview, Illinois, and London, Scott Foreman, 1989, 13.
2 Ibid.
3 Haycock, K., 'Research in teacher-librarianship: the implications for professional practice', *Emergency librarian*, **17** (1), 1989, 9 – 18.
4 Pain-Lewins, H., 'The education and training of public librarians working with children and teenagers', *Training and education*, **6** (1), 1989, 3 – 14.
5 US Department of Education, Office of Educational Research and Improvement, *Services and resources for young adults in public libraries*, Washington, National Center for Education Statistics, 1988.
6 Chelton, M. K., 'The first national survey of services and resources for young adults in public libraries', *Journal of youth services in libraries*, **2** (3), Spring 1989, 224 – 31.
7 American Association of School Libraries and the Association for Educational Communications and Technology, *Information power: guidelines for school media programs*, Chicago, American Library Association, 1988.
8 *Competencies for young adult librarians*, Chicago, American Library Association, Young Adult Services Division, 1989.
9 Yates, J., *Teenager to young adult: recent paperback fiction for 13 to 19 years*, Swindon, School Library Association, 1986.
10 Barker, K., *Bridging the gap*, London, The Book Trust, in association with the British Council, 1987.
11 Bradbury, R., *Fahrenheit 451*, London, Hart-Davis, 1954.
12 Chambers, A., *Breaktime*, London, Bodley Head, 1986.
13 Blosveren, B., 'Youth Review Board motivates young adults to read', *Journal of youth services in libraries*, **3** (1), Fall 1989, 54 – 8.
14 Klause, A. C., 'Booktalking science fiction to young adults', *Journal of youth services in libraries*, **3** (2), Winter 1990, 102 – 16.
15 *Hennepin County Library materials selection policy*, Bloomington, Minnesota, Hennepin County Library, 1988.
16 Reichman, H., *Censorship and selection: issues and answers for schools*, Chicago, American Library Association and Arlington, Vermont, American Association of School Administrators, 1988.
17 Carlsen, G. R., *Books and the teenage reader: a guide for teachers, librarians and parents*, New York, Harper and Row, 1967.
18 Donelsen, K. L. and Nilsen, A. P.
19 Schon, I., Hopkins, K. D. and Woodruff, M., 'Spanish-language books for young readers in public libraries: national survey of practices and attitudes', *Journal of youth services in libraries*, **1** (4), Summer 1988, 444 – 50.

20 Schon, I., *A Hispanic heritage, Series III: a guide to juvenile books about Hispanic people and cultures*, Metuchen, New Jersey, Scarecrow Press, 1988.

21 Davidson, J., 'Adolescent illiteracy: what libraries can do to solve the problem – a report on the research of the project on adolescent literacy', *Journal of youth services in libraries*, 1 (2), Winter 1988, 215 – 18.

22 'ALA policy manual', *ALA handbook of organization 1988/1989*, Chicago and London, American Library Association, 1988, 221.

23 'Young Adult Services Division', *ALA handbook of organization*, Chicago, American Library Association, 1989, 153.

24 Rosen, E. M., 'Inquiring librarians want to know: today's research questions', *Journal of youth services in libraries*, 2 (4), Summer 1989, 369 – 71.

# 6 Managing adult fiction collections in public libraries

*James H. Sweetland*

This chapter discusses the handling of adult fiction in public libraries, including the selection, preservation and eventual discard. The emphasis is on practice in the USA. This emphasis is important, since there are at least two important differences between the US and the UK public libraries. First, while the UK has less than 170 authorities[1] which operate public libraries, the US has over 9,000 independent public libraries, many with several branches.[2] Second, while the circulation of adult fiction in the UK tends to be between 60 and 70% of total circulation,[3] a figure which has apparently been growing,[4] its circulation in the USA has been declining from a high of 48% in 1940 to the present 31%.[5] Yet, at the same time, the proportion of adult fiction in the library collection is very similar, averaging about 45% in the UK[6] and about 40% in the USA.

This substantial difference in library business between the two nations has barely been remarked, let alone analysed, yet it may well help to explain some of the differences in the management of fiction collections which are noted in this chapter. In particular, the greater dispersal of purchasing authority and the relative unimportance of fiction may explain the considerable disparity in the literature on the subject. A review of the last 20 years in both the indexing sources (*Library and information science abstracts*, *Library literature*, *ERIC*, *Social sciences citation index*) and the general book catalogues (*National union catalog* [*US MARC*], *British books in print*, *Books in print*) clearly shows this situation. There is a considerable amount of work from the British and European point of view regarding adult fiction, including two books[7] (in addition to the present one). In the USA, on the other hand, most of the research involves children's material, with much of the remainder concerned with censorship. The US concern appears rather to be with *entertainment* material (fiction plus non-fiction) on the adult level, with a few exceptions.

Esther Jane Carrier has studied the place of fiction in the American public library from 1876 to 1950, examining the statements of librarians in books and journals, conference proceedings and library policy documents, and the results of research by both librarians and educators. Aside from a possible liberalization toward greater acceptance of some dubious formats (comic books were accepted in the middle of the twentieth century somewhat more readily than 'dime novels' had been in the late nineteenth), she found the basic principles, arguments made, and even many of the specific details of the arguments, to have changed very little over time.[8]

The basic arguments against having much fiction in the library can be summarized as these:

1  The budget is never adequate, and every purchase of fiction has an opportunity cost preventing purchase of more important and more needed material as well as other important library services.
2  Much new fiction is frankly poor, in literary quality, and often in physical quality.
3  While it is true that demand for fiction, especially light fiction, appears high, it is often indiscriminate (any title in a given genre will do) and is often very short term (everyone wants the current bestseller, but only as long as it is on the bestseller list).

The basic arguments in favour of fiction are these:

1  Public libraries are supported by taxpayers, who clearly want much fiction.
2  Not all current or popular material is 'bad'.
3  There is nothing wrong in having entertainment as a role for the public library.
4  By having currently popular material available, the library can attract non-users to it, and then gradually 'wean' them on to better material.

It is of interest that the current terms of the debate in the USA seem to have shifted, although the basic arguments stay the same. Presumably based on the actual use statistics, there is rather little concern, at least in the published literature, over *fiction per se*. Rather, the debate tends to be between 'important' or 'serious' material on the one hand, and 'entertainment' or 'popular' material on the other. Thus, current debate rarely singles out fiction, but rather lumps popular fiction with other material, including exercise tomes (usually 'written' by TV and movie stars), fad diets, advice on how to become rich overnight, biographies of currently popular rock musicians, and the latest advice on how to beat the Japanese in business, not to mention 'non-books' of cat cartoons.

Much of the practical discussion in the last decade has revolved around the Baltimore County Public Library (BCPL) and its 'give 'em what they want' policy. Under the leadership of director Charles Robinson and Head of Adult Collection Development Nora Rawlinson (now editor of *Library journal*), the BCPL in essence has redesigned its branch libraries in the guise of bookstores: face-out shelving, multiple copies of relatively few titles, and a strong emphasis on estimated user demand as the major selection criterion. This approach, implying the purchase of up to 700 copies of some popular titles, has increased the circulation and turnover rate of the average library.[9] Intriguingly, while many have attacked the library for pandering to the lowest common denominator, evidence suggests that this is not so. For one thing, the library system does rely on a central library and other forms of inter-library lending to obtain less popular materials when needed. And, there is clear evidence that 'wants' do include the classics of literature, as long as they are attractively packaged and displayed.[10] In any event, other larger library systems have also adopted the 'demand-driven' principle, even while trying to dissociate themselves from the perceived dangers of BCPL.[11]

An interesting variant of the 'what they want' thesis has developed in the writings of Thomas Ballard, also director of a metropolitan area library (in New Jersey). He notes that research shows most people generally support public libraries, and expect the library to have lots of print material, especially books, to check out.[12] However, he also opposes the BCPL approach because it appears to give too much emphasis to popular material.[13] He argues that taxpayers support the library because it is perceived as a public good with important social values. Thus, his ideal library, while meeting the public's demand for many books to check out, has a small reading area, little if any reference material or audiovisual material, and very little fiction. For example, in a suggested floor plan of 12,000 square feet in the library, about 400 square feet would be to house popular literature of all kinds, compared with about 8,000 square feet for 'serious' fiction and non-fiction.[14]

An important point seems to have come out as part of this discussion of entertainment versus the classics: the importance of display and promotion. BCPL has found that treating 'serious' fiction in the same fashion as 'light' fiction has increased its circulation. Similar findings have come from other libraries who have set up special displays, or produced *attractive* booklists.[15] Sharon Baker has examined the factors involved in fiction circulation, concluding that the most important factor in circulation is prominent display,[16] a point emphasized by practitioners,[17] and one which is taken further in the discussion on the marketing of fiction in Chapter 9.

Interestingly, outside the polemics, there is little evidence on the operational opinions of actual librarians. Hamilton and Weech are attempting to eliminate just this gap in knowledge by a scientifically designed survey which asks librarians to respond to a series of both 'quality-driven' and 'demand-driven' statements. To date, in a test of their method in the state of Illinois, they found generally stronger agreement with the latter, but a significant agreement with many of the quality-driven criteria, suggesting that librarians are in fact balancing their decisions.[18]

Clearly, all aspects of the debate noted above accept Ranganathan's first law, 'libraries are for use'.[19] Thus, an important factor in the consideration of fiction (or, for that matter, non-fiction) is the role of the public library within its community. The decision of the ALA Public Library Association to drop the idea of numeric standards in favour of a goal-setting and output evaluation process definitely has a role here. The PLDP (Public Library Development Process) begins by a library's consulting with its community in different ways to set general goals for the library service.[20] Crucial to this process is the assumption that few, if any, public libraries can meet all potential needs/wants of a given community, a point emphasized by the provision of a list of plausible goals. A typical library is expected to determine one (or perhaps two for large libraries) goals as its primary focus, and not more than two as a secondary focus, concentrating on these rather than trying to be all things to all its users.[21]

The Public Library Association has also begun collecting statistics regarding the measures recommended by the PLDP. The survey includes a question as to whether the library has developed goals following the 'goal-setting' procedure and what they are. In the most recent available report, for 1989, 125 libraries of all sizes indicated they had determined upon goals. By far the most popular was that of 'popular materials center', with 122 listing it as 'a' goal, and 95 ranking it as highest priority. The second most popular goal for these libraries was that of 'reference library', with 65 considering this of highest priority, and 117 listing the goal. The third most popular goal, by the way, with 118 libraries noting it, was 'pre-schooler's door to learning', but only 33 ranked it as first priority, 58 considering it as second priority.[22]

Possibly related to this process are a couple of articles arguing that there are a few, readily defined, different 'publics' for the library. In this view, there are significant differences between those who check out books and who use them in the library; between those who browse and those who use the catalogue to find materials; and even between those who seek print material and those who want other formats.[23]

This definition of different 'publics' may well be important for the use of fiction. In particular, given the usual treatment of adult fiction, we have in effect tried to separate the more or less serious from the rest. General practice has been to place the majority of literature and the more serious popular material in a sequence removed from the non-fiction, and arranged by author. In a collection of any size, this approach makes it difficult for the browser, unless he or she has a particular author in mind. However, most public libraries tend to arrange their light fiction in several genres, with science fiction, mysteries, and romance/gothics well-nigh universal,[24] although there are other possibilities. Thus, we almost force the browser to the light material, and the seeker after a given author to the 'serious' literature, while essentially ignoring the catalogue user and the subject reader entirely. The lack of subject approach to fiction has been dealt with at length in other places, but most typically in the context of classification. Sanford Berman, however, has long argued for improved subject access for both fiction and non-fiction for the typical public library, and in fact has implemented such an approach in the Hennepin County Public Library.[25] He has argued for many years for a wider application of this approach, making subject headings available through his library's own newsletter.[26] Possible acceptance of this approach, specifically with fiction, appears near with the acceptance of a set of recommendations of the Association for Library Collections and Technical Services Subject Analysis Committee, including formal 'Guidelines for subject access to individual works of fiction, drama, etc.'.[27] These include the recommendation that the Library of Congress (LC) assign both topical subject headings and genre/form headings to catalogue records where a fictional character or setting appears in at least three different works. Given the number of libraries who rely on LC cataloguing, either through jobbers, OCLC, or Cataloguing-in-Publication, acceptance of this recommendation would mean that users could, in a very few years, use the catalogue to find not only new 'detective novels' but also could look specifically for Sherlock Holmes, Mike Hammer or Miss Marple, among other favourites. The implications for improved use of the fiction collection through improved access are, to say the least, interesting.

Interestingly, although the role of fiction has caused considerable debate, there is little solid evidence on its actual purchase and treatment in US public libraries. That which deals with actual practice (outside of descriptions of the Baltimore County Public Library) very rarely deals with libraries in the USA. In hopes of partially remedying this situation I conducted a survey of medium-sized US public libraries in the spring of 1990 (see Appendix). For the sake of convenience, these were defined as libraries holding between 20,000 and 300,000 volumes, or about 44% of all public libraries. About 3% are larger than this, 53% having 20,000 or fewer volumes.[28] Lacking further information, it seems plausible that very large and very small libraries may treat fiction differently. For example, the small budgets and staffs of the smallest libraries would limit any collecting, while the very large staffs and budgets of the largest libraries, combined with their multi-building arrangement, would also seem to make their collection management practices distinct. Thus, all results which follow are still very tentative.

A major difficulty in conducting any study of libraries by size is the lack of standard data. For example, many libraries report only title or volume holdings, but not both, to R. R. Bowker, the compilers of the *American library directory*, while others do not report budget figures. For example, of respondents to the present survey, budget and volume data were available for 86%, title data for 48%. To avoid the immediate difficulty, the sample is based on either a volume or title count of 20,001 to 300,000.

Based on responses of the sample, we can say a few things about the average, medium-sized public library. (All figures given below are for the 'average', i.e. arithmetic mean, unless otherwise stated.) First of all, it has an annual budget of about $685,000 (£389,205) with a median of about $327,000 (£185,795). Its collection consists of about 112,000 volumes (a median of a little over 66,000). Of this collection, about 28% of its titles are adult fiction, 42% adult non-fiction, and about 29% children's material (fiction and non-fiction). Of the adult fiction, about 65% consists of 'light fiction' or 'entertainment' material, and about 24% is 'serious literature'. The remainder is composed of 'other' types of adult fiction. The responses to the latter question indicate the continuing nature of any discussion over 'serious' versus 'light' fiction: 18% of the responding libraries did not answer the question at all, and a number of them indicated that they objected to the question's categories as too vague. This inability to define the difference, if there is one, between types of fiction certainly helps fuel the debate on the role of fiction.

On another subject, however, the libraries were quite clear: about 75% do not buy any fiction titles in any language other than English. Of those which do, the average number of titles was only six.

Current additions to the collection are very important to any discussion of selection decisions. Again, of the responding libraries, we find considerable variation, but a general pattern emerges. The 'average' library bought about 1,600 new titles in the last year, and added about 150 titles as gifts in the same period. However, in this case averages or medians do not give a very good picture of the considerable deviation in number of titles added: two libraries bought over 10,000 new titles, while three bought less than 100 in the same year. Or, looking at this another way, 76% of the libraries purchased less than the 'average' 1,600 titles, and 96% bought 5,000 or fewer. Yet another way of looking at this situation is to consider that Nora Rawlinson has estimated that about 1,000 new titles are needed to satisfy users' demands for new fiction.[29] Of the sample, 46% of the libraries bought fewer than 1,000.

On the other hand, the role of gift books can be very important, especially for the smaller library. Thus, although the average number of gift fiction was 148, two libraries actually estimate receiving 1,000 or more titles. In fact, the total number of adult new titles added (purchase plus gifts) averages 1,626 titles. A number of libraries have indicated the importance of these gifts in specific genres, in effect freeing book funds for other genres or more 'serious' fiction. Since these gifts tend to be recent paperbacks, and since there is some evidence that the entertainment reader, in particular, seems to prefer paper to cloth covers, these gifts may well represent a substantial effect on circulation. On the other hand, the vast majority of libraries prefer to buy their fiction in hard covers. Not only did 82% of the respondents indicate they preferred the hard cover, only one (1.2%) preferred paper. One other library stated that 'it depends' and 10% said it made no difference to their decision. The hardcover versus paperback question continues to be an issue, in any event.

A comparison of the actual output of publishers with library practice may be useful. For example, all US publishers in 1987 (the most recent year for which final figures are available), issued 56,027 hardcover and trade paperback titles, of which 6,298 (about 11%) were fiction. Mass market paperback production, which generally contains popular reading, saw 3,916 new titles, of which 2,632 (about 67%) were fiction. British publishers in the same year issued 54,746 titles, of which 6,389 were fiction, again comprising about 12% of the total.[30]

The ways libraries actually add new fiction are clearly of considerable interest both to librarians and to the publishing industry. While specific criteria would be of extreme interest, these would be difficult to establish. For one thing, contrary to apparent British practice, US textbooks in collection management and development tend to say very little about fiction. For example, William Katz's text, which gives fiction the greatest emphasis, devotes about ten and a half pages to the topic,[31] while the very popular work by Curley and Broderick lacks even an index entry for the subject.[32]

Thus, perhaps the most important part of the survey asked the importance of a number of methods of selection. Based on the pilot study, libraries were asked to rank methods separately for hardcovers and for paperbacks. Again, the strong preference for cloth bindings is clear: more libraries indicate the importance of any selection method for hardcovers over paperbacks, with a number consistently stating they do not select paperbacks at all.

The first question asked about approval and standing order plans. In these plans, perhaps best known in an academic library context, a jobber or publisher, in effect, does the selecting for the library. The difference, of course, is that in the former, the material (or order forms for the material) is sent to the library 'on approval', giving the library staff the chance to look over the material, and decline to order if it is not what is wanted. The standing order, on the other hand, commits the library to purchase, but the material is sent automatically. In theory, based on conversations with a number of librarians, this method would be very useful for light fiction genres: knowing, for example, that users were interested in romances or westerns, a library could merely obtain a copy of every new release from specific lines of specific publishers. The facts, however, suggest that libraries still like their autonomy – approval and blanket order plans received the lowest rating of any of the methods studied, and were most likely to be marked 'do not use'. Interestingly, there was one category in which such plans received some favourable ratings – romance literature.

Related in a sense to approval plans are book clubs. Generally, these all follow the same pattern. Each four weeks or so, the subscriber receives an order card with a descriptive catalogue of some sort. Users who do nothing automatically receive the selection of the month, with a bill. Users also have the option of refusing to buy anything, or of selecting some other title from the month's offerings. As a form of promotion, book clubs often provide very large discounts and free books to new subscribers, and typically provide some sort of credit towards free titles for each purchase (e.g. one free selection for every four titles purchased). The 1990 *Literary market place* lists 25 clubs dealing with adult fiction.[33] Given the large number of speciality clubs, it seemed plausible that many libraries might rely on them, especially for lighter fiction. In essence the clubs have the advantages of approval plans with the addition of reviews of some sort, plus the attraction of free materials. And, in addition to the Book of the Month and similar 'literary' book clubs, there are many which specialize in light fiction genres. In fact, some libraries do rely on book clubs, especially in the areas of crime/mystery and science fiction, both of which have long-standing, strong, reputable clubs.

Although the questions specified only hardcover and paperback as formats, a number of responses indicate that large-print books are often treated separately from other 'normal-size' bindings. Several libraries wrote in particular about large-print book clubs/jobbers in response to this question. Other librarians made similar points in a free-form question. In short, it appears that many libraries do feel a considerable need for fiction in larger print, and use selection methods for this format different from that otherwise employed; in particular, they rely heavily on book clubs for this format.

Research going back at least to the turn of the century tells us that the preferred basis of library selection decisions has always been book reviews; this survey, as one might expect, confirms the research. Of all the methods studied, unquestionably reviews were ranked the highest, and by the largest number of libraries. Nearly all libraries ranked library/trade reviews as extremely important for hardcover purchase decisions, although nearly 10% indicated they did not use them at all for paperbacks. However, overall, reviews are the method of choice, especially for purchases of hardcover fiction.

Since the survey actually asked about two different types of reviews, it is possible to distinguish between the library/publishing trade reviews and the reviews in more popular media, including newspapers. When this distinction is made, there is a clear difference. Libraries definitely prefer the library/book trade review media, even for the popular genres. Of the media, there is no question as to preferences for specific titles. The survey requested, for fiction overall, as well as specific genres, the five most important review sources used. The most typical answer for respondents was to list two to five titles under the general heading 'fiction' and then merely to indicate that the same sources were used for all specific genres. And, the most popular sources used for fiction in particular were precisely the same as those libraries in earlier surveys indicated as most heavily used: *Booklist, Library journal, Publishers weekly, Kirkus reviews* and the *New York Times book review*.[34] An interesting addition to this standard list are the semi-review media produced by some book jobbers, with Baker and Taylor specifically listed a number of times.

Since these sources may be somewhat unfamiliar to a British audience, a few words about each would be appropriate. *Booklist* (1905 to date), published by the American Library Association, is aimed at public libraries and contains reviews of material in all formats and for all ages. Bound within is a separate review medium, *Reference books bulletin*, which reviews reference material for all types of libraries. *Library journal* (1876 to date), published by Bowker, is also aimed primarily at public libraries. It is a general trade/professional journal, not solely a book review medium, of course. *Publishers weekly* (1872 to date) is the premier US publishing trade journal, and primarily reviews for bookstores. *Kirkus reviews* (1933 to date) is solely a review medium, and tends to have longer reviews than the other sources listed here. In general, Kirkus tends to review more light fiction genres than the others. The one 'popular' review medium routinely used is the *New York Times book review* (1896 to date), which appears both separately and as part of the Sunday *New York Times*. Its reviews are often very long, and are generally aimed at the literate individual reader.

Another type of possible selection source studied is the list of recommended material either based on some sort of committee or bibliographer's work, or those winning literary prizes of some sort. Most review sources tend to have special lists of the 'best of the year' or similar; *Library journal* in fact has several such lists, including first novelists twice a year. And, of course, the several bibliographies produced by H. W. Wilson, especially the *Fiction catalog* series, would appear to be obvious sources of recommended material. As it happens, while most libraries did indicate some reliance on such lists, the most typical rank was solidly in the middle (3 on a scale of 1 to 5). The use of lists of prizewinners likewise tended to receive a middling ranking. In fact, a number of respondents indicate that they used prize lists only to the extent they found them in the review sources they usually read, as opposed to seeking such lists out specifically. *Literary market place* provides a reasonably comprehensive list of awards and prizes.[35] A count of the 1990 lists suggests that there are about 100 prizes available for adult fiction (excluding poetry and drama), including many in 'light fiction' genres such as mystery, romance and science fiction.[34] Given the apparent ease of using recommendations like these, the relatively low rank accorded them is curious. One possible explanation for this fact could be that prizewinners often tend to be heavily reviewed, with mention of the prize usually included after its award, so that reliance on reviews implies use of awards. Another explanation could be that librarians prefer to rely more on their own judgement, and thus, while taking awards into consideration, the further information provided by reviews is critical to a selection decision.

All of the above tend to be measures in some fashion of quality. Measures of demand include bestseller lists (as a measure of national demand) and specific user requests (as a measure of local demand). The survey enquired about both such criteria. Certainly the bestseller lists are important for the libraries in our survey, with 59% ranking these as very important for hardcovers, and no libraries stating they did not use them. The situation for paperbacks is very mixed, with 20% stating they did not use them and 32% ranking them as very important. Since one can usually assume that the more popular titles will tend to be reprinted in paper covers, it is possible that the lower ranking for paper is again the tendency of the libraries in the survey to avoid paperbacks for purchases.

User requests, on the other hand, are very important to nearly all libraries, ranking only a bit behind library/book trade reviews as selection sources. Considering the ongoing opposition to the 'give 'em what they want' school of thought, it is more than curious that most libraries in the survey appear to pay very close attention to user requests. Presumably, regardless of what a librarian might respond in theory, the simple fact of a local taxpayer requesting a specific title is hard to resist: after all, if libraries are for use, what better predictor of use than a specific request? And, if libraries are to serve the public, what better way than to respond to a specific request of a member of that public? In any even, it would appear that, within rather loose budget constraints, libraries will buy fiction on demand.

In recent years, there has been much discussion about the role of libraries within a 'community of information', including other outlets for reading, such as bookstores, as well as other libraries. These latter can include nearly any other library, given the extent of resource sharing networks. Thus, the survey asked libraries if, when considering the addition of fiction, they took any of these three potential sources of material. It is clear that local bookstores have little if any effect on purchase, with 65 respondents marking the lowest category, and 10 more the next, for a total of 93% stating local bookstores have little or no influence on their acquisition decisions. Local libraries have a bit more, but not much influence, with 50 libraries ranking them as 'no effect', 13 as a little, and 16 as moderate. Interlibrary loan is still more important, with only 34 marking as no effect, 19 as a little, and 18 as some. Thus, the bottom line is that, at least as far as adult fiction is concerned, potential availability has little to do with purchase decisions.

Another important issue with regard to fiction of all kinds is its long-term preservation. Again, the dichotomy of 'literature' and 'light fiction' is very relevant here, with the former both most likely to be preserved, and in a sense, least likely to need it. After all, the number of reprint editions of Shakespeare, or Steinbeck, or

Twain, not to mention the work of collectors, is sure to keep their works available.

The issue of preservation seems to have at least two aspects: conservation and preservation of material held, and the collection of the material in the first place. For most public libraries, the former work is at a very basic level, and rarely performed on fiction at all, other than simple repair and, perhaps, rebinding. Fortunately, the continuing work of organizations such as the Research Libraries Group in microfilming whole collections has included some older popular fiction, among other categories,[36] as has the work of the New York Public Library.[37] Surprisingly little attention has been paid to the role of the smaller public library, but a recent discussion of a programme in Wellesley, Massachusetts, may provoke further interest in this important work.[38]

The latter work, the collection of the material in the first place, has received very different treatment in the USA and the UK. The several regional Joint Fiction Reserves are fairly well known, and thus need relatively little detailed treatment here.[39] All are variations on the same theme: particular libraries in a given area are responsible for particular portions of all fiction, typically taking portions of the alphabet. Generally, these libraries will then lend such material to other libraries – however, often with some restrictions.

At least one state, Wyoming, has tried a similar approach, relying on three libraries.[40] Aside from reliance on the research collections, which may or may not lend material, another approach is the 'last copy center', where one library both tries to purchase new fiction, and acts as the depository for discarded fiction from all other libraries. Such a system has been working in Illinois for many years, with the Chicago Public Library as the depository.[41]

The major difficulty with either of these cooperative schemes appears to lie in their very cooperation. In effect, each library member agrees to buy (or, at least, store and service) material that its own clientele does not necessarily need, want or use. The only real reimbursement for this 'extra' work is the promise that other members of the consortium are doing their share as well, so that *if* a user of a given member library does happen to need something, it will be available on interlibrary loan from someone in the consortium. As budgets become tighter, such cooperation can become problematic. Or, as the local taxpayers might put it, 'why should we be stuck with things we don't really need just to support some other tax district?' Of course, once one member of such an agreement refuses to continue or reduces its commitment, the whole system begins to collapse.

One example of this phenomenon will suffice. The Milwaukee

Public Library is a member of the Milwaukee County Federated Library System. As it is by far the largest library in the system, it naturally receives heavy use by people who are not residents (or taxpayers) of the city. For this service, it received support from the county government as well. However, in late 1984 the county government determined, unilaterally, that it could not afford to pay for such service, and therefore essentially wrote the library out of its budget. It is important to note here that this decision was not based on any complaints about services, and in fact was made over the objections of the library community in the county. Given such a cut, the city library then restricted its information services to city residents (although anyone could still come into the library and access its collections). After considerable pressure by the library community and library users of all kinds, the funding was restored through the library system, and services were re-established.[42] A similar problem developed in Denver, again between the city and its surrounding communities.[43]

Consider that these problems have all arisen over 'serious' use of the library, not over fiction, and certainly not over popular fiction. The sometimes lukewarm support that resource sharing for fiction receives may not be so unreasonable.

One obvious solution is the traditional one: a particular library, seeing its role as partially the group memory of society, determines that part of its goal includes preservation of fiction − of any quality, so long as it is in a particular genre, or on a particular subject. At present, this more traditional approach seems to be the *de facto* one used in the USA, with a fairly large number of libraries maintaining collections of various genres of fiction. For example, the Russell B. Nye Popular Culture Collection at Michigan State University includes over 3,000 westerns and about the same number of romances and science fiction, plus over 3,500 detective/mystery novels and thousands of issues of 'pulp' story magazines. The J. Lloyd Eaton Collection at the University of California−Riverside has an extensive collection of SF and fantasy, with an emphasis on utopias and dystopias, gothic and horror fiction. Other extensive SF collections may be found at Pennsylvania State University and the universities of California, Los Angeles, Northern Illinois, and Kansas, among several others, not to mention the Dallas (Texas) and San Francisco (California) Public Libraries. Mysteries are collected by the San Diego (California) Public Library, Wofford College (Spartanburg, North Carolina), Brigham Young University, and Occidental College. Other horror and gothic collections may be found at Brigham Young and Occidental as well as the University of Wisconsin campuses at LaCrosse and Madison. A number of the aforementioned libraries also have significant collections of romances, as does the University of Oregon and the University of California–Fullerton. Examples of westerns may be found, among other places, at the universities of Arizona, Northern Illinois, Texas (Austin) and Texas–El Paso, as well as Colorado State, New Mexico State, and the State University of New York College at Oneonta. Several libraries also collect contemporary American writers, among them California State University–Northridge, the University of Texas–Arlington and the University of Northern Iowa. Some other examples of popular fiction collections include the University of California–Davis (Tom Mix, Buck Rogers, Charlie Chan, Popeye and the like), Emory University (English 'yellow backs'), and the University of Virginia (bestsellers). The Bowling Green State University collection of popular culture, of course, includes examples of all these genres. These are only a sampling of the larger collections, from which I have excluded dime novels, pulp magazines, general collections of American fiction, which usually include some popular material, and those libraries specializing in particular authors or publishers. Ash and Miller's *Subject collections* is a good starting place for seeking out such collections.[44]

The major difficulty with this approach, of course, is that the material is essentially being saved for research purposes. Thus, a given library cannot rely on these collections to meet the normal desires of its clients. In fact, many (but not all) research collections refuse to lend their materials, on the very good argument that they are both fragile and scarce (if not actually of great monetary value at the moment).

Connected with purchase of new titles is the elimination of older titles, known generally in the USA as 'weeding'. Fifty-four (64%) of the respondents indicated they had a formal programme for this activity; 26 (31%) indicated they did not have a formal programme, but a number of these included comments stating they did engage in the activity from time to time, generally 'as time permits'. The most extreme of this latter group was a library which indicated that it had not weeded at all in about 20 years, but which had finally begun to do so with the hiring of a new librarian.

As with other open-ended questions, the responses need more analysis, but a general pattern among the weeding programmes does emerge. Of libraries which weed, a regular schedule of one to three years examination is typical. The most common initial criterion for considering a book for discard is apparent use, defined as the number of times it has circulated. In particular, second and greater copies of books which seem not to have circulated 'recently' (a concept rarely defined by the respondents) are most likely to be removed, with one copy retained for potential future need. Interestingly, some libraries indicated they also retained 'classics' or 'high-quality' titles, even if the circulation was low, although few attempted to define these terms.

A number of libraries specifically mentioned the 'CREW' method in this context. Since this writer discusses the method in his collection management classes, unsolicited reference to it was gratifying (validation of the 'real-life' value of what you are teaching is always useful). In any event, a brief description may be useful to other libraries. The overall guidelines provide a basis for considering material for weeding based on the combination of copyright date, years since last circulation, and the 'MUSTY' formula for physical condition and contents. Books are candidates for weeding if they are Misleading (or factually inaccurate), Ugly (worn beyond mending or rebinding), Superseded (by a new edition or better book on the subject), Trivial (of little discernible literary or scientific merit) or 'Your collection has no need for this book' (irrelevant to the needs of your community). The specific years for the first two elements vary with Dewey class number. For fiction, the CREW guidelines suggest no particular copyright date, but circulation within two years. In other words, a work of fiction which has not circulated in over two years, and which meets one or more of the 'MUSTY' criteria, should be considered for weeding.[45]

It is hoped that this summary of 'typical' medium-sized public library practice in the USA will be useful, not only for the immediate purpose, but also for future discussions of the role of fiction.

## References

1   Capital Planning Information, *Trends in public library selection policies*, London, British Library, 1987, 8 (British National Bibliography Research Fund Report no. 29).

2   *American library directory* (42nd edn), Bowker, 1989 (DIALOG Information Services file no. 460, searched April, 1990).

3   Goldhor, H., 'Summary and review of the indexes of American public library statistics 1939–1983', Urbana, University of Illinois Research Center, 1985 (ERIC Document ED 264 879), 60.

4   Dixon, J. (ed.), *Fiction in libraries*, London, Library Association, 1986, 2.

5   Goldhor, H., 50; Johnson, D. W., 'Public library circulation holds steady in 1988', *American libraries*, **20** (7), 1989, 705.

6   Dixon, J., 6.

7   Dixon, J.; Atkinson, F., *Fiction librarianship*, London, Clive Bingley, 1981.

8  Carrier, E. J., *Fiction in public libraries 1876–1900*, New York, Scarecrow, 1965; Carrier, E. J., *Fiction in public libraries 1900–1950*, Littleton, Colorado, Libraries Unlimited, 1985.

9  Rawlinson, N., 'The approach to collection management at Baltimore County Public Library', in Serebnick, J. (ed.), *Collection management in public libraries*, Chicago, American Library Association, 1986, 76–80.

10  Rawlinson, N., 'Give 'em what they want!', *Library journal*, **106** (20), 1981, 2188–90.

11  'Tucson makes client demand central to collection development', *Library journal*, **107** (6), 1982, 586.

12  Ballard, T. H., *The failure of resource sharing in public libraries and alternative strategies for service*, Chicago, American Library Association, 1986, 121–69.

13  Ballard, T. H., 'A minority report on present book collection practices', in Serebnick, J. (ed.), *Collection management in public libraries*, Chicago, American Library Association, 1986, 81–90.

14  Ballard, T. H., *The failure of resource sharing*, 198–206.

15  Hermeneze, J., 'The "classics" will circulate', *Library journal*, **106** (20), 1981, 2191–5.

16  Baker, S. L., 'The display phenomenon: an exploration into factors causing the increased circulation of displayed books', *Library quarterly*, **56** (3), 1986, 237–57.

17  Hayden, R., 'If it circulates, keep it', *Library journal*, **112** (10), 1987, 80–2.

18  Hamilton, P. A. and Weech, T. L., 'The development and testing of an instrument to measure attitudes toward the quality vs. demand debate in collection management, *Collection management*, **10** (3/4), 1988, 27–42.

19  Ranganathan, S. R., *The five laws of librarianship*, (2nd edn), Bombay, Asia Publishing House, 1962, 26–79.

20  McClure, C. R. *et al.*, *Planning and role setting for public libraries: a manual of options and procedures*, Chicago, American Library Association, 1987.

21  McClure, C. R. *et al.*, 43.

22  Public Library Data Service, *Statistical report '89*, Chicago, American Library Association, 1989, 67–78.

23  De Gruyter, L., 'Who uses your library and what do they want?', *Public libraries*, **22** (4), 1983, 151–3; Webb, T. D., 'A hierarchy of public library user types', *Library journal*, **111** (15), 1986, 47–50.

24  Harrell, G., 'The classification and organization of adult fiction in large American public libraries', *Public libraries*, **24** (1), 1985, 13–14.

25  Berman, S., *Worth noting: editorials, letters, essays, an interview, and bibliography*, Jefferson, North Carolina, McFarland, 1988, 9–20.

26  Hennepin County Library, *Cataloging bulletin*, 1–40, May 1973 to May/June 1979.

27  American Library Association, 'ALCTS (Association for Library Collections and Technical Services) approves subject headings for fiction and drama', Press release, April, 1990.

28  Lynch, M. J., 'Volumes held by public libraries, Fall '82', in *Libraries in an information society: a statistical summary*, Chicago, American Library Association, 1986, 26.

29  Rawlinson, N., 'The approach to collection management', 79.

30  *The Bowker annual: library and book trade almanac* (34th edn), New York, Bowker, 1989, 425 – 6, 431 – 3, 442.

31  Katz, W. A., *Collection development: the selection of materials for libraries*, New York, Holt, Rinehart and Winston, 1980, 99 – 109.

32  Curley, A. and Broderick, D., *Building library collections* (6th edn), Metuchen, New Jersey, Scarecrow, 1985.

33  *Literary market place* (50th edn), New York, Bowker, 1990, 453–9.

34  Futas, L., *Library acquisition policies and procedures* (2nd edn), Phoenix, Oryx, 1984, xxii – xxix.

35  *Literary market place*, 1070 – 1101.

36  McClung, P. A., 'Costs associated with preservation microfilming: results of the Research Libraries Group study', *Library resources and technical services*, **30** (4), 1986, 363 – 74.

37  Dowd, A., 'The science fiction microfilming project at the New York Public Library', *Microform review*, **14** (1), 1985, 15 – 20.

38  Reynolds, A. L., Schrock, N. C. and Walsh, J., 'Preservation: the public library response', *Library journal*, **114** (3), 1989, 128 – 32.

39  Samways, A. J., 'The joint fiction reserve: an appraisal', *Journal of librarianship*, **12** (4), 1980, 267 – 79.

40  Collins, B., 'WLA fiction collective: how it works', *Wyoming library roundup*, **34** (3), 1979, 20.

41  Shroder, E. J., 'The last copy center for fiction in Illinois', *Illinois libraries*, **71** (1), 1989, 57 – 8.

42  'Libraries agree to compensation', *Milwaukee journal*, 23 May 1985 (NEWSBANK 1985, EDUCATION section, fiche no. 40, frame C2).

43  Akeroyd, R. G., 'Denver PL's nonresident fee policy', *Public library quarterly*, 4, 1983, 17 – 27.

44  Ash, L. and Miller, W. G., *Subject collections* (6th edn), New York, Bowker, 1985.

45  Segal, J. P., *Evaluating and weeding collections in small and medium-sized public libraries: the CREW method*, Chicago, American Library Association, 1980.

**Appendix: Summary of survey questions**

*Section 1: Importance of different selection methods*
Please rank the importance to you of each of the following methods
of selecting adult fiction by circling the appropriate number (1 =
do not use; 5 = extremely important) for paperbacks and for
hardcovers, separately (each question below was asked for each of
the following types of fiction);

Fiction in general
Crime/mystery/suspense
Science fiction/fantasy
Westerns
Historical
Romance, gothic, regency
Horror/supernatural
War, sea, naval
First novels/first stories
Experimental, alternative

Approval, blanket order plans (i.e. arrange with a publisher or
wholesalers to send a given class of books automatically as they
are produced, such as all new Harlequins).

Book club selections (i.e. either just take the automatic monthly
selection, or choose from the book club's list of alternate selections).

Reviews in library and publishing trade journals (for example
*Library journal, Publisher's weekly*).

Reviews in popular magazines and newspapers (for example
*Newsweek, New York Times*, local newspaper).

Bestseller lists (i.e. lists of fiction which are selling well, or which
are expected to sell well).

Best book, or recommended book lists (e.g. 'best new fiction of
the year', Wilson library catalogs).

Prizewinners, award winners (e.g. ABA awards, Hugo Awards).

User requests for a particular author or title.

*Section 2: Specific sources of selection information*
(Again, there was space to list the requested information for the
same list of fiction types as given for Section 1).

If you use reviews to assist you in buying fiction, please indicate
the five most important sources for those reviews.

If you use any blanket order or approval plans, please indicate
the plan(s) you use.

Some libraries use various types of rental plans, such as
McNaughton, to rent materials rather than buy them. If you use

such plans, please indicate them.

If you rely at all on awards or best book lists, please indicate the five most important for each type of material.

When deciding whether or not to *buy* a given title for your adult fiction collection do you consider any of the following (1 = makes no difference, 5 = extremely important):

Availability in local area bookstores
Availability in nearby libraries
Availability through interlibrary loan

Given a choice, do you prefer to *buy* your adult fiction in paperback/hardcover/makes no difference?

About how many new titles of adult fiction did you buy last year?

About how many new titles of adult fiction did you add through gifts and/or exchanges last year?

Do you try to add 'backlist' fiction (titles you did not buy when they were first published) to your library collection at all?

About how many backlist adult fiction titles did you buy last year?

About how many backlist adult fiction titles did you add through gifts and/or exchanges last year?

Do you add any adult fiction in languages other than English to your library collection?

About how many adult fiction titles in languages other than English did you add to your library last year?

If you added any, please list up to five of the languages which you obtained.

### Section 3: Size of adult fiction collection

Of your total library collection (including both adult and children's materials) about what percentage is

Adult fiction in general
Adult non-fiction
Children's fiction and non-fiction?

Of your adult fiction collection about what percentage is

Light fiction/entertainment reading
'Serious literature'
Other?

### Section 4: Deselection, 'weeding' of your adult fiction collection

Do you have a regular program for weeding your adult fiction collection?

Is this program any different from that you use for the collection in general?

In brief, what is your weeding policy for adult fiction?

### Section 5

Please feel free to add any explanation of your answers, comments on your fiction collection, or any other comments.

# 7 Organizing fiction for use

*Lyn Sear and Barbara Jennings*

## Introduction

This chapter is concerned with describing the various approaches to organizing fiction both on the shelf and via fiction classification schemes. However, it also looks at how readers themselves actually go about the process of selecting their fiction when in the library, and what the implications of this are for librarians in the way fiction needs to be arranged in the library if we are to help the user. If we do not understand and take account of user behaviour in a library's fiction arrangements, we will arrange it for administrative convenience rather than ease of use by the borrowers. The title of this chapter is, after all, organizing fiction *for use*.

Librarians' attitude to fiction provision is also a factor to be taken into account in a chapter on organizing fiction. There has often been ambivalence, if not actual animosity, concerning fiction. Savage wrote disdainfully 'how few novels are of cultural or literary value' and that he would prefer not more than 7% of the bookstock to be novels. He wished these to be placed in the literature class, 'the separate novel class being abandoned, as it ought to be'.[1] Twenty years later, C. D. Needham, also writing about the organization of fiction stock, criticized the categorization of fiction into reader interest arrangements (i.e. crime, romance, westerns) as 'alienating the serious reader. Pandering to a mass public can hardly do anything to support claims of more of the public's money for public libraries.'[2] This perhaps is at the root of librarians' ambivalence to fiction, always sensitive to the charge of 'Agatha Christie on the rates'.

This often has led to restrictive practices regarding fiction by some library authorities: the exclusion of certain genres, division of readers' tickets into fiction and non-fiction, the refusal of reserves for fiction, interweaving fiction and non-fiction arrangements so that the reader may stumble on a more worthy book than the novel he or she was seeking. Sheila Mackay, as a novelist, retaliates in her description in one of her novels of the library where old ladies are not allowed to choose their own books, and have Doris Lessing and

Simone de Beauvoir forced on them: 'When Luke came to have his books stamped out he heard the old lady in front of him whisper "I'm not really very keen on patio gardening and yoga, dear." "Never mind", the assistant whispered back, slipping two Mills and Boons furtively into her basket.'[3]

Certainly, the neglect and lack of attention to fiction organization can be compared with the effort that goes into the organization of non-fiction, such as 20 editions of a classification scheme, subject indexes, and professional cataloguers devoting their working lives to it. Users of fiction have to be content with stock ordered by the alphabet. A. W. McClellan writes: 'That the significance of fiction reading has been underrated is demonstrated by the apparent lack of experiment in ways of arranging it on library shelves and in methods of controlling the numbers and conditions of titles continuously to be found on those shelves.'[4] Yet fiction is acknowledged to be the bread and butter of public libraries, forming around 70% of the issues.

The lack of concern over the best way to organize fiction could be justified if there was evidence that readers of fiction know exactly what they want, and can find it without difficulty on the shelves. There have been, however, a number of studies over the last ten years that point to considerable difficulties experienced by library users in choosing fiction books. Peter Mann has been active in researching this field, and promoting research into this area of how readers select fiction. He comments 'for 2/3 people [surveyed] to want to find "any novel of interest" is surely an indicator of a lack of information about what to choose'.[5] These studies into fiction are summarized below, as understanding the ways our users go about selecting fiction is important to any discussion of the most effective method of arranging fiction for use. Also included is an account of some research we ourselves carried out in Kent County Library.

## Research

David Spiller in 1979 examined the pattern of borrowing of 500 library users in four library systems.[6] He distinguished between two methods of choice:

1  Novels for which the author's name or title was known to the reader, either actively sought or recognized as familiar during browsing.
2  Novels completely unknown to the reader and selected by browsing.

He found that 54% of novels selected were chosen by the first method, 46% by the latter. His study drew attention to the importance of browsing as a selection method for many readers of fiction. He commented that a 'browsing only' approach was often dictated by ignorance of what was published, or by an inability to remember authors' names: though for some people browsing represented 'freedom of selection, a conscious rejection of the critical establishment'.

Other research into fiction borrowing, mainly in the area of literary fiction, was carried out by Spenceley[7] and Day.[8] Their findings show that most fiction is chosen with little information and guidance, that the process is haphazard, indeed that readers find books *despite* the arrangement and not *because* of it. Most American studies into browsing have been concerned with academic libraries and their users, but there was a study by Goldhor in Illinois in 1972, somewhat earlier than the previous studies cited above, in which he observed the use of 119 fiction and non-fiction titles first scattered on the shelves, then in a special display.[9] The books were used far more in the latter period, and he noted that adult users of public libraries typically are not in search of specific titles but are looking for something good to read. He believed that whatever induces browsing will increase the use of books and whatever impedes browsing will reduce it.

We carried out a survey in 1985 of how people went about selecting fiction as users of Kent County Library Service.[10] We asked a sample of 135 readers in three libraries how they had actually gone about choosing the books they were just taking out. A prompt card offered users the following choices for describing their selection method:

1   I reserved this book.
2   I especially looked for this particular book.
3   I especially looked for books by this author.
4   I browsed and recognized this author's name.
5   I browsed and this book looked interesting.
6   I looked for books of this type, e.g. crime, romance, etc.
7   None of these.

The results were as shown in Figure 7.1.

*Managing fiction in libraries*

Numbers
of books

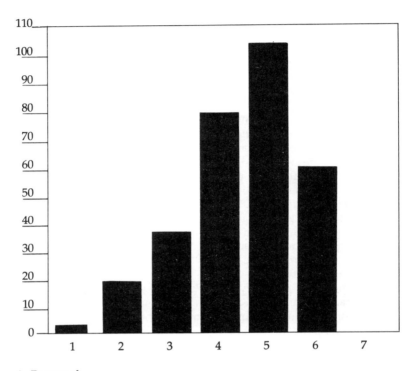

1  Reserved
2  Especially looked for this particular book
3  Especially looked for books by this author
4  Browsed/recognized author's name
5  Browsed/looked interesting
6  Looked for genre
7  Any other method

**Fig. 7.1  Method of choice**

Thus, as other surveys had shown, the most popular method of choosing was by browsing for that elusive 'something interesting'. Readers were asked why the book seemed interesting and reasons varied from the location of the story to the author's gender and the thickness of the book — but far and above the most popular reason was the 'blurb'. Most of the books chosen because they looked interesting were by authors new to the reader (85%). Clearly, browsing, not reading reviews, or looking at catalogues and lists, is the way readers discover new authors. This finding alone emphasizes the responsibility of libraries in helping readers browse to good advantage, and discovering the authors they will want to go on reading.

It was interesting that one-fifth of the books in our sample were selected by readers looking for a specific genre. At the time of the survey Kent County Library had a policy of not categorizing fiction. This was certainly a clear example of people finding books despite the arrangement! In Spiller's survey, 69% of his respondents said they often sought novels of a particular kind, indicating the usefulness of categorizing.

This does lead on to questions about ease of use of libraries. In the Kent survey, readers were asked to rate how easy or difficult, on a scale of 1–5, it is to pick fiction in a library (see Figure 7.2). It can be seen that most people opt for 'so-so'. In effect, one-third of the respondents admitted to having some difficulty in choosing fiction. This was due to not knowing what to look for, of it being a matter of chance as to what was in at the time. This perception by the readers of our survey that libraries are a lottery for selecting fiction does undermine any idea we might have as librarians that we provide a professional service as far as fiction provision is

Numbers
of people

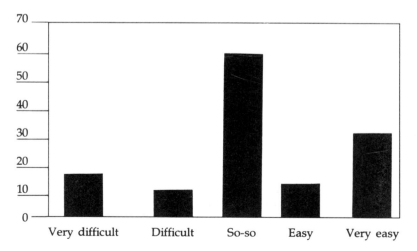

**Fig. 7.2 Is finding fiction easy or difficult?**

concerned. The three libraries in our survey carried stocks of fiction ranging from 17,000 books to 40,000, and at any one time people ought to be able to find on their visit to the library enough fiction books to their taste. But the arrangement was not seen as facilitating choice. It was left to luck for our users as to what they could come across on the small section of 'returned' shelves, or what might catch their eyes in the alphabetical sequence.

As well as looking at methods of selection, we attempted in the survey to correlate the method of choice with readers' satisfaction with the books selected (see Figure 7.3).

Percentage
of books
enjoyed

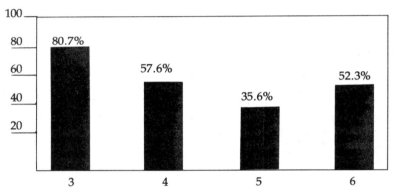

3  Especially looked for books by this author
4  Browsed/recognized author's name
5  Browsed/looked interesting
6  Looked for genre

**Fig. 7.3  Satisfaction rate**

It was found that those who had chosen books knowing something about the author enjoyed four out of five books taken out. However those who browsed and chose 'something interesting' enjoyed only one in three of their books. Thus the most popular method of choosing, i.e. browsing, appears to be the least successful in satisfying the reader. But the more information about a book the reader has at the selection stage, the greater the likelihood that it will be enjoyed. This was also found by Spenceley in his study of fiction browsing. This does not mean that we have to turn all our readers into purposive ones, only that more help and guidance is needed at the browsing stage. Though browsing can be pleasurable, it can also be bewildering. As Mann comments: 'There is a big difference between pleasant browsing along shelves stuffed with familiar goodies and wandering lonely as a cloud between banks of books which don't mean a thing to us.'[11]

We noted in the Kent study where books that were borrowed came from in the library. It was found that there was a heavy use of the returned section – 46% of the books in the sample had come from the returned section rather than the A–Z sequence on the shelves. This would seem to indicate readers' preference to choose from a smaller, more manageable range than the large unbroken alphabetic sequence. Goodall found about one-third of the books being taken out came from the alphabetic author sequence, the rest from the varied fiction arrangements in the library, the categorized shelves, paperback spinners or returned book section.[12]

All the surveys mentioned discovered that readers were reluctant to approach the staff for help (84% in Kent had never asked the staff for help, 93% in Spiller's survey), and a minimal use of the catalogue for fiction choice (in Goodall's survey 87% never used the catalogue, in the Kent survey 86%). So, concentrating help at the readers' advisory desk, or looking to catalogues to help the reader, will not be effective in reaching the majority of users.

Since the Kent study there have been other works on browsing for fiction, and Deborah Goodall has brought these together in a review of the literature.[13] Through these studies, public libraries need to recognize and accept that many of their users approach the stock through browsing, and that there is a need for a reappraisal of shelf arrangement to ensure accessibility of the stock, that libraries need to appear 'browser-friendly'. The following section looks at customary shelf arrangements in the light of the above research findings.

## Shelf arrangements for fiction
The essential debate in fiction arrangement on the shelves has been to categorize or not to categorize. Back in the 1930s in Britain, articles appeared in the *Library Association record* discussing the advantages and disadvantages of alphabetical arrangements which keep books by one author together, versus segregation into groups such as crime stories, romances or historical. Fifty years on these seem to have remained the main options open to libraries for organizing fiction.

### *Alphabetical sequence*
This is the time-honoured method of organizing fiction in one alphabetical sequence of authors' names. The advantages are:

1   There is just one place to look for specific titles – for staff and users.
2   Users will not confine themselves to a few categories, but will browse across the whole spectrum.
3   It will help in a general 'elevation' of reading habits as users will come across works of literary worth as well as popular titles.

Certainly, comments were made in favour of the A – Z sequence by readers in the Kent survey and in Goodall's survey, in terms of the arrangement being simple to follow, books being in their 'proper place', and, if authors were known, it being easy to find a book. But in the light of the research findings, this is not an arrangement that helps the majority of our readers who come in with no specific authors or titles in mind. Even those who do look for specific authors are often in the position of not finding those known authors on the shelves. In Kent it was found that 52% of those surveyed had looked for specific authors they knew and liked and not found what they had wanted. Readers are generally prepared to substitute, and it is at this stage that they need help to discover new authors, and to extend their list of known and liked authors. Browsing in the alphabetic sequence offers no guidance except a chance juxtaposition of authors. Spiller asks, 'How many Goldings and Goldmans have benefited from being shelved next to (or among) the works of William Golding?'

The provision of booklists describing authors who write in genres could be seen as a way of helping readers cope with the A – Z sequence, but in Kent the research showed that the majority of users (80%) did not make use of them and mostly were not aware of such guides, despite displays.

The most telling argument against the alphabetic sequence as a sole arrangement for fiction is perhaps the use made of it; borrowers in Kent were making as much use of the few bays of returned shelves as the tens of bays of A – Z fiction. The convenience factor of specific location for particular authors benefits only a minority of readers, and librarians' administrative arrangements. Libraries interested in making their fiction stock accessible and inviting to browse in need, therefore, to consider alternative arrangements.

### Categorization

This is the arrangement of fiction into genres or 'reader interest' categories; in the USA this is also referred to as fiction classification. Though being discussed in the 1930s, it has only really been since the 1970s in Britain that categorization has been introduced into libraries on any scale, for both fiction and non-fiction.

The approaches and methods of various British library authorities, e.g. Cambridgeshire, Hertfordshire, Surrey, East Sussex, are fully described in *Alternative arrangement: new approaches to public library stock.*[14] The common aim in all these library authorities was the desire to arrange stock to coincide more with readers' 'natural inclinations', to make their libraries 'user-orientated' rather than being arranged in line with the librarian's convenience. It was seen as a demystifying of systems which had been designed for the vocal minority of purposive users. The intentions behind the move to categorization were:

1 To make browsing easier and more fruitful.
2 To improve access to popular material.
3 To increase self-service potential.

Some authorities (e.g. Hertfordshire) found that issues increased as a result of this arrangement – by 167% at Hoddesdon. This would seem to show that borrowers find this arrangement easier to use, as it can be argued that ease of use is a prime factor affecting circulation figures.

The question for a library wishing to adopt categorization as a means of arranging its fiction stock is what categories to use, and how many categories of genre subdivisions are helpful. There are no definite answers to this, and further research is needed in this area. An array of dozens of categories could be as confusing and unhelpful for the reader as one alphabetic sequence. Gail Harrell's study of the use of genre classification in 47 libraries across the USA shows that three categories have proved themselves to librarians in America: science fiction, westerns and mysteries.[15] These were used by all the libraries in her survey. However, since 26 different categories were used by the libraries surveyed, it is clear there is not universal agreement on the rest! A list of categories used by British library authorities is included at the end of this chapter. There is also further research needed on the scale of categorization needed in a collection; this could range from a few bays to the entire stock.

Sharon Baker has carried out some research in this area in the USA.[16] She identifies the feeling of 'information overload' experienced by browsers – the frustration and confusion to which library users may be susceptible, while being expected to make their selection decisions from hundreds and thousands of items available for their use. She carried out some research on the use of categorized fiction areas in public libraries of various sizes: Denton with 2,500 books in its adult fiction collection, Thomasville with 6,000 and Lexington with 15,000. Her results show that in the larger libraries more people made use of the focus provided by categories; in the small library, use was not significant. She concludes that the guidance provided by classifying fiction is needed as collection size increases. Users at the larger libraries were very much in favour of fiction categorization, saying it made their selection easier and quicker, and enabled them to become familiar with other novelists in a particular genre.

In seeking to define categories, librarians need to ensure they are in touch with their readers' interests and be aware of trends. Subjective evidence can be gathered; Betts, writing in *Alternative arrangement* says that 'the only solution is for [category compilers] to back their judgement and try their ideas in practice. A practical constraint will be whether there is sufficient material to support the categories. Monitoring the use of fiction categories can also provide data for the allocation of funds for fiction purchasing, ensuring a closer fit between supply and demand'.[17]

A related idea is the shelving of some non-fiction with fiction as part of broad 'reader-interest' groupings (without the use of DDC) introduced at two East Sussex libraries in 1979. This has now been extended to all the county's small branches. Appropriate non-fiction is combined with fiction of particular genres (e.g. crime, war, adventure − but not historical), the rest of the fiction being in an alphabetical sequence.

As well as its enthusiastic advocates, categorization has its critics, often related to the connection of categorization with light fiction. Accusations of spoon-feeding readers and pandering to popular taste are made; that people will not venture outside familiar categories to 'improve' their reading habits. Even as recently as 1986, Dixon wrote of categorization as 'encouraging laziness' in readers.[18] These arguments are on the whole patronizing to our users, who should make their own choices about elevating their personal reading tastes. When readers, as opposed to librarians, are asked if they would prefer categorization as a stock arrangement, as in Spiller's survey and Baker's study above, the majority are in favour.

### Spine labelling of books

Some libraries have sought to combine the advantages of one alphabetic sequence with categorization, by using spine labels to indicate the genre of a book. Like many compromises this does not readily combine the advantages of both. It cannot give the reader an idea of the range of books available in the categories chosen, nor does it save the reader's time in searching the shelves through the whole stock collection. In any event it is now to a large extent a pointless exercise as the majority of genre fiction now being published is instantly recognizable from its cover, and from the publishers' series.

The degree to which these methods of organizing fiction are used in libraries has been studied by Gail Harrell.[19] Forty-six of the libraries (96% of those surveyed) divided their main fiction collections, at least in part, into smaller categories. There has been no equivalent British survey of libraries' methods in organizing fiction to date that we are aware of.

## Paperbacks

In some libraries, willingness to experiment with fiction arrangements is limited to paperback stock, perhaps grouped by categories or randomly shelved separate from the main sequence, often using special display racks or spinners.[20]

Although the debate over paperback provision, as fierce in its day as that over categorization, has now subsided, the nature of that provision may suggest underlying attitudes to paperbacks in libraries. When considered as an integral part of the stock, they are likely to be catalogued, processed and shelved like hardbacks. Paperback fiction provided as a concession or 'bait' (because it is informal, attractive and familiar) is likely to be uncatalogued and shelved separately and randomly – and is also likely to be extremely popular.

## Browsing areas

We have outlined the main approaches to organizing fiction on the shelves which have evolved over the years, and have tried to show that research on how libraries are used has implications not only for *what* is provided, but also for *how* it is provided. Librarians have been happily using the alphabetic fiction sequence for years, but research suggests that not all readers find it equally accessible. This is not to say that all public libraries should promptly rearrange their fiction stock, but that an increased awareness of the search strategies actually employed by readers and a willingness to experiment with arrangements could be productive, and are appropriate to an increasingly 'user-centred' approach, in which the librarian is seen as a provider rather than a custodian of materials.

This brings us back to readers actually choosing books from the shelf. Our 1985 Kent survey made us aware of the importance of browsing as a search method, and of the low use made of both catalogues and staff for help; if we were to assist people looking for books, we had to do it at the shelves. It would have been arrogant – not to mention pointless – to suggest that they should be using some search strategy other than browsing; we had to help them browse enjoyably and successfully.

So, in October 1987, we set up what we called a 'browsing area' at Sevenoaks Library, a large town-centre library which has an adult fiction stock of some 15,000 volumes. On four bays in the middle of the alphabetic sequence we provided a selection of fiction grouped by what we termed 'themes'. These themes were intended to bring together novels with a common background interest (e.g. Africa) or purpose (e.g. humorous novels), or which were united by some external factor (e.g. prizewinners, books made into films), to form a collection which would be attractive to the browser, stimulate and encourage choice, and 'suggest' new authors to readers.

We wanted the themes to be quite distinct from traditional genre categories, and to allow for a wide range of literary 'levels' and reading tastes. Half a dozen themes were on display at any one time, each identified by shelf-labelling, and the whole area was signed as 'Novel Ideas'. Reference works on fiction, back copies of the now sadly defunct *Fiction magazine* and a display of relevant posters were also provided.

We tried to pick up hints from the organization of bookshops – some face-out display and good clear guiding were two examples of their practices. Much book-borrowing, like much book-buying, is done on impulse, and both can be made enjoyable. As both the Kent survey and Goodall found,[21] many readers already have difficulties using the library; crammed shelves and poorly maintained stock are unlikely to help or encourage them.

Staff observation, self-completing questionnaires and interviews were employed to monitor the use of the area, and the experiment is described in detail in the report which followed it.[22]

We found that questionnaire respondents borrowed 40% of their books from the browsing area (which occupied about 12% of the fiction shelving), 60% of them found it easier to select from this area than from the alphabetic sequence, and 70% enjoyed using it.

A count of date stamps showed that the 'Novel Ideas' books had been well used. Only 24 of a total of 381 books had not been issued, and some titles had gone out after a long period without issues (demonstrating the well-known principle that displaying goods makes them more attractive).

Readers seemed to like the sense of a reduced, pre-selected stock (shades of the 'returned' trolley!) and the theme approach. They commented on finding authors new to them (a frequent and heartfelt demand), perhaps encouraged by the presence in the same theme of a familiar author, and on rediscovering authors whose names they had forgotten. A 'bookmark' questionnaire placed in each book asked readers to assess their enjoyment of the book. Fifty-six per cent of returned books were rated 'enjoyable' (compared, for example, with 36% of books returned by browsers in our 1985 survey).

Naturally, the browsing area did not suit all readers, but the enthusiastic and positive responses suggested that its presence had increased readers' satisfaction with their chosen books and their enjoyment of the selection process.

## Classification schemes

We have emphasized the need to help the reader at the shelves, and classification schemes for fiction represent another attempt to do this. Most readers' experience of fiction *classification* is limited to fiction *categorization* on the shelves, the provision of bookmarks or lists of authors within particular genres, or possibly the indicating of genre categories within an author/title fiction catalogue. Yet systems of fiction classification (i.e. analysing and representing the content of fiction) of varying degrees of sophistication have been developed throughout the past century. Some of these drew on existing schemes used for non-fiction or codified the genre categories, while others created an original, purpose-built scheme for fiction.

The Dewey Decimal Classification (DDC) is fairly typical of the most widely used classification schemes in allowing little scope for subject analysis of individual works of fiction (although there is provision for collections of fiction on specific topics); only language and historical period are indicated. One way to overcome this is to assess the subject matter of a novel and allocate it the appropriate main class Dewey number. This was the method adopted by Frank Haigh in Halifax Public Library in 1933, classifying the entire adult and junior fiction stock of one library by the 1889 edition of DDC, although retaining a separate fiction sequence on the shelves.[23] Detective stories were shelved at F365, novels with medical backgrounds at F610 – and *Jane Eyre* at F Biography. It proved a somewhat unwieldy tool as each novel could only be given one location. Geographical and historical features were given priority in such decisions (so westerns were classified as Travel and description – America).

Three years after Haigh, L. A. Burgess of Southampton Public Libraries produced his own decimal classification for fiction, intended to extend the benefits of classification to fiction and to help readers seeking substitutes for known authors.[24] He also suggested – not for 'any public record' – symbols of evaluation of literary quality to be assigned by librarians and used when advising readers. Burgess includes the familiar genres in detail, along with main classes such as Utopias and propagandist stories and novels of mood. Again, a book must be given one single classification, although a secondary interest may be indicated by adding a colon and the appropriate number.

McClellan's simpler scheme has 13 broad headings (e.g. Sea stories, Country life) and allows for 'Contemporary literary novels' and 'Classics', usually the left-overs in a categorized stock.[25]

The imperfections of these schemes bring out a significant point about the classifying of fiction, which is less easy than non-fiction to arrange in 'natural' subject groupings on the shelf. While a classification using notation can allocate alternative symbols to the same book within a catalogue, that book can only have one place on the shelf. Most novels require several access points to cater for the different ways readers might approach them – hence most fiction classification schemes have favoured an alphabetical sequence on the shelves and in a classified catalogue. The scheme which comes closest to overcoming these problems is that of R. S. Walker.[26] In his detailed, faceted scheme, the notation can encompass not just place and time, but also plot, style, theme and type of characters.

Perhaps the most flexible schemes for fiction, however, remain those that use verbal headings to provide a variety of potential access points. To take a straightforward example, *Fiction index* and *Fiction catalog* list a novel under each appropriate search term, e.g. A. N. Wilson's *Incline our hearts* is listed under Adolesence and England 1930–59 by *Fiction index*.

Scandinavian librarians have played an important part in recent work on the classification of fiction, and in particular in developing online subject searching of fiction, both adult and junior. The best-known scheme is that produced by Annelise Pejtersen in Denmark, which again combines an alphabetical shelf sequence with a classified card catalogue, and which has been used to compile the fiction database DANEBASE.

Pejtersen endeavours to retain the subjective factors inherent in choosing fiction, and to reconcile these with objective indexing criteria. Her AMP (Analysis and Mediation of Publications) classification scheme identifies four dominant 'dimensions' in readers' perceptions of what a novel is about:

1　Subject matter, e.g. events, description, social relations.
2　Frame, e.g. time, place, social setting.
3　Author's intention or attitude, e.g. humour, or criticism of contemporary values.
4　Accessibility, e.g. readability, size of typeface.

The novel is indexed accordingly, and a card giving the full annotation is placed at each access point for the book in the catalogue; there is also an alphabetical index.[27]

Pejtersen gives the following as one example of a full catalogue entry (translated from the Danish original):

FAST, Howard:    *Spartacus* (American) 1st ed. 1952.
Subject matter    *Action/course of events*: an extensive slave revolt, led by the gladiator Spartacus.
    *Social relations*: description of Roman society and relations between different social classes.
Frame    *Time*: ca 70 BC. *Place*: Italy − Rome and Capua.
Author's intention    *Emotional experience*: entertaining, exciting.
    *Cognition/information*: criticism of suppression and exploitation.
Accessibility    *Readability*: easy, large typography.
    *Bibliographic data*: 297 pp. − Spektrum, 1962.

The construction and use of the scheme are grounded in extensive research both at the Royal School of Librarianship and in Danish public libraries. Pejtersen reports that it has increased reader satisfaction by aiding choice, revived under-used bookstock by bringing it to people's attention, and improved librarians' professional knowledge of fiction.

The first criterion for judging any fiction classification scheme should be: does it help the reader find a book they will enjoy in the way they go about choosing? Does it give the reader improved access to the stock? Sapp assesses some fiction classification schemes and indexes, and argues the case that providing better subject access to fiction would improve services to readers.[28] We would suggest that fiction classification should not be seen as merely a pleasing intellectual exercise or an attempt to justify fiction's significance, and solely for librarians, but as a response to a genuine need on the part of readers. However, as long as classification schemes remain catalogue-based with alphabetical order on the shelves, and browsing readers 'unfortunately ... tend to choose fiction straight from the shelves'[29] and mostly to ignore catalogues and indexes, the usefulness of such schemes will depend entirely on their effective exploitation by librarians. A classification as detailed as Pejtersen's AMP would entail a lot more time being spent on fiction enquiries, and would also require the readers to be precise and articulate in their requests, which practising librarians might agree is not always the case.

Nevertheless, the Pejtersen experiment also shows that classification schemes can be worthwhile if librarians' attitudes towards fiction, discussed at the beginning of this chapter, are positive. Staff need to know their stock, encourage fiction enquiries (often very tentative), and use their catalogue to the full. Ideally, this would result in better-satisfied readers, better-satisfied librarians and a better-utilized stock – including improved booklists and displays.

Returning from contemplation of this rosy future to the question of reader demand for fiction classification, the simple questions, 'Have you any more books like this?' and 'Who else writes this sort of book?' are familiar. Two recent works try to respond to this need by creating what Peter Mann calls a 'browser's catalogue'. His *A readers' guide to fiction authors*[30] and Kenneth McLeish's *Bloomsbury good reading guide*[31] are intended to be used by readers, not just librarians.

*A readers' guide to fiction authors*, based on suggestions from librarians, is an alphabetical sequence of authors with alternatives to each one. It works on the simple 'If you like x, why not try y' principle. *Bloomsbury good reading guide* includes a brief description of an author's work and his or her main titles, and may divide alternatives according to which aspect of the author's work is most important to the reader. It includes reading 'menus' for a variety of topics.

The same underlying principle prompted the Kent browsing area experiment described above, which also tried to answer readers' demands for more 'names to look for'. Like these two books, it covered a wide literary range, the idea being not to confine readers to one restricted area. Narrowing a reader's range may be a risk with complex, perhaps computer-aided, schemes which search very precisely.

### Information technology

Following on from this discussion of classification schemes, it is worth looking at the potential uses of new technology in fiction retrieval. It has been stated above that research has indicated minimal use of catalogues and booklists by the public while selecting fiction. Therefore any use of new technology to aid retrieval of fiction books would have to offer something different to our users. Use of catalogues for fiction is normally based on the enquirer knowing the author or title; a computer database could offer different access points to the stock, via criteria the reader selects. If linked to an online issue system, the search could also be confined to those books on the shelves at the time of the reader's visit, thus overcoming one constraint of booklists!

The success of such an approach would depend on librarians being able to devise search criteria that match terms the readers would actually use. The 'dimensions' identified by Pejtersen, described above, are a possible starting point, as these were based on empirical analysis of users' verbal expressions of need. However, the considerable work involved in this level of indexing of our stock would have to be assessed against the anticipated value to our borrowers, and likely levels of use.

Douglas Betts of Surrey County Library has outlined some ways computer systems can assist self-service for library users. He suggests that catalogues carry synopses of fiction books that could be keyword searched by the reader. This gives a subject approach without constructing elaborate classifications. He states 'If you like sea-stories set in Napoleonic times, it shouldn't be too difficult to produce a set of user friendly questions to help readers do their own search, a little expert system'.[32] The information for the synopses could come from a variety of sources: pro formas at the selection stage, suppliers' information, staff's own reading.

Betts also suggests the building up of reader profiles; these could be used for the ultimate personalized service with printouts of new and existing stock matched against individual interests. If there were to be included in the database some linkages between authors' names along the lines of Peter Mann's or the Bloomsbury guide, you could even produce for readers a list of authors they might like to try, based on their previous reading history.

We may seem a long way from this use of technology to make our stock accessible in new ways to our users. But there are opportunities for experiment offered by the flexibility of computer databases. As Betts writes, 'If we are going to get real value out of computer processing then we should be thinking outside of librarians' creation of services towards what might be actually useful to our clients'.[33]

Here indeed is the key point. However we organize our fiction on the shelves, classify it, or catalogue it, our aim is surely to be of use to our customers, to guide people to books they want and will find worth reading.

## References

1 Savage, E. A. A., *A manual of book classification and display for public libraries*, London, Allen and Unwin, 1946.

2 Needham, C. D., *Organising knowledge in libraries*, (2nd edn), London, Deutsch, 1971.

3 Mackay, S., *Redhill rococco*, London, Heinemann, 1986.

4 McClellan, A. W., 'The reading dimension in effectiveness and service', *Library review*, 30, Summer 1981, 81.

5 Mann, P. H., 'Fiction and the reading public', in *Peebles '83: proceedings of the 69th Annual Conference of the Scottish Library Association, Peebles, June 6 – 9, 1983*, Glasgow, Scottish Library Association, 1983, 74.

6  Spiller, D., 'The provision of fiction for public libraries', MLS dissertation, Loughborough University of Technology, Department of Library and Information Studies, 1979.

7  Spenceley, N., 'Readership of literary fiction: a survey of library users in the Sheffield area', unpublished MA dissertation, University of Sheffield, Department of Information Studies, 1980.

8  Day, M. J., 'Selection and use of serious fiction in a public library system', unpublished MA dissertation, University of Sheffield, Department of Information Studies, 1978.

9  Goldhor, H., 'The effect of prime display location on public library circulation', *Library quarterly*, **42** (4), 1972.

10  Sear, L. and Jennings, B., *How readers select fiction*, Maidstone, Kent County Library, 1986 (Research and Development Report no. 9).

11  Mann, P. H., 'Libraries and the reading habit', in *Proceedings of the Library Association Public Libraries Group Weekend School, Sheffield 1982*, Penzance, Library Association Public Libraries Group, 1982, 18.

12  Goodall, D., 'Use made of an adult fiction collection', Undergraduate dissertation, Loughborough University of Technology, Department of Library and Information Studies, 1987, 79.

13  Goodall, D., *Browsing in public libraries*, Loughborough, LISU, 1989.

14  Ainley, P. and Totterdell, B., *Alternative arrangement: new approaches to public library stock*, London, Association of Assistant Librarians, 1982.

15  Harrell, G., 'The classification and organization of adult fiction in large American public libraries', *Public libraries*, **24** (1), Spring 1985, 13–14.

16  Baker, S. L., 'Will fiction classification schemes increase use?', *Reference quarterly*, **27** (3), Spring 1988, 366–76.

17  Betts, D. A., 'Reader interest categories in Surrey', in Ainley, P. and Totterdell, B., *Alternative arrangement: new approaches to public library stock*, London, Association of Assistant Librarians, 1982, 60–77.

18  Dixon, J. (ed.), *Fiction in libraries*, London, Library Association, 1986.

19  Harrell, G.

20  Cropper, B., *Going soft: some uses of paperbacks in libraries*, London, Branch and Mobiles Group of the Library Association, 1986, provides an interesting discussion on paperback provision.

21  Goodall, D., *Browsing in public libraries*.

22  Sear, L. and Jennings, B., *Novel ideas: a browsing area for fiction*, Maidstone, Kent County Library, 1989 (Research and Development Report no. 10).

23  Haigh, F., 'The subject classification of fiction: an actual experiment', *Library world*, 36, 1933, 78–82.

24  Burgess, L. A., 'A system for the classification and evaluation of fiction', *Library world*, 38, 1936, 179–82.

25  Atkinson, F., *Fiction librarianship*, London, Bingley, 1981, 45–6.

26  Discussed in Dixon, J., 162.

27  Pejtersen, A. M. and Austin, J., 'Fiction retrieval: experimental design and evaluation of a search system based on users' value criteria', *Journal of documentation*, **39** (4), December 1983, 230 – 46 (Part One); *Journal of documentation*, **40** (1), March 1984, 25 – 35 (Part Two).

28  Sapp, G., 'The levels of access: subject approaches to fiction', *Reference quarterly*, **25** (4), Summer 1986, 488 – 97.

29  *Library and information science abstracts*, abstract 88/1045.

30  Mann, P. H., *A readers' guide to fiction authors*, Loughborough, CLAIM, 1985.

31  McLeish, K., *Bloomsbury good reading guide*, London, Bloomsbury, 1988.

32  Betts, D. A., *Borrowing and the fiction reader*, London, Branch and Mobile Libraries Group of the Library Association, 1987.

33  Ibid.

## Appendix
Some categories in use in British libraries:
Adventure
Contemporary literary novels
Country life
Crime
Detective stories
English classics
Family sagas
Fantasy
General fiction
Historical
Horror
Humour/satire
Romance
Science fiction
Sea stories
Short stories
Spy stories
Teenage
Thrillers
Translations
War stories
Westerns

# 8   Fiction information: sources and services

*Michael Greenhalgh*

## Introduction

This chapter examines a range of UK (with selective reference to US) sources of information on adult fiction likely to be needed by librarians in providing an effective service and by library users in wishing to advance their knowledge. The writer is conscious there will always be other and new sources: this is therefore an indicative guide which attempts to foster a critical approach.

A survey is offered here of material sources to which any public library system might reasonably be expected to gain access. There are others. The library supplier will have standard and new fiction lists. Both Spiller[1] and Dixon[2] warn against over reliance on these but one supplier has pointed out that while his role is to supply anything libraries will buy, this is 'very predictable'.[3] Reviews broadcast on radio or television are not normally preserved in a form to which subsequent reference can be made and their validity checked. Another influential yet similarly immaterial source, deserving more documentation and scrutiny, is requests from individual users; attending to these will fulfil that portion of service concerned with expressed demand but will not stimulate progress in the less tangible aspects of service, unexpressed and unactivated demand.[4]

Sources of information on fiction are necessarily so widely scattered in libraries that a pamphlet pointing this out would be an appropriate means of promoting their use and, more importantly, their collation. Bibliographical sources tend to live at the readers' adviser's side of the counter. Current reviews are dispersed over the periodicals area; retrospective reviews are found in the literary criticism section. Some biographical material will be in the reference section, some in the sequence of biographies, some within literary criticism. Bringing these diverse information sources together, through the medium of an explanatory leaflet, would be of considerable help to the enquiring reader of fiction.

## Bibliographical sources

*Whitaker's books in print (WBIP)*, 1874— (the US equivalent of which is Bowker's *Books in print*), whose annual four-volume cumulation appears in April, is more currently accessed through its monthly microfiche or BOOKBANK, its CD-ROM version. This is the British book trade's, as well as librarians', guide to in-print fiction and its dates of publication. There are both author and title entries. *WBIP's* weekly periodical format, *The Bookseller*, is rendered more digestible through its subject arrangement, in which fiction is presented in the categories general, historical, mystery, romance, science fiction, short stories, war and western, while the final pages list the current bestsellers. There are two bumper versions, the Spring books issue and the Autumn books issue which, as showcases for publishers' plans for the next six months, allow librarians some prescience in collection development. Advertising dominates, yet this can bring an awareness of lesser-known publishers not readily encountered through library suppliers. The 1989 figures given for fiction are 1,148 cloth-bound titles published, a 4% increase on 1988, at an average price of £10.98.[5] The 1988 figures – more indicative of the total output, if not necessarily library interest – were 6,496 titles, 47% of which were reprints and new editions, and 4% translations.

The *British national bibliography (BNB)*, 1950—, weekly, with quarterly and annual cumulations, available in hard copy, microfiche, CD-ROM (1950–85 backfile, 1986– current file updated quarterly) and online through BLAISE, provides the most systematic listing of UK material. Its sister publication *Books in English*, 1971—, bi-monthly snowballing cumulations, with 1971–80 and 1981–5 retrospective cumulations, available in microfiche, extends coverage to English language titles worldwide. *BNB* main entries are presented in Dewey Decimal Classification (DDC) order, thus observing the distinction, for instance, between novelists prolific before and after 1945, and between not only UK and US novelists but, enriching DDC's capabilities, those of many other nations writing in English. Separate listing is also given to short stories and anthologies. The most popular categories' extensiveness in relation to review coverage is surprising. In 1989 there were 2,846 UK novels of post-war writers and 1,478 US novels; 247 UK novels of pre-war writers and 131 US novels; and 118 UK short story collections of post-war writers. Australian culture gets next best representation, with 91 novels, while Canada offers 61. There are 60 US short story collections by post-war writers, but it might be deemed equally significant in collection development and the production of lists by author provenance that there are 37 novels by New Zealand writers, 27 by South African writers and 25 by Indian writers.

This is to emphasize the retrospective value of the annual cumulation, while the CD-ROM backfile for 1950–85 is of more interest for tracing the output of individual authors. But the weekly issues form the basis of practical current collection development. The question of timeliness then arises. Thanks to Cataloguing in Publication, whereby an entry is created from pre-publication information from the publisher, this is fair. A sample of 20 titles was taken from the September to December 1989 period and compared against *Whitaker's books in print* and *The Times literary supplement (TLS)* coverage. The *British national bibliography* was found to be, on average, five weeks behind *Whitaker's books in print*, but the overall picture was that 4 titles appeared the same month, 4 appeared earlier in *BNB*, 11 later in *BNB* (1 appeared in *BNB* but not *WBIP*). In comparison with *The Times literary supplement*, *BNB* was found to be, on average, eight weeks ahead, yet the overall picture here was that 3 titles appeared the same month, 8 appeared earlier in *BNB*, 3 later in *BNB* (6 appeared in *BNB* but not *TLS*). So, while *BNB* is not the best source for current awareness, this cannot be achieved comprehensively without regular reference to it, *WBIP* and reviews.

Another feature of entries which is of both scholarly and practical collection development significance is the clarification of the existence of an earlier edition of the book, often under a different publisher, or a different format such as paperback or large print. The debate whether fiction should be accorded full descriptive cataloguing[7] has raised at national level the development of a policy which has sometimes resulted in scant information on fiction holdings at local level. Should full entry only survive if it can be commercially viable through sufficient sales by the British Library for direct input to local catalogues? Rationalization of holdings is similarly being raised as an issue,[8] a reminder of the present advantage that all titles listed are permanently retained and may be consulted at the British Library in London.

*British book news*, 1941–, also available on microfilm, has both a prospective and retrospective value. Its forthcoming books section of titles to be published the following month provides briefly annotated entries (15–50 words) and, though the concentration on plot has no critical basis and lacks consistency of detail, its better examples have something of the stimulating quality of blurbs – but without their questionable plaudits. The quantity of coverage is itself valuable, with 1,284 titles appearing in 1989. Although the entries are not categorized, crime, historical, and short stories may be readily identified in skimming and, to a lesser extent, science fiction, fantasy, adventure, animal stories and romance. There is useful noting of series and sequels, award winners and reissues. The retrospective feature is its book surveys which are succinct yet thorough overviews of, in 1990, crime fiction, Agatha Christie at her centenary, science fiction, short stories and, in December, the year's literary novels. Invaluable for librarians' stock revision, they will also be appreciated by library users for their informed yet user-friendly manner.

The remainder of this section turns from general to specific bibliographies. *Prizewinning literature: UK literary award winners*[9] is an enumerative bibliography of all prizewinners of current awards since their inception. Without annotations, its use is not so straightforward for the general reader as the librarian, who can then put together thematic lists, exhibitions, or display works by theme.[10] With 1989 in-print availability indicated in hardback, paperback and large print, as well as ISBNs or *BNB* numbers for original editions, the specialized categories of historical fiction and science fiction provide markers for stock selection and revision, even though only represented by one award each; but the ten awards for regional fiction, seven for first novels, three for crime fiction and three for romantic fiction offer more ample scope. The distortion factor is that the context of the award, that is the quality of the opposition at the time, is no longer apparent, except when shortlisted novels are cited for the Booker Prize and also the *Sunday Express* Book of the Year, as are runners-up of the Betty Trask Awards, *Yorkshire Post* Awards and silver as well as gold dagger Crime Writers' Association Awards. The author index makes salutary reading with regard to frequent Booker shortlistings and perhaps one success: is there an élite of Booker writers of arcane literary merit but limited general appeal?

*PLR in practice*[11] provides information on consumer take-up of fiction in libraries through an intentionally nationally representative sample of 20 libraries, whose variability in response is itself noted.[12] The 100 adult fiction titles scoring the highest loans are listed,[13] with the caveat that this is not wholly representative of the popularity of authors whose many titles do not individually receive as much borrowing. Nevertheless, the 100 top adult fiction titles come from only 23 authors, the earliest dating from 1970. There is also a statistical analysis[14] of 19 categories of adult fiction, with reference to 12 titles specified in every category, an affirmation that if fiction is selected in accordance with an awareness of the socio-economic characteristics of the community, uniformity and thus cost-effectiveness of issues may be achieved. As if to illustrate this point, regional fiction has a wider appeal outside its geographical area than might be supposed.[15] What is offered here is a national average by which an individual library authority's performance might be estimated; but it is more important to acquire and analyse local issue figures and in particular to consider the reasons for lack of borrowing.

To refine the focus still further, from popular to specialized consumption, *Out on the shelves: lesbian books into libraries*[16] is a select annotated bibliography (blurb-like summaries of up to 100 words with a smattering of critique) of positive discrimination to counter the pussyfooting of library suppliers. The following categorization of contemporary fiction and numbers of representative titles are featured: the last 20 years (36 titles); lesbian thrillers (18); lesbian romance (13); science fiction (8); short story collections (6); fiction for young (in essence teenage) women (6).

*Tale of the future*[17] is a bibliographic spin-off, or working plan, for a retrospective analysis in that its chronological listing of stories located in time future to that of their date of publication was the starting point for the author's analysis of the origins and development of these works.[18] The publication period covered is 1644 to 1976 and it is instructive to trace the growth of this fiction, for instance from 11 entries in 1950 to 250 in 1975. One-sentence annotations provide only a brief indication of the main theme of the narrative but there is scholarly and useful attention to variant publication dates and titles between UK and US editions and the appearance of translations in relation to the originals. For US coverage particularly, there are fuller (75–100 word) annotations in *Anatomy of wonder*.[19] British publishers of science fiction are singled out in a wider-ranging US readers' guide, *Genrereflecting*,[20] which surveys westerns, thrillers, romances, fantasy and horror, looking too under all these categories at themes and types, and also noting sources of films. It is prodigal in expressing the librarian's constant desire to further classify, but also a model of user friendliness.

*The Glasgow novel*[21] combines bibliography and critical survey, which is also reflected in the succinct evaluation of the works' quality by annotations to the bibliography; these also clarify the nature of the Glasgow connection and the fidelity with which the life, character or atmosphere of the city is conveyed. Sequels are noted in the entries. Publications from 1771 to 1985 are featured in nine period groups, alphabetically by author, an arrangement more convenient for the overviewing critic than ready reference bibliographer; but there are also chronological, author and title indexes plus a useful, unexpected biographical source in a list of biography and criticism of 29 individual authors.[22] Here is an example of a localized publication which in its thoroughness and comparative recency proves of national and cultural utility. There is also reference to fuller treatment of the Glasgow detective story.[23]

## Indexes

Indexing is, or should be, concerned with accommodating characteristics from multiple yet feasible viewpoints. The *Fiction index*[24] offers the fullest example, with annual volumes supplementing the five-year cumulations whose coverage began in 1945.[25] The principle in this is clear cut: an entry giving author and title under a heading which may be a concrete entity (a place, person, occupation, subject, named period of history), an abstract theme (like love) or a genre. Headings with several entries may themselves provide a basis for annotated guides or displays. Without an author/title index readers cannot, however, link a work they have enjoyed to one in the same category; yet the reader's adviser familiar with this index may be able to effect that link and even signal it on an OPAC. The most popular categories and number of 1988 entries are: thrillers (125), family life (88), love (83), detective stories (82), murder (72), fantasies (62), family chronicles (60), England: twentieth century (58), macabre stories (47), science fiction (45), World War Two (44), short stories (42), spy stories: twentieth century (42). The popularity of thrillers is further respected and extended by the use of the suffix 'x' to indicate thriller type material whose primary focus occurs under another heading, such as 'drug traffic'. In the cumulated volumes[26] 12 types of crime fiction are distinguished, though it is admitted these are not necessarily exclusive. There are 45 headings which in the 1988 volume featured ten or more titles. It might be objected that some of these categories are vaguer than others and subsume a number of very different works, approaches and attitudes; but the lists at any rate provide a start for more refined listings according to the interests of the local community, while it is a canon of literary criticism that a novel is a synthesis of different qualities of interest[27] and so may be approached through focusing on individual qualities. Multiple viewpoints are thus catered for; whether these are all feasible viewpoints and highlight more than the basic and perhaps least interesting characteristics of a work (and whether the more interesting are capable of indexing of this simple kind) is another matter. There is helpful detail with regard to specific countries, places, historical periods and figures, novels based on television series with the series cited, pastiches and parodies with the originals cited. Quasi-biographical information is also valuable: a list of detectives (72 in 1988) with cross-reference to authors, and in the 1987 volume but not the 1988, a list of 259 authors of romances, 20 of historical romances and 64 of westerns.

Beside *Fiction index*, trim and to the point, a US survey of one year's production, *Olderr's fiction index 1987*,[28] seems bulky and cumbersome. The difference lies in the further access points Olderr provides: as well as subject (based on the Library of Congress thesaurus), by period the work covers, place, central characters, title and series title, all presented in the dictionary format of a single alphabetical sequence. Beginning with subject headings for dates, whose precision is helpful. There are main entries under author which give UK publishers and variant titles, though a check of the first 25 revealed only three UK publishers and these were for works originating in the UK. This index attempts to double as *Book review index (BRI)* in its inclusion of citations to reviews in *Booklist, Library journal, Publisher's weekly* and adult books deemed suitable for young adults by *School library journal* reviewers. Further, but not necessarily better than *BRI*, it converts reviews to a four-star rating system made more complex by plus and minus suffixes, though the appended 369 best books list (those which at least one review gave what was considered the highest rating) is useful for collection development. A closer US parallel to *Fiction index* is to be found in *Short story index*,[29] which for 1987 indexed 4,167 stories, 87% of which appeared in collections, the rest (but welcome guidance to further access to authors' writings) in periodicals. Entries are under theme and author, though with so many individual stories in collections the constant repetition of collection title is irksome.

*Sequels*,[30] whose first edition was published in 1922, adopts a suitably liberal definition which allows the grouping of sequences of novels with the same central character (most commonly a detective), or characters, theme, historical or geographical connection, chronologically under author. The annotations sort out the precise bedfellows in omnibus editions, backed by an index of series and characters. In the latest edition entries are from around 1950, except for long-running series still in print, to the end of 1988, and this seems to be a growth area in fiction. There is attention to alternative titles, paperbacks (rife in science fiction and fantasy) with dates of subsequent publication in hardback, and to differences between UK and US publication. A sophistication and an interesting theme for booklists and displays is the continuations of the 'family sagas' of classic novels by other writers: see under Jane Austen, Charlotte and Emily Brontë, Charles Dickens and, most popular, Conan Doyle.

*Filmed books and plays: a list of books and plays from which films have been made, 1928 – 86*[31] is self-explanatory but no less useful for that, with a film title index, author index and change of original title index.

*A readers' guide to fiction authors*[32] is an index in which authors considered to be similar to others by over 600 practising librarians have been analysed by computer to produce over 900 names linked with each other. The idea, that by this means readers who have exhausted the library's stock of their favourite authors, may find others similarly satisfying, is worthy – but its execution is suspect at this level of generality.[33] More professional opinion does not mean better, but rather the offering of more diffuse and idiosyncratic views. To have the comparisons without a reasoned explanation, which is the foundation of critical practice, is to compound the felony. The excitement of fiction reading and browsing is for the reader to discover his or her own idiosyncrasy and its distinctive quality is that no one author is quite like another. That there are 58 authors suggested as being like Barbara Cartland disavows the compiler's own survey[34] of author loyalty in romantic fiction. There is a refinement, or confusion, of three-star grading for gauging the strength of recommendation, in addition to the basic listing and it would be recognizing the guide's pragmatic value if librarians pull the highest matches out (in the Barbara Cartland example, Clare Darcy and Netta Muskett) and cross-refer on an OPAC.

More helpful in its detailed citation and clarification of works of a similar level and style is the *Bloomsbury good reading guide.*[35] Its outstanding feature is its wealth of cross-references, with every right-hand margin invitingly headed 'read on'. There are over 300 main author entries of authors worldwide writing in English, with good coverage of literary and middlebrow, but only selective coverage of popular authors. A paragraph about the author's work and style in general is followed by an enthusiastic description (a ready-made model for librarians' annotated lists) of a selected characteristic work, with suggestions for further reading of the same and other authors: in all reference is made to over 3,000 titles (US variant titles are cited after UK ones). There are two further levels of cross-referencing. Seven or eight books of a similar kind are grouped in 'menus' of suggested reading under a theme which is sometimes straightforward yet interestingly selective, like 'old dark houses', at other times complex enough to require annotation itself, like 'only connect' (people emotionally ill-at-ease)'. There are 81 of these 'menus' and again these could form the basis for librarians' fuller lists, though the inclusion of two lists each for 'politics' and 'Roman Catholicism' indicates a belief that small is beautiful or that any suggestion of information overload is to be avoided. The third way this guide makes connections is through 'skeins' in which a specific book like Iris Murdoch's *An unofficial rose* is related to other titles in different aspects of association, in the Murdoch example articulated as novels about women alone (six titles compared, with brief explanatory annotations), novels about searching for self (six more titles) and novels about the lure of the exotic (six more titles). There are 19 such skeins which are arguably too subjective and contentious as models for indexing, yet equally may activate more sophisticated readers' advisory work. The *Bloomsbury good reading guide to science fiction and fantasy*[36] is a further guide in the same format, featuring nine new skeins.

A brief mention, finally, of some general and specialized US indexes. *Book review index*, 1965 – , offers issues every two months as well as annual cumulations and indexes *The Times literary supplement* and *London review of books*, which *An index to book reviews in the humanities*, 1960 – , annual, does not, though it covers fiction. *Science fiction and fantasy literature: a checklist, 1770 – 1974*[37] is welcome for its series index and the *Index to science fiction anthologies and collections*[38] for its books contents, that is subject, index. Logasa's *Historical fiction*[39] is arranged by place, then chronology.

## An approach to reviews

The material surveyed so far occupies the relatively safe and objective territory of listing and categorizing, although even here the critical consideration of whether the categorization matches the likely users' approach and whether the listing, for the users, appears an off-putting information overload, are factors which the librarian ought to consider in the presentation of guides to fiction, whether directly through pamphlets, bookmarks or readers' advisory services or indirectly through an OPAC. While it is a good principle and attitude that all sources of information on fiction should be visible and accessible on the open shelves rather than behind library counters, encouraging their use might be a more subtle and long-term matter, which it should be accepted with some users will never materialize. Reviews are initially more attractive for users because they give more significant information on which to make a judgement, albeit that information is more subjective and liable to bias. Users will also have expressed some partiality by their choice of reviewing periodical which, consciously or unconsciously, conforms to their approach to fiction. The librarian, with the responsibility of a less partial judgement, ought to compare reviews where this seems justified or devise other expedients such as reviews by colleagues or users. The existence of a clear collection development policy will assist in this process, but equally important is a clear understanding of what should be expected from reviews, a critical checklist for external ones which will double as a specification for internal reviews.

The literature on the analysis of reviews will repay attention. Dixon[40] offers a checklist of desirable features with reference to UK adult fiction. Of particular interest to the librarian are identification of the category of a work, the type of readers it will interest (which the librarian may be able to match with a community profile) and the physical bulk and likely durability of the book. Of interest to librarian and library user are the subject and its treatment, period, locality, author's approach, comparison with other books by the author and/or on the subject. Style and characterization are more the province of literary criticism and of interest mainly to the reader pursuing education of some kind. Of interest more to the reader than the librarian will be details on the author and likely effect on the reader, though this may be considered partly the librarian's responsibility in the context of bibliotherapy. Dixon raises awareness that the range of issues with which librarians are concerned is greater than that of particular journals. Nevertheless, the acid test of a review of fiction ought still to be literary: its focus on the extent to which a unique contribution or insight is achieved by a given work.

Should there be an effort to create local sources of information on fiction through panels of reviewers, both library staff and users? As a means of raising the profile of, interest in and debate about the fiction service, librarians' advisory capability and self-help activity by community groups, this would seem to be well worth the organization time and resourcing requirements of dissemination. There would need, however, to be agreement as to what specifically a review should cover. Emphasis on fiction perceived as not attracting much review coverage, like romances, historical romances, westerns, would be particularly suitable. Librarians may compile indicative, but not over critical, abstracts from reviews, always bearing in mind the user is more concerned with the impact and readability of the story than literary quality. Such abstracts can also be compiled quite quickly from skimming a book, if major dimensions are looked for, like Pejtersen's subject matter, frame, author's intention and accessibility,[41] but the overview obtained by or via a complete reading is preferable. In any public library system are there not staff and readers waiting for the opportunity to whet their critical faculties, articulate their experience of fiction and give back something of their pleasure?

Palmer,[42] having studied the influence of reviews on the acquisition of Canadian fiction by US public and academic libraries, found that five core journals largely determined public but not academic library purchases, which were more influenced by faculty recommendations or approval plans (the UK equivalent of these latter would be library suppliers' lists or blanket coverage to a specification). He also discovered that, for several libraries, publishers' catalogues or current lists such as those already surveyed in this chapter were the main source of acquisitions. There is scope for a study of publishers' catalogues as information sources: Moorbath[43] raises the issue in the medical field that publishers produce these largely for libraries yet do not take librarians' requirements into account.

### Current reviews

*The Times literary supplement*, 1902 –, weekly, gives the most comprehensive coverage, with 395 fiction titles reviewed in 1989. There is a sense of august authority, a steeping in tradition and sense of literary culture, while the combination of this with streamlined and journalistic presentation would probably be more welcome to busy librarians and readers than extensive critical analyses. Nevertheless there is also a certain neutrality, a tendency to avoid excessive praise or blame. Works are, however, generally scrupulously placed in the context of the author's development, with references to earlier works useful for stock revision. The majority of reviews are of single works, about 750 words, allowing proper concentration on the individual author and avoiding the danger of distortion resulting from having to link separate authors, though this is practised occasionally in features on one geographical and cultural area. International coverage is unsurpassed, with 63 translations (16% of reviews) in 1989, often comparisons with earlier reviews in the original language (which, incidentally, do not figure in the grand total above), with the flattering assumption that many readers have the fluency to tackle these. Short stories are also well represented, with 44 (11% of reviews) in 1989. Other notable features were 27 first novels (7%) and 27 crime novels (7%), though the latter are only brief, in the main enthusiastic, annotations from a single reviewer – in 1989 T. J. Binyon. In terms of timeliness, however, the *TLS* overall lags a little behind *Literary review*. To be specific, of the 124 reviews which appeared in both periodicals in 1989, 37% came out in the same month, but 43% appeared earlier in *Literary review*, while only 20% appeared earlier in the *TLS*.

*Literary review*, 1979 –, monthly, is intended to provide coverage which is not so academic or 'stuffy' as the *TLS*, nor with a total of 259 reviews in 1989 is it as comprehensive. But reviews are generally longer, around 1,000 words, predominantly of one work by one author and accompanied by a photograph, though this is not dated so the reader can only assume it relates to the author when writing the work. The reviews are more lively than those of the *TLS,* sometimes quite vituperative, and their positive advantage, for readers particularly, is that their first concern is to convey the experience of reading the novels rather than trying to place the works in some literary canon. Crime reviews are of the same 100 word variety as in *TLS* but feature more consistently every month and with 78 for the year make up 30% of the grand total. Again one reviewer, in 1989 Philip Oakes, is used and his emphasis on recounting the plot would easily transfer to librarians' production of annotated lists or even extracting and filing these review pages separately for readers' consultation. Coverage of translations is not so strong as *TLS* with 24 (9% of reviews) in 1989 but the international fiction category, previously titled – and still largely – American fiction, comprised 33 titles (13%) in 1989. Only 13 collections of short stories (5%) were reviewed in this period, with about the same attention to women's fiction and popular fiction, which at least suggests a broader range than *TLS.*

The *London review of books,* 1979 – , bi-monthly (the English counterpart of the *New York review of books,* 1963 – , bi-monthly) has all the appearance of a hybrid of the *Literary review* and *TLS.* On the one hand it is more formal and academic than the *Literary review,* more readily seduced by the obsession as to what constitutes a true novel; on the other it is more reflective and serendipitous than the *TLS* in its liking for reviews which cluster three or four novels together. There is a feeling of spaciousness, even though only about 400 words are generally given per novel – because over 2,000 are for those rarely permitted single reviews. But it is considerably more selective anyway, with 128 fiction titles featured in 1989, of which about 7% were translations, 5% short stories and 4% crime. Indexing is poor, so one feels no expectation of retrospective reference. A commendable feature is the citation of date of publication of novels reviewed, suggesting perhaps the length of time the reviewer has had to make judgement, sometimes as much as eight months. In terms of timeliness *LRB* is indistinguishable from *TLS:* to be specific, of the 90 works both reviewed in 1989, they appeared in the same month in 36% of cases, the *LRB* review appeared earlier in 31% but later than *TLS* in 33% of cases.

*London magazine,* 1954 – , every two months, has a more restricted coverage still, but is interesting for its mannered approach, in particular trying to distil features of quality and very much concerned with the nature of expression. This self-consciousness is pardonable in a publication mainly devoted to creative expression in the form of short stories, poems and art criticism in the wider sense. There is a preference, however, for reviews which cluster novels or short stories, so one book will only be accorded about

200 words. In 1989 a total of 78 titles were featured, of which 19 (24%) were short stories and 13 (17%) translations. With regard to timeliness, for the 40 titles matched with *TLS*, *LM* reviews appeared on average a month later, with 15% appearing the same month, 22% earlier than *TLS* but 63% later. Other reviews are to be found, of course, in the quality (and sometimes local) daily and Sunday newspapers and general cultural periodicals, which will all prove sources of user requests but do not give the wide-ranging coverage and depth of assessment that render them worthy of retention as retrospective review sources in the larger public and academic libraries. As fiction is increasingly presented and accessed in audiovisual form, one hopes that reviews of this will increase in quantity and quality. At present *The Gramophone*, 1923–, monthly, is the most consistent source for brief notices on and advertisements of talking books, while *Video today*, 1980–, monthly, offers critical reviews of videocassettes.

**Retrospective reviews**
Once writers become established or notorious enough, there is no shortage of critical and biographical studies of individual authors, though perhaps the location of these in a collection, as in the *British national bibliography*, is too readily divorced from the writings themselves and they are accordingly easily overlooked. With OPACs the librarian has the opportunity to alert a reader's attention. Compendia, however, are both more likely to feature a wider range of authors and themselves be even less regarded and indexed, not least because the task of indexing is more extensive and intricate, yet may pay dividends.

Some indicative examples begin at the general level. *Bestsellers*[44] is a handy encapsulation of the phenomenon in all its genre guises through the 1970s. It attempts to account for the success and fairly puts in perspective the achievements which may prove an indicator of likely continued popularity. Quotations add flavour; checklist by title makes for ease of reference.

*Crime and mystery: the 100 best books*[45] is a good example of a promotional guide for a genre. The title is just catchpenny but the demonstration of an enthusiast's, more welcoming than an authority's, selection and format of around 750-word appraisals of individual novels presented in chronological order (1845–1986) combines the appeal of the blurb with some placing of the works in context, some reference to other works and citations of first UK and US editions. There is a judicious mix of anecdote, and of criticism unsupported by evidence to make it seem overmuch erudition. Yet this highlights the qualities of particular books, as well as the significance of the author's contribution. Arguably, the best published criticism is ingenuously such a blend of journalism and enjoyed exploration. Perhaps the librarian should consider harnessing the energies of colleagues and users to review fiction with the same desire to convey the positive quality of the experience.

*Contemporary women novelists*[46] sees itself as a guide to current literature and its issues, looking at ten writers in their cultural milieu and (of more interest and value to the librarian and readers) supplying succinct yet concentrated analyses of 20 specific texts. The appendix of biographical information, of about 150 words per novelist, is a model of its kind.

*Shadows of the past in contemporary British fiction*[47] is of interest as a critique of ten specific novels by nine authors, and is concerned with the way these are both influenced by and exploit a sense of the past, not only personal and cultural, but also literary. It thus alludes to earlier literature, a fundamental of literary criticism which enables it to be a promoter of sources and hence library collections as the means of making interconnections. Some interview material with the authors is incorporated – but arguably overmuch on the critic's terms and selection.

*Short stories and short fiction 1880–1980*,[48] in expounding the historical development of various literary techniques and themes which are tellingly expressed through this medium, quotes liberally from what are deemed significant works. Thus it is a shop window and its bibliography becomes a kind of mail order checklist, provided that the author's thesis is accepted or at least considered a fair basis for further exploration. The US *Critical survey of short fiction*[49] devotes three volumes to established authors and one to current writers, listing principal works and including signed analyses of the individual authors' contributions.

## Biographical material

*Contemporary novelists*[50] has been commented upon with somewhat bemused admiration by Sutherland,[51] who appreciates its comprehensiveness in terms of little-known authors of high literary accomplishment, but is amused by its panel of advisers' refusal to admit popular authors. These latter are, however, suitably served by *The writer's directory*[52] which, based on information from the writers themselves, gives brief biographical details and lists works chronologically of over 16,000 living writers in English worldwide. It also includes a subject index, but the groupings under which fiction writers appear are mostly too general to be helpful: 'novels/short stories, mystery/crime/suspense, historical/romance, westerns/adventure, science fiction/fantasy'. For popular novelists there is also plenty of popular periodical coverage, and if their popularity continues biographies can be expected. *Who's who* also provides a reliable reference point, with Eleanor Hibbert appearing in all her guises as Jean Plaidy, Eleanor Burford, Ellalice Tate, Elbur Ford, Kathleen Kellow, Philippa Carr and Victoria Holt. She also appears in the *Dictionary of British women writers*[53] among 400 others. This dictionary's entries comprise a biographical sketch, signed discussion of key works and themes placing the individual writer succinctly in context, a chronological listing of works and helpful citations to criticism. This is as thorough as, and more user friendly than, *Contemporary novelists*, though the latter's listing of uncollected short stories and sometimes comments by the novelist are bonuses. Both these works are a very efficient path to an author's world, though one hopes not the only one and that the availability of fuller and broader critical assessment is heeded.

Collections of interviews of authors are uncommon, yet provide a valuable means of bridging the gap between popular journalism and the fascinating detail but sometimes rather tortuous introspection of autobiography. *Novelists in interview*[54] gives us an insight into 14 contemporary novelists as individuals, briefly sketched in their environment, talking extensively on the themes that interest them and the way they choose to articulate them. Neither the vein of literary criticism, quotations from reviews, nor the interviewer obtrude. The detailed discussion of specific works might, however, usefully be referred to under these works on an OPAC. Thus this chapter closes with the affirmation, not for the first time, that the librarian should be creating references which clarify unexpected sources of information on fiction and provide that fresh access which truly enhances user satisfaction.

## References

1　Spiller, D., *Book selection: an introduction to principles and practice* (4th edn), London, Bingley, 1986, 157.

2　Dixon, J. (ed.), *Fiction in libraries*, London, Library Association, 1986, 147 – 9.

3　Kipling, G., 'Only connect: libraries, fiction and the reading public – a report of the Branch and Mobiles Group one day meeting, June 1987', *Service point*, 37, 1987, 18 – 21 (the quotation is from Lance Wetherall, Marketing Director for John Menzies).

4　Totterdell, B. and Bird, J., *The effective library: report of the Hillingdon project on public library effectiveness*, London, Library Association, 1976, 16 – 17.

5　*The Bookseller*, 23 March 1990, 940.

6　*The Bookseller*, 3 February 1989, 374 – 5.

7   Lewis, P., 'The future of the National Bibliography', *Library Association record*, **89** (10), 1987, 516, 519 – 20.

8   British Library, *Gateway to knowledge: the British Library strategic plan, 1989 – 94*, London, British Library, 1989, 24.

9   Strachan, A., *Prizewinning literature: UK literary award winners*, London, Library Association, 1989.

10   Jennings, B. and Sear, L., 'Novel ideas: a browsing area for fiction', *Public library journal*, **4** (3), 1989, 41 – 4 (exemplifies practice at Sevenoaks Library, Kent County).

11   Sumsion, J., *PLR in practice*, Stockton-on-Tees, Registrar of Public Lending Right, 1988.

12   Ibid., 58.

13   Iibd., 144 – 9.

14   Ibid., 58 – 71.

15   Ibid., 56.

16   Allen, J., *et al.*, *Out on the shelves: lesbian books into libraries*, Newcastle-under-Lyme, Association of Assistant Librarians, 1989, 5 – 26.

17   Clarke, I. F., *Tale of the future: from the beginning to the present day* (3rd edn), London, Library Association, 1978.

18   Clarke, I. F., *Voices prophesying war*, London, Oxford University Press, 1966 (a history of the imaginary wars of the future); Clarke, I. F., *The pattern of expectation, 1644 – 2001*, London, Cape, 1978 (surveys the evolution of futuristic literature).

19   Barron, N. (ed.), *Anatomy of wonder: a critical guide to science fiction* (2nd edn), New York and London, Bowker, 1981.

20   Rosenberg, B., *Genrereflecting: a guide to reading interests in genre fiction*, Littleton, Libraries Unlimited, 1982.

21   Burgess, M., *The Glasgow novel* (2nd edn), Motherwell, Scottish Library Association, 1986.

22   Ibid., 16 – 20.

23   Whyte, H., *Glasgow crime fiction: a bibliographic guide*, Glasgow, Mitchell Library, 1977.

24   Hicken, M. E. (comp.), *Fiction index 1988: a guide to works of fiction available during the year and not previously indexed in the Fiction Index series*, Newcastle-under-Lyme, Association of Assistant Librarians, 1989.

25   Cotton, G. B. and Glencross, A. (comps.), *Cumulated fiction index 1945 – 1960*, London, Association of Assistant Librarians, 1960; Smith, R. F. (comp.), *Cumulated fiction index 1960 – 69*, London, Association of Assistant Librarians, 1970; Smith, R. F. and Gordon, A. J. (comps.), *Cumulated fiction index 1970 – 74*, London, Association of Assistant Librarians, 1975; Hicken, M. E. (comp.), *Cumulated fiction index 1975 – 79*, Chesterfield, Association of Assistant Librarians, 1980; Hicken, M. E. (comp.), *Cumulated fiction index 1980 – 84*, Chesterfield, Association of Assistant Librarians, 1985.

26  Hicken, M. E. (comp.), *Cumulated fiction index 1980 – 84*, Chesterfield, Association of Assistant Librarians, 1985, vii (for example).

27  Forster, E. M., *Aspects of the novel*, London, Arnold, 1927 (for example).

28  Olderr, S., *Olderr's fiction index 1987*, Chicago and London, St James' Press, 1988.

29  Yaakov, J. (ed.), *Short story index: an index to stories in collections and periodicals*, New York, H. W. Wilson, 1988 (for example).

30  Hicken, M. E., *Sequels: volume 1, adult books* (9th edn), London, Association of Assistant Librarians, 1989.

31  Enser, A. G. S., *Filmed books and plays: a list of books and plays from which films have been made, 1928 – 86*, Aldershot, Gower, 1987.

32  Mann, P. H., *A readers' guide to fiction authors*, Loughborough, CLAIM, 1985.

33  Kearns, C., 'Eccentric guide', *Library Association record*, **87** (10), 1985, 415.

34  Mann, P. H., *A new survey: the facts about romantic fiction*, London, Mills and Boon, 1974, 17, 21.

35  McLeish, K., *Bloomsbury good reading guide*, London, Bloomsbury, 1988.

36  Zool, M. H., *Bloomsbury good reading guide to science fiction and fantasy*, Bloomsbury, 1989.

37  Reginald, R., *Science fiction and fantasy literature: a checklist, 1770 – 1974*, 2 vols, Detroit, Gale, 1979.

38  Contento, W., *Index to science fiction anthologies and collections*, Boston, G. K. Hall, 1978.

39  Logasa, H., *Historical fiction: guide for junior and senior high schools and colleges, also for general readers* (9th ed.), Brooklawn, New Jersey, McKinley, 1968.

40  Dixon, J., *op. cit.*, 140.

41  Pejtersen, A. M. and Austin, J., 'Fiction retrieval: experimental design and evaluation of a search system based on users' value criteria', *Journal of documentation*, **39** (4), 1983, 230 – 46 and **40** (1), 1984, 25 – 35.

42  Palmer, J. W., 'Factors responsible for the acquisition of Canadian fiction by US public and academic libraries', *Library acquisitions: practice and theory*, **12** (3/4), 1988, 341 – 56.

43  Moorbath, P., 'Why do publishers send out their catalogues?', *Aslib proceedings*, **41** (6), 1989, 213 – 16.

44  Sutherland, J., *Bestsellers: popular fiction of the 1970s*, London, Routledge and Kegan Paul, 1981.

45  Keating, H. R. F., *Crime and mystery: the 100 best books*, London, Xanadu, 1987.

46  Alexander, F., *Contemporary women novelists*, London, Edward Arnold, 1989.

47  Higdon, D. L., *Shadows of the past in contemporary British fiction*, London, Macmillan, 1984.

48 Hanson C., *Short stories and short fictions 1880–1980*, London, Macmillan, 1985.

49 Magill, F. N., *Critical survey of short fiction*, 7 vols, Englewood Cliffs, New Jersey, Salem Press, 1981.

50 Vinson, J. (ed.), *Contemporary novelists* (4th edn), London, Macmillan, 1986.

51 Sutherland, J., *op. cit.*, 3–4.

52 *The writer's directory 1990–92* (9th edn), Chicago and London, St James' Press, 1990.

53 Todd, J. (ed.), *Dictionary of British women writers*, London, Routledge, 1989.

54 Haffenden, J., *Novelists in interview*, London, Methuen, 1985.

# 9  Marketing fiction services

*Deborah Goodall*

## Introduction

Fiction is a pre-eminent art form. As we enter the 1990s books are seen as 'glamorous, dangerous, and news'[1] in the publishing and bookselling world. We are in the age of the paperback, a visually aware time, in which both the number of titles coming on to the market and the number of retail outlets have increased dramatically. Neither publishers nor booksellers seem to be deterred by the fact that book sales have remained static for the past two years. Both are now increasingly concerned with visual impact and style as ways to entice new buyers and readers. As one publisher said: 'there's nothing wrong with books looking sexy if it widens the net of people who are going to buy.'[2]

In contrast, many public librarians have developed, or perhaps retained, their cautious attitude towards fiction. Faced with a declining book fund and a greater selection of titles they often adopt an anti-marketing strategy, restricting buying to popular authors and old favourites. This reactive approach must be replaced by the 'go for it' proactive attitude of the commercial world if libraries too are to survive, and flourish, in the 1990s. Choice, image and impact are the key words for the new decade.

*Choice*, because, as librarians, we must ensure that we make the right choices when buying our stock so that what we have to offer is appropriate and attractive to the people with choice, that is, the choice not to read. As Betts noted some time ago, whether we like it or not, we are operating in a market-place, competing for people's time against other activities, and, particularly where fiction is concerned, against other sources of entertainment.[3] The sooner we realize this and take positive steps to exploit the situation to our advantage, the better.

*Image*, because the commercial world is acutely aware of the value of a positive image. Contrary to popular belief, librarians are responsible for their own image and the fact that the unfavourable stereotype still persists indicates that not enough is being done to improve public and professional perceptions of the library service.

*Impact*, because in times of financial restraint and increasing competition it is more important than ever for libraries to adopt a structured approach to service provision and make the best use of limited resources. One of the aims of the library service must surely be to make an impact on the community, if not society, with a well-presented, high-quality service which is appropriate for, and responsive to, the needs of its users. In achieving this, such success not only generates more success but also ensures survival in a changing and often unfriendly environment.

The obvious question which arises from the above points is 'how?' How do we persuade people to choose books, how do we project a positive image, and how do we make an impact with the library service? A marketing approach, whilst not being a panacea, will certainly improve libraries' chances of success and survival. And such an approach is equally applicable to the whole service or just one aspect of provision.

## A marketing viewpoint

To consider fiction promotion from a marketing viewpoint it seems wise to first define what is meant by marketing, to look at the elements of the marketing cycle, and to assess its relevance to the library service. Although traditionally associated with advertising and selling, marketing is essentially an attitude of mind which places the user at the centre of any activity. It is often referred to as 'customer satisfaction engineering' and has been formally defined as 'a systematic approach to planning and achieving desired exchange relationships with other groups'.[4]

### *Marketing definitions*

Marketing is a two-way process of communication between user and service provider which relies on designing services in terms of users' wants and needs rather than in terms of the service provider's wants and needs. Kotler writes that: 'The central principle upon which marketing rests is that the benefits derived by the receiver take precedence over gains to the supplier. The key feature of the marketing mode is its emphasis on satisfying first and foremost the needs of the client. This is rather different from selling, which has to do with maximizing the supplier's profits or gains.'[5]

So, marketing is more than just selling: it is an all-embracing activity concerning how a library operates in relation to its users. Above all, it is to do with improvement rather than growth.

Marketing should be a central function of library management which is used to achieve defined objectives. It is a circular process which is dependent on having defined management objectives and begins by inspiring the right attitude in staff and working from sound information. The actual marketing approach involves a set of techniques, and associated jargon, namely 'product', 'design', 'price', 'place' or distribution, and most visibly, 'promotion', both of a service and the library service, which work together to give a marketing mix appropriate to the situation and people that you are trying to reach. It must be noted that we have to market to the whole environment in which the library operates as well as to defined markets of users and prospective users. This necessitates identifying and segmenting our market: 'market segmentation'. Librarians generally are extremely reluctant to prioritize – we want to do everything and we do nothing particularly well. Market segmentation is simply a process of categorization. Clearly, to be successful it is necessary to market your service to a well-defined section of the population which is measurable (i.e. we know who they are), accessible and viable. This can often be achieved by experience but a more informative way of determining the library's relationship with its market is by undertaking 'market research' or 'user studies'.

### Market research

Market research is simply a tool for analysing the groups that form the market. It is something that 'at best . . . will reduce uncertainty around decisions though it can never eliminate it . . .'[6] and is often defined as 'a quantifiable analysis of a market in terms of its size and trends and of its structure'.[7] This information is used in determining the balance of the 'marketing mix'. Admittedly, this whole process is not one that comes naturally to librarians who, traditionally, make a quixotic attempt to serve all. However, market research is essential in planning services and, in keeping with the overall process of marketing, market research must have clear aims and be well designed.

The techniques of market research are varied and are well documented.[8] Briefly, it is possible to work from primary or secondary data – the latter usually already exist in the library service, for example, issue statistics, which are cheap and quick to acquire though not always appropriate or reliable. Primary data can be obtained on an *ad hoc* basis or continuously, using observation or survey techniques involving, for example, interviews, questionnaires and user panels. Each method has associated advantages and disadvantages and it is necessary to choose that, or those which will most appropriately satisfy your needs for information, though possibly restricted by the time and resources available.

## Service development

Having discovered who we are serving we can then develop the appropriate service by using the marketing techniques mentioned previously. In marketing terms the product is not books but a much wider concept encompassing ideas, information, entertainment, etc. We are marketing reading, not the form in which it can be made to appear, and effective marketing is user-orientated rather than book-orientated. It is essential that the stock and service is appropriate and attractive to users, which is why user studies are needed before beginning to market a service. Marketing cannot be used as an excuse to impose a product that is unwanted on our customers.

## Price

Price is often seen as a flaw in the marketing process for most non-profit organizations, but price does not necessarily have to be in monetary terms. The use made of a service is voluntary, so we have to offer a service that is both attractive and appropriate to the target market. In this context marketing can be seen as the philosophical alternative to force, where the library seeks to offer benefits to the target group of sufficient attractiveness to produce a voluntary exchange in order to maximize library objectives.

Marketing seeks to optimize the value of activities occurring in libraries by matching capabilities and resources to needs and wants. Increasing awareness, timeliness, and the availability of fiction can change its value from nothing to infinity for users. But as well as attracting use in terms of people's time and energy and interest libraries must also attract funds and support at the political level and this is where the marketing approach is particularly relevant. In the past it has been too easy to choose not to realize that libraries operate in a market-place in which demand and supply are relevant concepts. This is no longer the situation today.

## Distribution

Having the right product in the right place at the right time is a crucial aspect of marketing and one in which libraries have the intrinsic advantage of having numerous service points and community outlets. In the case of mobile libraries we can take our service directly to potential users, though obviously physical access and availability are not enough to ensure use.

## Promotion

Promotion occurs after the aims have been decided, needs have been identified, and services have been designed appropriately.

Promotion is only a tool, albeit one of the most visible, which exploits all of the other activities of marketing and is used when it is time to communicate with the market, to create awareness and visibility. It is important to realize that promotion is not just media publicity. Libraries are not selling products but are offering a very distinctive range of services so any publicity that the library develops must be related to the overall aims of the library service.

Promotion is expensive in staff time and money and can be difficult to justify in terms of financial constraint. Promotion must be professional, with methods agreed and defined, targets identified and practical, and the message to be conveyed appropriate and effective. This is not always the case in practice and indeed British Library Report 5470 identified some of the problems with promotion in public libraries – for example, few libraries specially earmark funds for promotional activities and even fewer assign staff with special responsibilities for it.[9] Generally, there are very wide differences in the level of finance between different library authorities and the quality of promotional material varies, with the best being very good indeed. The report also found little evidence that the effectiveness of the material was being assessed in relation to the set objectives of the library service.

Promotion is pervasive and numerous activities come under the heading of promotion, but essentially it can be considered as involving personal contact, the published word, say in the form of publicity materials and 'atmospherics' or 'image'. Promotion via personal contact happens all of the time in libraries, and involves all staff, from those working on routine daily duties to those participating in special activities or events, or having the role of fiction librarian. This is where engendering the right attitude in staff is essential, as staff need to be approachable and competent. As well as providing relevant staff training for dealing with the public it is also necessary to promote the fiction service to the staff, for example, by using internal newsletters.

The use of publicity material is commonplace now in libraries, varying from day-to-day informative notices to specially commissioned publicity and promotional packages designed for special events. The materials used to promote fiction festivals, for example, are becoming increasingly stylish, with Leicestershire Libraries winning an award for the quality of their publicity material for the 'Fiction Addiction' promotion in 1989. Wherever possible it is sensible to utilize the services of professional graphic designers for written promotional material, as presentation really is everything. The purpose of promotional graphics is to increase public awareness, to stimulate interest and curiosity, and to achieve maximum visibility for the library. Unfortunately in the UK we lag behind the USA, and some of the European and Nordic countries, where much more importance is given to library graphics. Little is done nationally here, probably due to the decentralized nature of the services as well as a lack of production and distribution facilities – though at one point Cronin advocated a national graphics resource centre for the UK.[10]

In contrast, more and more library authorities are asserting their individuality with the use of a strong corporate image. No matter how good services are we have to attract our customers before we can demonstrate the library's intrinsic quality. Library services are very diverse and librarians often fail to give a clear image, which is unfortunate as the success of a marketing approach depends on the ability to create a positive image of libraries. A corporate image can be used to gather together the component parts of an organization into a single unit which can be clearly recognized. A library service has an image whether it is worked at or not and we must ensure, through marketing, that the image is a positive one. The aim of developing a corporate image is to create a professional view of the organization. This involves the effective communication of the objectives of the organization, the development of efficient services, and a pleasant environment. We must be, and appear to be, a capable and coherent organization – both to staff, users and the outside world.

The most difficult group to project a positive image to are the general public. Users are all individuals whose image of the whole library system is often based on their use or knowledge of one particular aspect of the library service, and when this fails them the whole service fails in their eyes.

Obviously first impressions of the library service are important in determining future use, but, also, if people are regular users then the danger of over-familiarity may arise. So, image clearly has an impact on use, both for potential users and current users. This is illustrated in the commercial world where companies use a corporate image to cope with competition and promote what they stand for, in addition to using a corporate image to instil loyalty and develop a corporate feeling amongst staff. A good corporate image also creates a favourable impression with financial providers and other professionals, as well as society at large.

Developing a corporate image involves much more than creating a graphic identity. However, a corporate image does have visual advantages for promotion – though it is important to realize that image is much more than a logo or having coordinated stationery. The library has to be efficient as well as appearing to be efficient and, for example, a good graphic image must be supported by equally good staff training.

Finally, while it is possible to change an image, and this often occurs in the retail sector, it is important to work to maintain a good corporate image. Even in times of financial stringency it makes sense to increase, not decrease, the promotional effort. To decrease expenditure on promotional activities and maintaining image may allow short-term savings but the long-term loss in credibility and visibility will not be made up so easily.

One of the hardest parts of marketing is achieving the balance in the marketing mix. Just as coordination is essential in carrying out a user survey or promotional activity, coordination of the whole marketing process is vital. However, once a service has actually been marketed there is still one more procedure, that of evaluation.

### Evaluation

Evaluation is carried out to ensure that the marketing process is effective and efficient. Evaluation is not an easy process but must be attempted to provide feedback which can then be considered when planning how services should develop in the future. It is generally easier to measure the overall impact of a marketing policy than to discover which aspect of the marketing was particularly effective for any one group of users. Although often difficult, a detailed evaluation is important as resources are limited and all aspects of marketing have a cost, either a direct financial cost, for example the cost of having publicity material printed, or indirectly, such as the cost of staff time and energy.

All of the different elements in the whole marketing process are linked by a constant flow of information, with the total marketing cycle planned and tailored to suit the needs of the situation.

Marketing is applicable to all those offering a professional service. Some aspects can be applied directly to the non-profit sector and some cannot and have to be modified, so there may be restraints on methods but not on the use of marketing. Though it can be argued that more money is needed in the bookfund rather than for marketing services, marketing is relevant to public libraries because it encourages the library to be more user-orientated – and the more user-orientated you are the more users you can reach. This support should ensure that the library survives financial and social crises.

Though the aim of market research is to learn about users to satisfy their needs better, one has to be wary of charges of wasting public money and being obtrusive. Librarians must always be ready to explain the benefits of marketing – especially those to do with a richer understanding of the library's role and an awareness of new opportunities.

Adopting a marketing approach ensures that objectives are set and achieved and provides a structure for decision making. As evaluation is a major part of the marketing process the service should be continually changing to meet demands and needs through the development of carefully formulated and controlled programmes, rather than developing haphazardly. Additionally, marketing activities are based on the use of management information to ensure that the greatest impact is achieved. Because funds are often inadequate it behoves the librarian to achieve maximal efficiency and effectiveness in marketing activities.

Today, librarians should be interested in marketing because they are involved in it whether they are conscious of it or not. Involvement is not the issue, but rather *how* they should be involved. In the past librarians relied on traditional, minimal marketing where demand was simply assumed to be there because the library service was available. This gave a reliance on current users and word-of-mouth promotion which is inappropriate and *not* dynamic enough for today. Nor should the aggressive hard-sell approach of the commercial world be advocated where production is continuous and goods and services must be sold. Rather, non-profit organizations must aim for balanced marketing which blends all elements of the marketing mix to give high user satisfaction and high use of the product or service.

Despite the adoption of this appropriate and unthreatening approach there are still some objections to marketing a library service, most of these essentially stem from a wrong attitude which is often engendered when marketing professionals are brought in to market a service. Though we have to use professional techniques to be credible it is much easier, and in the long run more effective, for librarians to learn about marketing rather than involving outside consultants.

Because of increasing competition within the public sector for resources, librarians have to adopt effective marketing techniques to survive, and this also applies within libraries, in the fight for bookfunds, materials and space, etc. What is more, we are competing with people who are adroit in using the techniques of marketing, not least the booksellers. According to Tim Waterstone, 'with more than 50,000 new titles out each year and the struggle for people's leisure time growing ever keener, the importance of hard selling is increasing and is unlikely to diminish'.[11] This is illustrated by the rise of the Charter Booksellers, who are a group of about 400 shops who aim to provide a basic range of services for their customers, including trained and helpful staff who are able to advise, if required, and help customers make a choice.

Additionally, the shops stock the largest possible selection of titles for their size and will endeavour to obtain books not in stock. They also produce numerous published items, for example a books magazine which contains reviews, adverts and extracts, bookmarks and booklists for summer reading.

Faced with this type of organized competition it is being acknowledged more and more by public librarians that they too are going to have to be professional about marketing activities. The whole process is second nature to large businesses, and even groups of large businesses operate together to market a product, whereas in libraries we tend to market as a 'gut reaction', using *ad hoc* methods and so lose out on the valuable information gained at the fact-finding and evaluation stages. As resources get scarcer, and the competition tougher, marketing will inevitably become more, not less, important for libraries.

**Fiction services**
The next section of this chapter aims to illustrate how a marketing approach has been applied to fiction services in a number of library authorities in the UK.

Before any service can be marketed there has to be a firm belief in the value of that service. In the past, fiction provision was often seen as a second-rate service or a loss leader in the library. Now it has become apparent that more and more library authorities have realized that they are seriously in the business of encouraging fiction reading, if only through enlightened self-interest. Betts believes that 'the library is the place for fiction ... our provision of fiction is, if not the most important thing we do, then on a par with anything else we do ...'.[12] In deciding to promote fiction we have to decide not only to give each type of fiction its due but also whether to increase support for fiction at the cost of other material. Librarians have been reluctant to prioritize but we must now be less defensive about our role and positively promote the cultural, social, psychological and informational benefits of fiction in our society.

*User studies*
Finding out about readers and borrowers is a prerequisite to providing any service, as was discussed in Chapter 1, and many user studies have been carried out in the USA to investigate this. It would appear that American librarians are much quicker to make use of consumer research techniques. For example, Baker examines the problem of 'overload, browsers and selection' and the 'display phenomenon'.[13] The concept of overload originates from the retail sector, where consumers are overwhelmed by the large numbers

of purchasing options. It is felt that this can occur in libraries with browsers, who, because of the unfocused nature of browsing may become overwhelmed and confused if they are presented with too many choices. To resolve this problem the research recommends the strategy of 'exposure', which exposes a large number of borrowers to a relatively small set of books – by narrowing choice and focusing attention the choice is, effectively, increased for browsers. In practical terms this can be achieved by book displays and booklists, and the research rather obviously concludes that displays and booklists are most effective when they are highly visible and readily accessible, requiring little effort from the user. Whilst the results from this consumer research are really rather bland it is interesting to see how traditional market research techniques have been applied, almost directly, in libraries.

A reasonable amount of research has been carried out in the UK on browsing and book selection,[14] and although on a smaller scale, work has been done in considerable depth, even making progress towards measuring customer satisfaction. In Kent a number of user studies have been conducted which examined how people are using the library service. Some of the most widely reported are those of Jennings and Sear.[15] In 1985 they carried out a survey of three libraries in Kent to find out how readers went about the process of selecting their fiction and in particular how often they browsed. They also looked at user satisfaction and the use made of existing guidance and how this could be improved.

The research used standard personal survey techniques and 135 interviews were carried out using a schedule of prepared questions. The results showed that contrary to popular belief readers did not find it easy to choose fiction, and those using the most common method of selection, browsing, rather than looking for known authors' titles, were most likely to be dissatisfied with their choice.

Interestingly, their research was prompted by a sense that fiction in libraries is often under-rated and a feeling that readers were given little guidance despite the great quantity of use made of the service – so, clearly, they were aiming to be more user-orientated.

Using the information they obtained about people's habits and needs Jennings and Sear then made a number of suggestions as to how the library could respond and be more user-orientated. For example, they recognized that low use was made of reservations and the catalogue and that people were interested in what was on the shelf at the time of their visit, and consequently it was felt that work had to be done on stock presentation, especially genre categorization and thematic displays. It was also recognized that the bookseller's technique of face-out display would help people to find that elusive 'something to read'. The surveys revealed that if people knew something about the author then they were more likely to enjoy reading books by that author, which gave rise to a number of possible courses of action, from pinning up reviews to producing booklists and guides, etc., and inviting authors to speak and read.

Clearly the whole ethos of their research was finding out about user needs, primarily in this case recognizing that browsing is a search strategy, and then adjusting the service provision to cater for these needs. It is particularly pleasing to see that this work has been continued, that the results were used to define aims and decide on action which was then implemented and evaluated. More recently the situation was reassessed; for example in 1989 Jennings and Sear[16] reported how, in the light of the results of the original survey, a comfortable and attractive browsing area was set up in Sevenoaks Library, and this is described in Chapter 6. Again, their aims were clear: to increase effectiveness rather than efficiency, so that people would enjoy the books they borrowed, rather than borrowing more books. The browsing area was monitored to establish if the process of choosing was made easier for the browser, if users were more satisfied with the books chosen, and if readers were discovering new authors, as many respondents in the original survey had complained of not knowing how to find new authors. Monitoring was not easy and a range of techniques was utilized to look at satisfaction and ease of use – areas which are difficult to quantify. The success of self-completion questionnaires as evaluation devices was poor so the researchers used observation techniques and personal interviews as well as examining issues on a comparative basis. Thus a database of quantitative and qualitative management information was compiled.

Considering the research results only from a marketing viewpoint, it is interesting to note that the need for forceful publicity for any new venture was readily recognized. Also, plenty of practical information was gained, such as the need for attractive presentation of stock and good signing, etc., to encourage people to spend time browsing in the library. All of this illustrates the importance of getting the product right for the audience and then regularly checking to see that the product is still appropriate to the demand. Another valid point to note is that Jennings and Sear were conscious of having to market the browsing areas to library staff too and they did this by taking account of comments made by staff in the management of the browsing area. Again, this reiterates the importance of inspiring a positive attitude in staff towards their organization and its work.

## Fiction promotion

Once services are designed then they need to be promoted, and in recent years fiction promotions have been becoming increasingly more visible across the country. Some, though not all, activities and events are based on a sound knowledge of readers' wants and needs. Sometimes this information has been obtained by the research methods just described, though in many cases the promotion relies on a combination of professional knowledge, a feeling for the community, and much enthusiasm.

In Nottinghamshire, fiction promotion initially evolved from a feeling that there was need for such work.[17] Now, its importance is formally valued, to the extent that promotional work is an integral part of staff training and is built into the management structure of the authority. For example, there is a stock promotion group supported by the standardized buying of serious fiction. Although major fiction events are coordinated centrally, much work is still under the control of district representatives, which ensures local initiative and continuity in promotional work. The authority is clearly aware that it is essential to maintain impact to sustain interest and also to have local relevance when marketing a library service.

Much promotion is concentrated on serious fiction, which is appropriate, as various pieces of research over the years, notably by Spenceley[18] and Mann,[19] have highlighted the need for the promotion of literary fiction as this tends to be one area where readers are more than likely to flounder. Spenceley's research showed that if the author and title of a serious novel are known then there was a very good positive reaction to the book.[20] If the author only was known then there was a two to one chance of a positive reaction. But if the book was selected simply by browsing, as indeed the majority of serious fiction books were in this study, then it was unlikely that the novel would be enjoyed by the reader. Nottinghamshire County Libraries are clearly trying to avoid this problem by working to promote and impart information about such novels and their writers. Nottinghamshire's aims are to lead people away from obvious authors but without being too highbrow; for example, a very successful event is the 'Angel Row Authors' which started in Nottingham in 1985. Each series lasts about ten weeks each autumn and consists of five contemporary authors reading from and discussing their books. Nottinghamshire are pleased with the level of interest generated; indeed, there is a strong hard-core of followers, with audiences regularly numbering 30–40 per session, but it is still felt that there is potential for improvement and to this end audiences are being surveyed and information obtained will be used when planning future events.

So, in contrast to what is happening in Kent, promotion in Nottinghamshire tends to be concentrated on what the library thinks should be promoted, i.e. quality writing, though attention is paid to public demand, particularly in light of the fact that such events have definite costs and charges. Such financial implications have ensured that the marketing policy is very well coordinated: booklists are produced and links are established with local bookshops for each event to encourage a positive response. Additionally, Nottinghamshire also realizes the value of tapping into what is already happening in the community and to this end a literature development worker is employed, financed by the East Midlands Arts Council and Nottinghamshire County Council Arts Division. Such work with other organizations can benefit the library service, for example, with sponsorship or more wide-reaching publicity. For example, a 'poetry on the buses' scheme was useful in reaching those who did not use the library service.

Whilst the work in Kent was useful in illustrating the market strategy of 'market penetration', i.e. encouraging more use of the existing service by present users, the Nottinghamshire promotions go some way to developing new services for the present user groups and also delivering present services to new markets. There is also the marketing strategy known as 'diversification', which involves developing new services for new markets.

Whatever the type of promotion it has to be supported by the appropriate stock. There is no use in working hard to generate interest if the materials to satisfy the demand are not available. This is where libraries, ironically, often fail in the marketing field. In Nottinghamshire this problem has been avoided by allocating part of the bookfund for purchase of promotional stock. Not surprisingly such organization requires much advance planning and at least some of the necessary management information can be provided directly from a marketing approach.

On a larger promotional scale there is an increasing number of fiction festivals taking place all over the country; for example, Birmingham's Readers' and Writers' Festival, which is now in its sixth year and is one of the most substantial literary festivals in the country, with over 180 events in 1989, providing about 350 hours of entertainment by about 200 writers and artists. Similarly, Leicestershire's 'Fiction Addiction' which started in 1989 combined literary events with competitions and used 'theme months' to introduce people to new areas of fiction. The success of this promotion is possibly due to a combination of striking publicity material and plenty of relevant stock. Much of Sheffield City Library's promotion of fiction has been spurred by the belief that 'libraries offer a miraculous facility and an eminently marketable one too'.[21] In 1984 Chris Meade and Rachel Van Riel were appointed to develop community arts in Sheffield libraries. The idea was to bring new users into the libraries and to offer new cultural informational services to all who visit them. They were responsible for developing the 'Write Back' scheme[22] – a highly innovative way to promote creative reading and writing which makes libraries not just places to borrow other people's words but also to share your own; for example, over 20 branch libraries have special 'Write Back' display boards where people can pin up poems and stories. Also, cut-price photocopying allows small-scale publication and larger manuscripts are bound and displayed for borrowing in libraries, plus some of the libraries have their own publishing programme.

The success of 'Write Back' led on to 'Opening the Book' – an eight-day festival of reading and writing which reflected a wide range of tastes and utilized theme days combined with author talks and readings, plays, meals, etc., all of which promoted the whole library service as well as marketing the fiction service. To continue to encourage creative writing in the community there was a series of workshops and also a book of the festival was produced.

The value of such events for raising the profile of the whole library service, not just the fiction service, is immense. Such events require much planning and coordination and a truly professional approach as they invariably involve obtaining finance and sponsorship.

To return to the example of Sheffield, many of the events were charged for and funds were raised for the event from commercial sponsors as well as the City of Sheffield and the Arts Council. As mentioned previously when discussing the problems of marketing a non-profit-making organization, some would argue that such actions may undermine the free public library service. The response from Sheffield would seem to be that while the library service should be kept free, and while accessibility and openness are essential, the word must still be spread.

Chris Meade felt that it was still not an automatic reaction to promote services in libraries, but being conscious that people choose to use libraries he was convinced that we must encourage use.[23] Above all, it would appear that Sheffield are aware of the value of doing something that is useful and appropriate for the community: just as stock and services vary in libraries then methods of marketing and promotion must also be appropriate for the community. In Sheffield this means getting people involved and offering them 'a good deal', or as their slogans put it, offering 'much more than books'. This type of promotion, like that of Nottingham-shire, which widens people's literary/reading horizons is clearly the way forward for public libraries. We will have to compete to retain our current users and go out to attract present non-users.

Librarians must not be deterred by the fact that early marketing attempts may fail as the audience is not always receptive. For example, the initial displays in the fiction area in Coventry generated little interest as borrowers were simply not used to seeing fiction promoted in that way. Once this climate was established the take-up from displays and exhibitions increased immensely. Again, this demonstrates the need for a constant information flow in the marketing cycle and above all that the whole process is a learning experience.

### Promotional techniques

Numerous promotional ideas have already been mentioned in the course of the chapter, and although it is not the aim of this chapter to describe in detail how to promote a fiction service there are plenty of techniques which are applicable to any library service. Briefly, some examples: bookmarks can be produced in-house and can be used for promotion and to provide information. Leicestershire had an attractive one entitled 'If you've read all of Catherine Cookson now try . . .'. Generally, the aim is to lead people away from the established authors to new or different authors. And similarly one can use annotated booklists and Spiller gives some straightforward guidelines for producing booklists.[24] Guides such as Peter Mann's *A readers' guide to fiction authors*[25] or Bloomsbury's *Good reading guide*,[26] as well as the more traditional guides to literature and fiction indexes, are also useful for providing ideas for themes and displays and for giving people that extra bit of information. It is also helpful to pin up information such as reviews and interviews with authors in an attempt to broaden interests.

This type of work is being done increasingly in bookshops. Libraries can also learn from bookshops about display techniques; indeed Taylor and Johnson drew attention to the fact that readers who visit the library for a specific book will require a different sort of provision from the reader, often a fiction reader, who is basically looking for any good book to read. They comment that these people 'will be more susceptible to, and will welcome, any display techniques that show . . . at a glance, or with minimum effort, a wide range of books that may be of interest. This applies to all sizes of libraries and is of no particular importance at larger libraries where the number of books is likely to be bewildering and confusing for those who have no specific requirement in mind.'[27] Furthermore they recommend that 'it should be the aim of librarians to make users aware of books . . . which they would not otherwise seek out.

This requires more facilities for the display of books ... and the best bookshop practice could be studied with advantage.'[28]

As well as developing internally generated marketing and promotion it is also important for librarians to be aware of what is happening in the wider environment – both so they can take advantage of local and national events and activities and so that they can market the service to those wielding the financial and political power.

On a local basis personal contacts are vital and librarians should always be ready to promote their service at any opportunity, for example, by liaising with local publishers, magazines, writing groups, etc. More unusually, it is also possible for library authorities to work together to promote fiction. A very successful example of joint fiction promotion is the 'Well Worth Reading' scheme based in Berkshire, Dorset and Hampshire which aims to 'encourage the reading of quality contemporary fiction, to use local media in order to reach non-library users and to build links with the local trade for joint promotions and mutual support, both financial and otherwise'.[29] It is primarily supported by Southern Arts, with a budget of about £10,000 for promotional materials. Librarians from three widely differing county library authorities work together, combining enthusiasm, author knowledge and bookfunds. It is interesting to note that the whole operation is coordinated by a marketing firm – Direct Contact.

Each promotion under the 'Well Worth Reading' umbrella is based on a theme and each novel that is promoted has an annotation or a review written by a volunteer librarian so that the novels have genuine personal recommendation. Each theme has been supported by 500 posters, 13,000 newsletters, and where possible 35,000 bookmarks. The newsletters are the foundation of the scheme and comprise a mix of about a dozen reviews, author photographs, book jacket illustrations and a further reading list. Design and artwork are recognized as being a crucial part of the scheme. Each library buys as many multiple copies of the book as possible, usually in paperback. In Hampshire's case it is reported that they began with a budget promotion of about £1,500, which was enough to send displays around about a third of the county's libraries. To an extent Hampshire have become a victim of their own success and there is pressure to buy more sets of books for other parts of Hampshire and also to stock the further reading titles in multiples, so that budgets are now closer to £2,500 for each display. Displays have included 'thrillers', 'growing pains' (about adolescence), 'the empire writes back' (post-colonial novelists), and 'just for laughs'.

The reviews for each theme are handled by one authority working from basic ground-rules about what to include and exclude. It can often be hard to achieve an appropriate content balance when such activities have a funding body such as an arts association. Southern Arts are keen to raise the intellectual and literary level as high as possible, whereas the librarians realize that the scheme will fail through lack of public interest if it involves too much experimental fiction. Pleasingly though, it is reported that 'lists have ended up a comfortable mixture of intellectual and literary levels, with some tempting bait for our readers and a hope that we can lead them on to higher things'.[30]

Barry Kempthorne commentated that 'the size of the financial commitment from Southern Arts and the library authorities, together with the substantial amount of business we were giving to the book trade meant that we felt more than justified in looking for book trade sponsorship'.[31] This was not easy to obtain but with persistence Sherratt and Hughes, as well as being sponsors, ran the 'just for laughs' displays concurrently with local libraries, and in Winchester both the shop and library had such a runaway success that there was desperate re-ordering of stock all round. The promotion has continued to receive financial support from the government under the Business Sponsorship Incentive Scheme and there has also been interest from a major publisher. The impact of the scheme has been assessed with questionnaires for readers and staff, as well as systematic statistical monitoring in terms of measuring the borrowings of a title in a library with the promotion against one where the book struggles for a living in the normal A – Z sequence. There were some striking results, with some novels getting seven loans in two months when promoted, compared with their normal issue rate of one or two. It is felt that the whole scheme is proof that 'literary fiction will get borrowed and read, with only a little extra effort from the library world'.[32]

National initiatives may not always be suitable for readers, but the added impact to be achieved from participating in national events such as Library Promotion Week or exploiting national media interest, about book prizes for example, can be tremendous. Additionally, involvement with outside professional agencies often enables libraries to keep up with the competition from bookshops as well as providing a source of fresh ideas.

The Book Trust is an independent educational charity which promotes reading and books amongst all types of people. It claims to be 'the independent voice for readers'. Some of the ways it encourages more people to read more books is through encouraging sponsorship for books and through administering 14 literary prizes, including the Booker, major book events and media campaigns, exhibitions and publications. Its other activities include a book information service, bestseller lists and campaigning against any threat to the book.

A recent example of the work of the Book Trust dealt with contemporary fiction – a touring exhibition of 82 titles by 56 authors which was available for hire complete with publicity material and an informative and well-produced booklist. It was hoped that the books chosen would reflect recent changes and innovations in English writing and cover a wide range of styles. At only £27.50 to hire this was a bargain, especially as staff time involved was fairly minimal if one was simply content to fill a display space.

The Book Trust also issues a guide to literary prizes, grants and awards – there are over 200, with prizes ranging from an illuminated scroll to £25,000. Book prizes are becoming more prolific, with the greatest number for fiction; and winners often make front page news. The Booker, though not the largest literary award, is the one which has most caught public attention and is most successful in promotional terms, with its £20,000 prize and extensive media coverage – choosing the winner has been televised since 1981. More than 100 novels are submitted each year and novels benefit simply by being named on the short-list. The winner generates worldwide demand and it is not surprising that winning the Booker prize can add 50,000 to hardback sales and 150,000 to paperback sales.

The motive behind many prizes is promotional and many firms have followed Booker in sponsoring the arts. However, libraries have to be wary in attempting to do this, as commercial firms and businesses will want to see a visible return for their money.

Despite the increasing amount of commercial marketing of the Booker Prize there can be no doubt that the Booker Prize has succeeded beyond expectation in its aim to increase the readership of serious fiction. The short-list gives a manageable recommended reading list from the tens of thousands of novels published each year. Libraries should latch on to this type of event, as much of the hard work in generating interest is done by the media and all libraries have to do is effectively feed from it.

### User education

A marketing approach can be used in other areas of library management. Marketing to particular user groups is important if you want to reach new users or develop new services for users, for example to children and young people. Public libraries are increasingly involved in user education which is often just a diluted style of marketing. User education is particularly important in the light of recent changes in the education system in this country with the development of individualized learning and a greater reliance on project work. Particularly for younger people, it is becoming more important to understand how to use a library, and most library authorities have well-established schools instruction services and hold library instruction sessions, either formally or informally, for schools or other groups; for example, in Coventry the Scouts are regular visitors. The aim is to break down any barriers, generate enthusiasm and interest in the library and impart some information about using the library. Such work is very labour intensive and librarians have to continually keep in touch with current demands.

Additionally, it is important to market services to other sections of the community, for example, the partially sighted or those whose first language is not English. Such user education often involves talks supported by the production of guides and leaflets to establish the value of the library service to that particular group of users. The aim in the public libraries is not necessarily to make users self-sufficient as is often the case in an academic library, but rather to improve perceptions and encourage greater use of the service on offer.

Clearly, the boundaries between user education and marketing are blurred, as both processes have a number of similarities: the need for aims and target groups to be identified, an appropriate and effective message which is supported by relevant materials, coordination of all activities, and above all a procedure for getting feedback, if a user education programme is to continue to be successful. User education is simply a way of increasing awareness, with guidance being both educational and promotional.

Applying a marketing approach to user education programmes often highlights libraries' weaknesses in that we tend to see user education as an end in itself, whereas it is really only equivalent to the promotional element of marketing. To be successful user education programmes need to grow out of a service which is already user-orientated. For example, it is easy to give a good verbal introduction to the library but this needs to be followed up on a practical basis, for example, with a worksheet for children, or with leaflets for adults and encouragement to talk to library staff. Thus we have to consider the place of user education in the whole organization: do we want people to be self-sufficient or do we want to encourage them to consult the staff, who are trained in customer care? We also have to be willing to link in to the work of other organizations such as education and social services. In the past the relationship between user education and the provision of a service was not always recognized, just as the link between promotion and the full marketing process is not always realized.

## Conclusion

In conclusion, then, this chapter has illustrated both the principles and practice of marketing fiction. The examples have deliberately not been restricted to libraries because marketing is a pervasive activity which occurs throughout society. The choice for librarians is not whether to market services but how to market services well in an increasingly competitive environment.

Research has shown that people are not aware of the services that a public library provides, and that public libraries need to make more effort to go out and publicize their services and to present a positive image to the public. Awareness is connected to the image of the library in society and its perceived relationship with other information and entertainment providers. Additionally, surveys of book reading in society in general show that the library is only one of many sources of books, and indeed the public library is interdependent with booksellers so it should attempt to work with them to increase reading. Marketing should not be anathema to librarians: it is simply a way of becoming more user-orientated. We can no longer just put books on shelves and think that our responsibility ends there. We have to market and promote and make available: our aim should be to get people to read more satisfying, not necessarily 'better' books.

## References

1  Bragg, M., 'A hard sell', *The Sunday Times, review section C*, 10 December, 1989, 1.

2  Day-Ellison, G., 'Putting on the style', *The Guardian, weekend supplement*, 28 January, 1990, 20.

3  Betts, D. A., *Borrowing and the fiction reader*, London, Branch and Mobile Libraries Group of the Library Association, 1987.

4  Kotler, P., *Marketing for non-profit organizations*, New Jersey, Prentice-Hall, 1975, 13.

5  Ibid.

6  Yorke, D. A., *Marketing the library service*, London, Library Association, 1977, 15.

7  Ibid., 14.

8  For example, Luck, D. J. and Rubin, R. S., *Marketing research* (7th edn), London, Prentice-Hall International, 1987.

9  Woodhouse, R. G. and Neill, J., *The promotion of public library use*, Newcastle-on-Tyne Polytechnic, Department of Librarianship, 1978 (British Library Research and Development Department Report no. 5470).

10 Cronin, B., 'Nationally co-ordinated library promotion', *Journal of librarianship*, **13** (4), 1981, 223–51.

11 Bragg, M.

12 Betts, D. A., 2.

13 Baker, S. L., 'Overload, browsers and selections', *LISR*, 8, 1986, 315–29.
   Baker, S. L., 'Display phenomenon: an exploration into factors causing the increased circulation of displayed books', *Library quarterly*, **56** (3), July 1986, 237–57.

14 Usefully summarized in Goodall, D. L., *Browsing in public libraries*, Loughborough, LISU, 1989.

15 Sear, L. and Jennings, B., *How readers select fiction*, Maidstone, Kent County Library, 1986 (Research and Development Report no. 9).

16 Sear, L. and Jennings, B., 'Novel ideas: a browsing area for fiction', *Public library journal*, **4** (3), 1989, 41–4.

17 Personal communication with John Boyd, Assistant County Librarian, Nottinghamshire County Libraries, December 1989.

18 Spenceley, N., 'The readership of literary fiction: a survey of library users in the Sheffield area', unpublished MA dissertation, University of Sheffield, Department of Information Studies, 1980.

19 Mann, P. H., 'Fiction and the reading public', in *Peebles '83: Proceedings of the 69th Annual Conference of the Scottish Library Association, June 6–9, 1983*, Glasgow, Scottish Library Association, 1983.

20 Spenceley, N.

21 Meade, C., 'Opening the book: putting libraries on the map', *British book news*, January 1990, 20–1.

22 Ibid.

23 Personal communication with Chris Meade, Coordinator of 'Opening the Book', Sheffield City Libraries, January 1990.

24 Spiller, D., 'The provision of fiction for public libraries', MLS dissertation, Loughborough University of Technology, Department of Library and Information Studies, 1979.

25 Mann, P. H., *A readers' guide to fiction authors*, Loughborough, CLAIM, 1985.

26 McLeish, K., *Bloomsbury good reading guide*, London, Bloomsbury, 1988.

27 Taylor, J. N. and Johnson, I. M., *Public libraries and their use*, London, HMSO, 1973, 22.

28 Ibid., 62.

29 Kempthorne, B., 'Well worth reading: an experiment in fiction promotion', *New library world*, February 1989, 25–6.

30 Ibid., 25.

31 Ibid., 25.

32 Ibid., 26.

# 10 Education and training for fiction management

*Margaret Kinnell*

## Introduction

Managing the fiction resources in public libraries involves librarians in a wide range of professional activities. As we have seen from previous chapters, the effective management of fiction demands considerable versatility. Librarians need to be skilled in: assessing the wide variety of users' needs and preferences for fiction; knowing the range of fiction and its information sources; designing acquisitions systems; organizing fiction appropriately; and promoting the reading of fiction. And all of these activities must complement the librarian's many other management functions.

In this chapter therefore, the delivery of this complex mix of skills and knowledge will be considered, with the emphasis very much on relating fiction management to other areas of the librarian's professional role. One central question is the relationship between initial professional education and continuing education through in-service training and short course provision. A further issue is that of generalism versus specialism. Public librarians are increasingly expected to combine several areas of specialism and the management of the fiction collection is likely to be only one of the many professional tasks demanded of them. Also, there are certain skills which are transferable across several activities: here too, links with the wider demands on public library managers will be considered.

The chapter will begin with an assessment of the knowledge and skills needed by librarians in managing the fiction collection in a public library service. As library users are frequently helped by non-professional assistants, and theirs is also an important role in collection management, the skills needed by non-professional staff will also be discussed. From this analysis will follow a discussion of fiction management in initial education programmes for professional librarians and then a section on training programmes for both professional and non-professional staff. The examples given will be from the UK situation, but the analysis should also be of relevance to educators and trainers in the USA and in many European countries.

### Skills and knowledge analysis

Educators and trainers first have to decide on the mix of skills and knowledge needed for librarians working with fiction. One approach to defining education and training needs for librarians, competency-based education (CBE), has the merit of ensuring that programmes are designed to meet the needs of the task in hand, and that employers can have some confidence that their staff really do have the range of knowledge and skills required to perform particular duties.[1] Such an approach takes the design of teaching programmes into a detailed consideration of the specific competencies required to perform a particular job, and moves on from the initial broad-brush assessment of areas of knowledge and skills needed. A drawback is that CBE looks at the job as it appears *now*, not as it might develop in the future. Competency-based education is also not helpful for defining the necessary attitudes and personal qualities that go hand in hand with the acquisition of skills and knowledge to perform jobs effectively. These qualities are, however, essential and it seems important therefore to begin by considering them. Public libraries are seen by users as places for borrowing books, and of all the books borrowed around 60% are adult fiction. This fact of library use is sometimes underestimated at a time when librarians are heavily committed to providing for so many other information needs. A good read, offered by friendly and helpful staff in a pleasant environment, is what most users want. The *Which?* report on public libraries (1989) found that library staff were generally well thought of and 'came in for plenty of praise, rated 'good' or 'excellent' by 80% of adults'. However, libraries' stocks were less well rated: 'the main reason for both adults and children being dissatisfied was the poor range of books available'. The cuts in bookfunds in recent years had made their mark on the public's perception of their library service.[2]

This survey emphasizes that people want a decent range of books, together with the professional service they have come to expect and that the education of librarians for public library careers must take account of this, in curricula that relate users' needs to the imparting of professional skills.

User orientation in a library service means many things, from well-planned buildings, convenient opening hours and relevant stock selection to the range of service delivery, but importantly, staff attitudes and behaviour towards them are seen by the public as two of the more important aspects of their libraries. While difficult to encompass in the term 'competency', nevertheless the attitude of staff is an essential prerequisite to professional *and* non-professional skills in providing for users' fiction needs. Placing users at the centre of all activities as valued 'customers' for the service stems from the awareness of staff that their behaviour is important in defining the quality of library provision. While ensuring access to a broad range of fiction is a priority of the service, immediate responsiveness to a reader's request for assistance, a friendly and helpful telephone manner, and a proactive but non-intrusive approach to users, further reinforce the service through proper customer care. This attitude to users as customers of the service should inform everything that staff do in the library, in relating all activities to meeting users' needs. It means that books are not only selected with the user in mind. They are also organized and displayed appropriately and promoted effectively. The reservation system is constantly reviewed for its effectiveness, stock is regularly 'weeded' and books kept in good condition. In short, the library is seen by its staff as a matter for pride in the service offered.

It is on this foundation of a pervasive attitude to user orientation that specific skills and knowledge should be built. What then do staff need by way of skills and knowledge, in addition to adequate financial resources, to manage and exploit a fiction collection effectively?

## Professional librarians

The professional librarian either responsible for or working with the fiction collection in a public library will require the 'core' skills and knowledge of library management, together with specialized skills and knowledge in relation to fiction provision.

### Core skills and knowledge

There is much debate on what constitutes the core curriculum in library and information science,[3] as the subject field is changing so rapidly at present. It is worth noting, however, that there has been a 'crisis' in deciding the content and method of delivering library education for at least the last 20 years,[4] and further, that change is something endemic in a field that deals in information as its stock in trade. What *is* new relates first to the pace of change in the area of information technology. Secondly, librarianship increasingly is related to other subject fields: management studies and computer science in particular. The pace of change and the need to take account of related disciplines have thrown open the question of precisely the core of knowledge and skills needed by librarians in a dynamic employment market in which information management skills are in great demand.

The difficulties in determining this core of skills, despite the moderating procedures of the professional associations, have long been argued. One alternative has been to concentrate on the kinds of *objectives* the professional librarian should achieve 'in order to become the kind of person who is intrinsically, intuitively and effectually a librarian whatever the current circumstance and state of the art in which he finds himself'.[5] With this view of the skills of librarianship, the argument turns full circle and we are back with attitude.

Despite these problems of definition the Report of the Transbinary Group on Librarianship and Information Studies, which was set up to look at the curriculum in the light of the developing information market, has offered a synthesis of recent practice and thinking which moves beyond this closed circle. They first listed areas of knowledge required by professional librarians and information scientists:

● The nature and value of the total information resource
● The role of information in society and in particular organizations
● The transfer of information from originator to user by whatever means, and the economic, legal and political issues to which the flow of information gives rise
● The design and management of information services (from traditional libraries to electronic networks)
● The contexts (i.e. social, commercial, political, etc.) in which information services operate
● The applications of information-processing technology
● The levels of individual and organizational responsibility and operation for the information manager.

They then offered a listing of skills:

● An ability to relate to people and to understand their information needs
● An ability to retrieve information from the whole range of sources, including printed material, non-book media and electronic information services
● An ability to analyse and distil information for particular needs
● An ability to communicate information in an effective and appropriate form
● An ability to select and organize collections of information using technology as appropriate
● An ability to manage an information service including management of personnel, finance and the information resource itself

- An ability to promote information services and to influence decision makers in supporting their development.[6]

However, the Transbinary Group's outline only provides a curriculum framework for educators. From these broad areas of knowledge and skills further analysis is needed of the jobs librarians do to produce the kinds of competencies that can be worked into a core curriculum. For example, the design and management of information services (knowledge area) and an ability to manage an information service (skills area) would include, among the competencies demanded of librarians, effectiveness in:

- Planning library buildings/departments for specified services
- Allocating resources to take account of service priorities
- Budgetary control to ensure effective use of resources and, where appropriate, provide accurate forecasting
- Manpower planning to ensure optimum staffing levels
- Recruiting staff to meet the specific needs of the library service
- Training staff to ensure effective service delivery
- Developing stock-acquisition policies and systems to ensure efficient use of resources
- Developing stock-editing policies and procedures to ensure effective collection development; and so on.

A similar analysis for each of the broad areas of knowledge and skills results in a comprehensive core curriculum. However, one difficulty with the competency-based approach, in addition to those already identified, is the sheer number of competencies that result from this kind of iteration, and another is deciding the level of competency required in the jobs undertaken by new recruits to the various library/information professions. This can make analysis in terms of developing educational programmes a complex undertaking. (One study for a school librarianship curriculum has identified 108 such competencies from an analyis of some 29 study programmes).[7]

Nevertheless, however difficult, this level of analysis becomes more important as employers demand an ever greater variety of skills in library and information science graduates; and schools of library and information studies develop programmes to meet the needs of flexible career paths. Students intending to pursue careers in the 'emerging markets'[8] are being educated alongside those aiming for public library work. Also, students moving into specialized areas of 'traditional' librarianship, like school librarianship, are increasingly being offered largely generalist educational programmes.[9] Some means of identifying detailed competencies is therefore essential to balance the range of needs in the curriculum. Certainly from the example above of some competencies needed for managing a service, the range is obvious. Staff managing a large public library service have different needs to those managing a small information unit. However, a 'core' of management competencies is common to them both: planning the task; acquiring and allocating resources; budgeting; human resource management; collection management; and performance review, are essential to all librarians and information managers.

### Specialized skills and knowledge

The public librarian specializing in fiction services will also require particular competencies in addition to the 'core' needed by all library and information managers. Deciding on these is, however, less fraught with contradictions. The context, the public library, is a constant, and this considerably simplifies the analysis of areas of knowledge and skills from which competencies for the new professional can be derived. The user communities are of course very variable – if we are to assume that our fiction specialist is concerned with the spectrum of child, adolescent and adult users. The ability to relate fiction services to these varied needs will add to the breadth of knowledge and analytical skills required.

Areas of knowledge could be defined as:

- The nature of fiction – its characteristics for children, adolescents and adults
- Genres of fiction
- The fiction industry – authors, publishing, bookselling, library supply
- Readership – the characteristics of reading needs across user groups
- Selection and acquisition – policies, procedures
- Organization – cataloguing, classification, categorization
- Promotion
- Information sources – bibliographic, biographical, statistical

Skills could be described as:

- The ability to discriminate between different genres and levels of fiction
- The ability to analyse the fiction needs of the various groups in the community (including children, adolescents, ethnic minorities, handicapped readers)
- The ability to select and acquire books for the varied needs of the user community
- The ability to classify, catalogue and index fiction; to write indicative abstracts and more extensive reviews

- The ability to organize fiction in the library and to mount displays
- The ability to promote fiction through organizing events, producing booklists, book talks and relevant activities for user groups
- Retrieval of information on fiction
- Communication to users on fiction enquiries

These areas of knowledge and skills could form the basis for curriculum design; but, as we saw above, each of these requires analysis to ensure consideration of the varied competencies that employers expect. Some competencies will be transferable across the curriculum – and these will require identification to ensure reinforcement rather than repetition: interpersonal and communication skills are particularly relevant for all professional activities. It is equally important to consider the needs of trainee librarians in all of this. As well as ensuring the new professional has adequate competencies for their first professional post to meet the needs of employers, a competency-based education should also satisfy the needs of new entrants to the profession.[10]

For it is vital that new professionals are given confidence in their knowledge of such a wide field and are encouraged to develop their skills 'on the job' and, most significant of all, are prepared for flexibility in the future and to see their knowledge and skills acquisition as a lifelong process.

### Non-professional staff

There has been much less attention paid in the professional literature to the education and training needs of 'non-professional' staff. The distinction between the qualified professional and the non-qualified assistant is a particular concern of public libraries in the UK. Special libraries and school libraries have often employed staff in a professional capacity who have no formal librarianship qualifications. Employers in these sectors have been more concerned with specific skills than in paper qualifications and there is consequently a less clear distinction between 'professional' (i.e. with librarianship qualifications) and non-professional (i.e. without) staff. However, it is important to recognize that so-called non-professional library assistants in the public library will frequently provide the reader's first contact with library staff. They project the library's image to users. Assistants also gain a tremendous amount of knowledge of readers' book preferences and of the library's stock over the years and may have a wide knowledge of fiction from their own reading experience. Library assistants in smaller service points may also be much more in touch with the local community than a peripatetic professional librarian.

All of these capabilities should not be underestimated by library managers. When considering the knowledge and skills needed by the non-professional, not only the basic technical skills of serving users and organizing stock are of importance. Assistants should be aware of the range of services and stock in the library; of the reference tools to answer simple enquiries; and should understand the context in which their library operates. They need to be skilled in dealing with all kinds of reader, in answering enquiries, and knowing when to refer a reader on for the specialist skills of the librarian. They need above all to be encouraged to make the most of their abilities in the job they do, and to feel their contribution is valued. Many library authorities, recognizing this value to the service of their non-professionals' knowledge, skills and on-the-job experience, have involved them to some extent in professional activities like book selection, by taking account of their knowledge of users' needs, reading trends and new books.[11] Skills involving relating readers' needs to the existing collection and future demand are also therefore of importance. In summary, there is a need for the education and training of non-professionals to achieve 'a thorough knowledge of and a general insight into the background and information of librarianship'.[12] The result will be a well-informed and a highly motivated staff, further enhancing the attitudes of user orientation which are so important for the success of the service.

**Initial education programmes**
Initial education for librarians is now much more integrated with that for information scientists than in the past and, it is now increasingly argued, 'often in such a direction as to bring them closer together in terms of skills required'.[13] The core curriculum outlined by the Transbinary Working Group reflects the reality of this developing merger of the information and the so-called 'traditional' library skills in schools of library and information studies (LIS) in the UK. The impact of information technology has shifted much of the emphasis in curricula to IT-based teaching methods and content. This is just as important for the public librarian involved with the fiction collection as it is for the information scientist. Books are today acquired and catalogued using computerized systems of the kind described in Chapter 3; and budgeting in large authorities often involves the use of financial software packages. Also, the housekeeping systems for membership records and the issuing, reserving and stock control of books are now heavily computerized. Librarians need to understand how these systems can be optimally used, for example to undertake marketing research to investigate use of materials by particular groups, or to identify gaps in coverage

and to assist in performance review. The fiction librarian, as we have seen, needs more, however, than the core of library and information management skills outlined by the Transbinary Group. Librarians need to understand the characteristics of fiction and its readers, to know about information sources and how best to respond to enquiries in the field of fiction, and be able to develop promotional programmes and techniques to maximize the reading of fiction – if they are to meet the needs of library users. Some of the most exciting developments in fiction provision by public libraries have involved the mounting of fiction festivals which require wide-ranging marketing skills, as we learned in Chapter 9. Sheffield's Opening the Book Festival in 1989 ran 77 events in eight days, and Hertfordshire's Fiction Festival in 1989 was similarly ambitious. There were 20 public lectures, a two-day writers' workshop, and a Fiction Day.[14] All of this demands a high level of organizational ability and an understanding of the techniques of marketing, to ensure the optimum use of the library's resources. Courses that include a marketing component are therefore of considerable value.

In some UK library schools specialist courses in fiction librarian-ship have been offered, either on undergraduate or postgraduate courses, to develop competencies in fiction collection management and the development of this type of proactive fiction service. Specialist courses are also offered for work with children and young people, often particularly geared to the provision of fiction and the development of reading skills through materials provision, promotion and information skills development. However, there appears to be a worrying decline in commitment to these courses in some library schools. One result of the closing gap between information science and librarianship has been a dilution of the commitment to book-orientated specialisms.

There have been two relevant surveys of these areas – one on fiction librarianship in general, the other on library services to children and young people, including children's literature. In 1984, Michael Greenhalgh conducted a survey of all library schools in the UK and Eire, to ascertain what was being offered in fiction librarianship, and the distinctions between undergraduate and postgraduate students. His findings were encouraging to an extent, but rather confirmed the view that fiction librarianship 'was accorded low priority in professional practice'.[15] Out of the 17 schools, some elements of fiction librarianship were evident in all of the curricula, but usually subsumed in a 'core' of library/information knowledge and skills. There is a suspicion from reading the various responses of educators' unwillingness to admit neglect of such an important area, despite the only minimal input by some schools. There is too a defensiveness apparent in some respondents, when all that can be said is, 'students . . . may choose to do a dissertation on some aspect of fiction provision in libraries'.[16] Truly *specialist* courses containing most of the elements identified for a course specifically on fiction in libraries were only apparent in three schools. However, one difficulty with the findings was the interpretation of what schools offered in their core. Some made more of fiction in teaching the management of public libraries than did others. Sheffield University, for example, involved their (all postgraduate) students in a realistic stock-selection exercise in conjunction with Sheffield City Libraries, and also included a session on reader interest categorization. However, Leeds Polytechnic, another school which only offered fiction librarianship within the overall core, offered their postgraduates an element called 'the book trade', rather than linking fiction to public library management issues.

It could be argued that, if all students were offered something, however sketchy, on issues relevant to fiction librarianship in core courses like these, surely this would be better than marginalizing the subject and only providing it as an option for the few. Ideally, however, with flexibility of career path so important today, an introduction to the major issues relating to fiction provision in libraries would be offered to all students, with the addition of an option in fiction librarianship for those wishing to pursue this specialism.

The UK library schools were contacted again in March 1990, in an attempt to update Greenhalgh's survey for the purpose of writing this chapter. Of the now 16 schools, there were responses from ten, itself perhaps an indication of the way in which fiction in libraries is viewed. The range of provision was wide, and varied. There was the minimalist approach of a department devoted solely to inform-ation science and information technology, where a respondent commented that 'although there is one hour on humanities inform-ation sources, probably all that is taught on fiction librarianship is one sentence in my lecture on the UK library scene, viz. "Public libraries are largely regarded by many of their users as a source of a 'good read'"'.' A positive view of fiction at any rate.

And there was the more focused approach to fiction within the LIS curriculum offered by some responses. Ealing College of Higher Education has retained its commitment to the subject with an 'Imaginative Literature and Information Transfer' option and eight of the schools did offer an element in their core courses relating to fiction management in public libraries. However, only three of the schools which responded were providing specialist courses in fiction librarianship. My own department at Loughborough

University, which has offered an optional course in the past, is no longer (March 1990) doing so, although fiction management is now subsumed in the core undergraduate and postgraduate courses and there is a specialist course in children's literature.

One of the most interesting features of this follow-up survey was the comments from colleagues, many of whom described situations in their institutions that underlined the movement away from 'the book' in library school curricula. Institutional reorganization was an important factor. Some library schools had been relocated in information technology faculties and the names of departments give the clue to current curriculum concerns and the images they seek to project. 'School of Information Science and Technology', 'Department of Information Science', 'Department of Information Studies and Technology', 'School of Information Studies', 'Department of Information Studies', 'Division of Informatics' were some of the names responding. Only the University College of Wales Aberystwyth, Loughborough University and Manchester Polytechnic, of those responding, have retained the word 'library' in their titles. There appears to have been a retreat by institutions from librarianship, at the very least in the images they seek to project.

If these departments have largely committed themselves to an IT orientation, and to the new markets opening up for information professionals, nevertheless there are still opportunities for the study of fiction management. One of the more heartening comments made was that the 'modularization' of courses could mean a revival in the book-related specialisms, fiction librarianship and children's literature/librarianship in particular. Offering courses 'institution-wide' was seen by one respondent as a way of developing the fiction specialism. Much curricular development was taking place with this modularization of courses in mind and it will be interesting to see how this eventually affects the teaching of fiction librarianship, and indeed other specialisms in the library and information studies curriculum, in UK library schools.

Another positive aspect of provision was the student choice of undergraduate project or postgraduate dissertation. All of the respondents held this out as a way in which students could develop their interest in the subject. However, as argued above, this is hardly a substitute for a commitment by educators to providing at least some measure of input to students in their taught course elements.

Helen Lewins' findings from her survey of provision for teaching in the children's specialisms in 1986, and her follow-up survey in 1988, present a similar picture for library work with children, including the study of children's literature.[17] She related her findings to IFLA's recommendation that 'the education of children's librarians must be an integrated part of all library education (1/70 of the course)', and that 'library services for children must be available as an opportunity for specialized studies within basic education (3/70 of the course)'.[18] While undergraduate students fared reasonably well in their core courses for children's or school librarianship (13 schools), children's literature only appeared in the core in three schools. Postgraduates did rather worse, presumably because of the packed nature of their one-year course schedules. Only three schools offered them anything on children's or school librarianship, and no school offered their postgraduates children's literature in the core. Optional courses for postgraduates on either children's/school librarianship or children's literature were available at only four schools, while optional courses for undergraduates were offered by seven schools.

Since these surveys, the situation has worsened, with two schools now completely without specialist teaching in the children's field; the move to IT being a major factor.[19] Public library work with children, and children's literature, would seem to be endangered as components of librarianship courses in the UK.[20] Only modularization offers some hope in the present climate. The children's specialisms have never enjoyed high status, either within the profession or academically, and without this kind of development the present headlong impetus towards information management as a result of market pressures appears almost irresistible and all-consuming.

Initial education of any kind for non-professional staff is limited in the UK. Most library assistants wanting some form of qualification will usually first obtain a post, undergo in-service training and then consider a course such as the Business Education Council Public Administration Course, which has library options, or the City and Guilds course for library assistants. The Library Association/School Library Association Certificate in School Library Studies is a further possibility for teachers or clerical assistants working in school libraries. There was a suggestion in the Transbinary Report that Loughborough Technical College, then a school of librarianship offering a Diploma in Higher Education, could consider providing advanced courses for paraprofessionals, but nothing has come of this. Most of the burden for training these staff falls on library authority training programmes.

It would also appear that in-service education and training for professional librarians is similarly now the principal vehicle for staff gaining the kinds of specialized competencies identified as necessary for fiction management at the beginning of this chapter.

**Training programmes**

As well as the training programmes provided by library authorities, either singly or cooperatively, the professional associations also contribute greatly to continuing education and training for professional staff and initial training programmes for non-professionals. The Library Association's continuing education programme and the courses offered by local groups of the Association of Assistant Librarians are often geared to some aspect of fiction management, and the exploitation and promotion of resources.

Other significant UK professional groups providing courses as an adjunct to in-service training in this field are: the Youth Libraries Group; the School Libraries Group; the Publicity and Public Relations Group – all Library Association groups, but responsible for their own short course programmes. Staff should also be encouraged to consider Workers' Educational Association classes, courses run by the extramural departments of local polytechnics and universities and the Open University; their Arts Foundation Course, the Nineteenth-Century Novel and its Legacy, and special study packs on individual writers, are very relevant to library staff wishing to broaden their knowledge of fiction. Distance learning of one kind or another is becoming an attractive option for both aspiring non-professionals, and those professional librarians wishing to develop their knowledge. There are many possibilities.[20] Continuing education is not only about developing the functional skills of librarianship, it should also aim at widening and deepening the liberal education of staff in their chosen subject field. Internal training is of limited usefulness for this, and training officers need an awareness of these possibilities for individual development through the kinds of courses available beyond the workplace. Writers on in-service training usually see continuing education as an activity separate from training. However, continuing education is often pursued on a part-time basis whilst working and there is no easy distinction between staff applying the skills they have acquired on workplace in-service training and relating the fruits of continuing education pursued elsewhere, to the job in hand. In the present economic climate opportunities for this kind of study within work time are inevitably limited, but it may become more important as libraries complete for dwindling numbers of young people that they provide extra educational incentives within the job package they offer. The old traineeship schemes, which sent students off to library school on a salary and a guaranteed job at the end of their course, may be revived in a new and more flexible format that takes account of employees' alternative aspirations.

In deciding on training programmes internally within a library authority there will be several levels of need. First will be the need for induction courses for new professional and non-professional staff. Secondly will be the importance of continuing training for professional and non-professional staff in particular jobs and skills. Thirdly, and less readily definable, will be the need to encourage staff to develop their higher management skills by means of a variety of possibilities: including professional involvement in a range of organizations, specialist short courses, higher degree programmes, and the kind of continuing education in an alternative field referred to above. In her report on *Training and management development in librarianship*, Sheila Ritchie found that management and computing were particularly mentioned as needs by respondents – although it ought to be noted that respondents preferred the delivery of this type of education and training to be job-based.[21]

### Induction courses

All new staff, professional and non-professional alike, require a sound introduction to the organization, and the quality of their induction will show in their subsequent effectiveness in the job.[22] The nature of induction courses varies between library authorities. Some provide only a brief general introduction to the service, and the individual's particular job. Other programmes are more thorough and systematic, using a checklist for each individual to ensure everything is covered – particularly important since the pre-licentiateship regulations came into being. These would include a comprehensive introduction to the various services. This should normally be delivered by a range of senior staff to ensure a good spread of participation, and ensure the new entrant is introduced to as many staff as possible, but with one 'supervisor' of the new employee to ensure continuity in the delivery of the programme.

Full-time training officers who are able to spend all their time dealing with training are rare in UK public libraries.[23] However, most local authorities have training departments which provide some centrally organized courses, either at the induction level or for continuing job training.

As with all training programmes, a 'needs analysis' must precede the design of the programme. Like the analysis that precedes competency-based education, this should ensure that training provides the employee with those skills and knowledge that are relevant to the job in hand. What does this person need to know? What do they know already? This enables trainers to identify the 'training gap'. Then follow questions on: how shall we teach them; who will do it; what is the timescale; how will we evaluate it?[24]

Every such analysis should disclose the need for some basic

introduction to the fiction service offered by the library: the catalogue, book-stock arrangement, issuing, return and reservation routines, book acquisition routines, weeding procedures – important even for new *professional* staff.[25] The further level of detail will then depend on the individual's job. Most important of all, the culture of the library service should be inculcated at this early stage, and the user orientation of the service stressed to the new employee. The induction forms the base on which further training is built and 'getting it right' is an important means of safeguarding the library authority's considerable investment in its human resource. Having developed an induction programme and delivered it over a period of (usually) between one and three months, it is therefore vital that its efficacy should be evaluated. Has the employee performed the tasks satisfactorily as a result of the training; does the employee understand the wider organizational implications of their job; how user-orientated is the employee in dealing with the public? The employee also needs to be able to comment on the induction programme. Evaluation should be a two-way process.

**Continuing training**
The continuing job training offered to staff within UK public libraries is very varied. Much depends on the resources available. One problem noted by senior librarians, in addition to their lack of money and a full-time training officer, is the lack of sufficient numbers of staff available for release on to training programmes.[26] Inevitably, a lack of resources means that internal courses will often be of general rather than specific applicability: communications skills, handling users and marketing are some of the most widely taught subjects. Less funding for training purposes also means that fewer staff are able to attend external courses run by professional groups, library schools or other bodies.

Despite this retrenchment there is a considerable range of interesting in-service training in fiction librarianship. Courses on stock management, on working with children and teenagers and in bibliographical materials for fiction are all of importance to the development of fiction services. As we saw, the generalist tendency of courses in departments of library and information studies means that such in-depth in-service training provision will become even more significant. Staffordshire County Library, for example, has run a one-day workshop on fiction that provides a detailed training session for staff;[27] Sheffield Libraries' 'Opening the Book Unit' have run a seminar for other librarians on how to run fiction promotion events; and because of the increasing recognition that children and teenagers' reading needs are of vital importance some library authorities are now combining their training courses for library staffs with that for teachers and education support staff.[28] Such cooperative ventures offer the greatest scope in specialist fields for in-service trainers with limited budgets. The South West Association of County Libraries Training Officers' Group (SWACL) found that courses on reading development, children's literature, book selection and other book-related courses would be particularly relevant on a regional scale and likely to receive strong support from within their authorities.[29]

The structure of courses, their level and, importantly, their evaluation will vary according to need. The training needs analysis which precedes all training programmes should address these issues. Determining the effect of training on the way in which jobs are performed is difficult and it has even been argued that 'to measure the effect of training on the organization is to attempt the impossible'.[30] Given the scarcity of resources in libraries today, evaluation must be attempted nevertheless, to argue for the benefits of continuing training activities.

## Conclusion

In concluding this chapter on initial education and in-service training, it should be said that there appears insufficient acknowledgement by educators of the centrality of fiction to the public library service and its significance in the curriculum. Everything the library service does for the public only serves to emphasize the continuing importance of fiction provision in the minds of the public, and this simply cannot be ignored in initial education. It appears that library trainers are filling the gap.

The next phase of education and training development should now be concentrating on the marrying of information management skills with those of librarianship, to enhance the development of the library/information studies curriculum and promote the importance of fiction services. Understanding the complexity of the knowledge and skills required of the librarian in managing fiction resources is a first step, and a competency-based, analytical approach to both education and training should help in providing the substantive content of both curricula and training programmes. The means of delivery depend on resources, which in turn demand professional and political commitment to fiction services — a further and more intractable complexity.

## References

1 Griffiths, J.-M., 'A survey of competency requirements for library and information science professionals', in Armstrong, C. and Keenan, S. (eds.), *Information technology in the library/information school curriculum*, Aldershot, Gower, 1985.

2 'Public libraries', *Which?*, February 1990, 108–10.

3 Meadows, A. J., 'Educating the information professional', in Oppenheim, C., Citroen, C. L. and Griffiths, J.-M. (eds.), *Perspectives in information management I*, London, Butterworths, 1989, 169–86.

4 Bundy, M. L., 'Crisis in library education', *Library journal*, **96**, 1971, 797.

5 Burrell, T. W., 'Curriculum design and development in education for librarianship and information science', *Education for information*, 1, 1983, 229–61.

6 UGC/NAB Transbinary Working Group on Librarianship and Information Studies, *Report of the Transbinary Group on Librarianship and Information Studies*, London, British Library, 1986, 63–4.

7 Abdel-Motey, Y. Y., 'Education for school library media specialists in the State of Kuwait: a competency based approach', unpublished PhD thesis, Loughborough University Department of Library and Information Studies, 1989.

8 McLelland, D., 'Education for school librarianship: the Scottish perspective', *International review of children's literature and librarianship*, **5** (1), 1990.

9 Moore, N., 'Employment market for information specialists in the UK', *Journal of information science*, **13**, 1987, 327–33.

10 Grant, G. *et al.*, *On competence: a critical analysis of competency-based reform in higher education*, San Francisco, Jossey-Bass, 1979.

11 Nottinghamshire County Council Leisure Services, 'Adult book selection: a policy document', Nottingham, Nottinghamshire County Council, 1988 (unpublished).

12 Casteleyn, M., *Planning library training programmes*, London, Deutsch, 1981, 89.

13 Meadows, A. J.

14 'The Hertfordshire fiction festival', *Library Association record*, **92** (4), 1990, 268–9.

15 Greenhalgh, M., 'The role of the library school', in Dixon, J. (ed.), *Fiction in libraries*, London, Library Association, 1986, 201.

16 Greenhalgh, M., 198.

17 Pain, H., 'Professional education and children's and school librarianship', *Library Association record*, **89** (3), 1987, 131–5.
Pain-Lewins, H., 'The education and training of public librarians working with children and teenagers', *Training and education*, **6** (1), 1989, 3–14.

18 Glistrup, E. (ed.), *Education and training of librarians in children's librarianship*, Ballerup, Bibliotekscentralens Forlag, 1986.

19 McClelland, D.

20 Kinnell, M., 'Children's literature and the role of libraries: delivering services', paper delivered at the Symposium on Children's Reading in Europe: the British – German experience, Goethe Institute, London, 14 March, 1990.

21 Ritchie, S., *Training and management development in librarianship*, London, British Library, 1988 (Library and Information Research Report no. 34), 64.

22 Jones, N. and Jordan, P., *Staff management in library and information work* (2nd edn), Aldershot, Gower, 1987, 220.

23 Bird, J., *In-service training in public library authorities*, London, Library Association, 1986 (BLR&D Report 5898/LA Research Publication no. 23), 22.

24 Luccock, G., 'Induction training', in Prytherch, R. (ed.), *Handbook of library training practice*, Aldershot, Gower, 1986, 3 – 36.

25 Jones, N. and Jordan, P., 221.
Luccock, G., 18 – 212.
Akers, N., 'Training in school libraries', in Prytherch, R. (ed.), *Staff training in libraries: the British experience*, Aldershot, Gower, 1986, 107 – 20.

26 Bird, J., 35.

27 Stanley, S., 'Information sources', in Prytherch, R. (ed.), *Handbook of library training practice*, Aldershot, Gower, 1986, 207 – 76.

28 Parker, A., 'New skills, new opportunities: the role of in-service training', *International review of children's literature and librarianship*, **1** (1), 1986, 1 – 21.

29 Byrne, P., 'SWACL: public library staff training in the South West', in MacDougall, A. and Prytherch, R., *Cooperative training in libraries*, Aldershot, Gower, 1989, 111 – 20.

30 Conyers, A., *The evaluation of staff training* (2nd edn), London, Library Association, 1986 (Guidelines for Training in Libraries 2).

# Bibliography

Abdel-Motey, Y. Y., 'Education for school library media specialists in the State of Kuwait: a competency based approach', unpublished PhD thesis, Loughborough University, Department of Library and Information Studies, 1989.

Adult Literacy and Basic Skills Unit, *Literacy and numeracy: evidence from the national child development unit*, London, ALBSU, 1983.

Adult Literacy and Basic Skills Unit, *Literacy, numeracy and adults*, London, ALBSU, 1987.

Ainley, P. and Totterdell, B., *Alternative arrangement: new approaches to public library stock*, London, Association of Assistant Librarians, 1982.

Akeroyd, R. G., 'Denver PL's nonresident fee policy', *Public library quarterly*, 4, 1983, 17 – 27.

Akers, N., 'Training in school libraries', in Prytherch, R. (ed.), *Staff training in libraries: the British experience*, Aldershot, Gower, 1986.

'ALA policy manual', *ALA handbook of organization, 1988/1989*, Chicago
and London, ALA, 1988.

Alexander, F., *Contemporary women novelists*, London, Edward Arnold, 1989.

Allen, J. *et al.*, *Out on the shelves: lesbian books into libraries*, Newcastle-under-Lyme, Association of Assistant Librarians, 1989.

American Association of School Libraries and the Association for Educational Communications and Technology, *Information power: guidelines for school library media programs*, Chicago, American Library Association, 1988.

American Library Association, 'ALCTS [Association for Library Collections and Technical Services] approves subject headings for fiction and drama', press release, April 1990.

*American library directory* (42nd edn), Bowker, 1989.

Arthur Young, *Book retailing in the 1990s: the Arthur Young Report*, London, Publishers Association, 1989.

Ash, L. and Miller, W. G., *Subject collections* (6th edn), New York, Bowker, 1985.

Atkinson, F., *Fiction librarianship*, London, Bingley, 1980.

Baker, S. L., 'Display phenomenon: an exploration into factors causing the increased circulation of displayed books', *Library quarterly*, **56** (3), July 1986, 237–57.

Baker, S. L., 'Overload, browsers and selections', *LISR*, 8, 1986, 315–29.

Baker, S. L., 'Will fiction classification schemes increase use?', *Reference quarterly*, **27** (3), Spring 1988, 366–76.

'Balancing act', *Assistant librarian*, **79** (11), 1986, 149.

Ballard, T. H., *The failure of resource sharing in public libraries and alternative strategies for service*, Chicago, American Library Association, 1986.

Ballard, T. H., 'A minority report on present book selection practices', in Serebnick, J. (ed.), *Collection management in public libraries*, Chicago, American Library Association, 1986.

BARB, *The month's viewing in summary, four weeks ending 25th February 1990*, London, BARB, 1990.

BARB, *The week's viewing in summary, week ending 25th March 1990*, London, BARB, 1990.

Barker, K., *Bridging the gap*, London, the Book Trust in association with the British Council, 1987.

Barron, N. (ed.), *Anatomy of wonder: a critical guide to science fiction* (2nd edn), New York and London, Bowker, 1981.

BBC Broadcasting Research Department, *Annual review of BBC broadcasting research findings, no. 15*, London, BBC, 1989.

Berman, S., *Worth noting: editorials, letters, essays, an interview, and bibliography*, Jefferson, North Carolina, McFarland, 1988.

Betts, D. A., *Borrowing and the fiction reader*, London, Branch and Mobiles Group of the Library Association, 1987.

Betts, D. A., 'Reader interest categories in Surrey', in Ainley, P. and Totterdell, B., *Alternative arrangement: new approaches to public library stock*, London, Association of Assistant Librarians, 1982.

Bird, J., *In-service training in public library authorities*, London, Library Association, 1986 (British Library Research and Development Department Report 5898/LA Research Publication no. 23).

Birn, R., 'Effective togetherness in mapping a market', *The Bookseller*, 26 January 1990.

Blenkin, S., 'Moulding the mind: book selection for children and young people', unpublished MA dissertation, Loughborough University of Technology, Department of Library and Information Studies, 1989.

Blosveren, B., 'Youth Review Board motivates young adults to read', *Journal of youth services in libraries*, **3** (1), Fall 1989, 54–8.

*The Bookseller*, 1986–1990.

*The Bowker annual: library and book trade almanac* (34th edn), New York, Bowker, 1989.

Bradbury, R., *Fahrenheit 451*, London, Hart-Davis, 1954.

Bragg, M., 'A hard sell', *Sunday Times, review section C*, 10 December 1989, 1.

British Library, *Gateway to knowledge: the British Library strategic plan, 1989–94*, London, British Library, 1989.

Bundy, M. L., 'Crisis in library education', *Library journal*, **96**, 1971, 797.

Burgess, L. A., 'A system for the classification and evaluation of fiction', *Library world*, 38, 1936, 179–82.

Burgess, M., *The Glasgow novel* (2nd edn), Motherwell, Scottish Library Association, 1986.

Burrell, T. W., 'Curriculum design and development in education for librarianship and information science', *Education for information*, 1, 1983, 229–61.

Burroughs, R., 'Selling children's books in the mass market', *Publishers weekly*, 19 January 1990, 66–70.

Burroughs, R., 'Targeting the hard-sell', *Publishers weekly*, 19 May 1989, 52–4.

Byrne, P., 'SWACL: public library staff training in the South West', in MacDougall, A. and Prytherch, R., *Cooperative training in libraries*, Aldershot, Gower, 1989, 111–20.

Capital Planning Information, *Trends in public library selection policies*, London, British Library, 1987 (British National Bibliography Research Fund Report no. 29).

Carlsen, E. J., *Books and the teenage reader: a guide for teachers, librarians and parents*, New York, Harper and Row, 1967.

Carrier, E. J., *Fiction in public libraries 1876–1900*, New York, Scarecrow, 1965.

Carrier, E. J., *Fiction in public libraries, 1900–1950*, Littleton, Colorado, Libraries Unlimited, 1985.

Carter, C., 'Young people and books: a review of research into young people's reading habits', *Journal of librarianship*, 18, January 1986, 1–22.

Casteleyn, M., *Planning library training programmes*, London, Deutsch, 1981.

Cawelti, J. G., *Adventure, mystery, and romance: formula stories as art and popular culture*, Chicago, University of Chicago Press, 1976.

Central Statistical Office, *Social trends 20*, London, HMSO, 1990.

Chambers, A., *Breaktime*, London, Bodley Head, 1986.

Chelton, M. K., 'The first national survey of services and resources for young adults in public libraries', *Journal of youth services in libraries*, **2** (3), Spring 1989, 224–31.

CIPFA Statistical Information Service, *Public library statistics 1978–79 actuals*, London, CIPFA, 1980.

CIPFA Statistical Information Service, *Public library statistics 1988–89 actuals*, London, CIPFA, 1990.

Clarke, I. F., *The pattern of expectation 1644–2001*, London, Cape, 1978.

Clarke, I. F., *Tale of the future: from the beginning to the present day* (3rd edn), London, Library Association, 1978.

Clarke, I. F., *Voices prophesying war*, London, Oxford University Press, 1966.

Clee, N., 'The rising cost of the golden hello', *The Bookseller*, 29 September 1989, 1056–60.

Collins, B., 'WLA fiction collective: how it works', *Wyoming library roundup*, **34** (3), 1979, 20.

*Competencies for young adult librarians*, Chicago, American Library Association, Young Adult Services Division, 1989.

Contento, W., *Index to science fiction anthologies and collections*, Boston, G. K. Hall, 1978.

Conyers, A., *The evaluation of staff training* (2nd edn), London, Library Association, 1986 (Guidelines for Training in Libraries no. 2).

Cope, C. and Mann, P. H., *Public library statistics 1978–1988: a trend analysis*, Loughborough, LISU, 1989 (Report no. 3).

Cotton, G. B. and Glencross, A., *Cumulated fiction index 1945–1960*, London, Association of Assistant Librarians, 1960.

Cronin, B., 'Nationally co-ordinated library promotion', *Journal of librarianship*, **13** (4), 1981, 223–51.

Cropper, B., *Going soft: some uses of paperbacks in libraries*, London, Branch and Mobile Libraries Group of the Library Association, 1986.

Curley, A. and Broderick, D., *Building library collections* (6th edn), Metuchen, New Jersey, Scarecrow, 1985.

Davidson, J., 'Adolescent illiteracy: what libraries can do to solve the problem: a report on the research of the project on adolescent literacy', *Journal of youth services in libraries*, **1** (2), Winter 1988, 215–18.

Davies, S., 'The hare and the tortoise', *The Bookseller*, 2 February 1990, 363–71.

Day, M. J., 'Selection and use of serious fiction in a public library system', unpublished MA dissertation, University of Sheffield, Department of Information Studies, 1978.

Day-Ellison, G., 'Putting on the style', *The Guardian, weekend supplement*, 28 January 1990, 20.

De Glas, F., 'Fiction and bibliometrics: analyzing a publishing house's stocklist', *Libri*, **36** (1), 1986, 40 – 64.

De Gruyter, L., 'Who uses your library and what do they want?', *Public libraries*, **22** (4), 1983, 151 – 3.

Dennis, G. (ed.), *Annual abstract of statistics No. 126*, London, HMSO, 1990.

Dessauer, J. P., *Book publishing: what it is, what it does* (2nd edn), New York, Bowker, 1981.

Dixon, J. (ed.), *Fiction in libraries*, London, Library Association, 1986.

Donelsen, K. L. and Nilsen, A. P., *Literature for today's young adults*, Glenview, Illinois and London, Scott Foresman, 1989.

Donoghue, M. (comp.), *Schools' and children's libraries in England and Wales*, Loughborough, AMDECL, SOCCEL, LISU, 1989.

Dove, R., 'Teleordering and EDI in the book trade', *The Bookseller*, 30 March 1990, 1074 – 8.

Dowd, A., 'The science fiction microfilming project at the New York Public Library', *Microform review*, **14** (1), 1985, 15 – 20.

EIU, *Retail business*, 290, April 1987.

EIU, *Retail business*, 377, July 1989.

EIU, *Retail business quarterly trade review*, 10, June 1989.

England, L., 'Is there life after Adrian Mole', *The Bookseller*, 13 March 1987, 977.

Enser, A. G. S., *Filmed books and plays: a list of books and plays from which films have been made, 1928 – 86*, Aldershot, Gower, 1987.

Euromonitor, *The book report 1989*, London, Euromonitor, 1989.

Fishwick, F., 'The economic implications of the Net Book Agreement', *The Bookseller*, 28 April 1989, 1470 – 89.

Fishwick, F., *The market for books in the Republic of Ireland*, Dublin, Book House Ireland, 1987.

'The Fishwick Report', *The Bookseller*, 28 April 1989, 1470 – 8.

Forster, E. M., *Aspects of the novel*, London, Arnold, 1927.

Futas, L., *Library acquisition policies and procedures* (2nd edn), Phoenix, Oryx, 1984.

Geare, M., 'Bestsellerdom without hype', *The Bookseller*, 18 and 25 December 1987, 2372 – 3.

Glistrup, E. (ed.), *Education and training of librarians in children's librarianship*, Ballerup, Bibliotekscentralens Forlag, 1986.

Goldhor, H., 'The effect of prime display location on public library circulation', *Library quarterly*, **42** (4), 1972.

Goldhor, H., 'Summary and review of the indexes of American public library statistics: 1939 – 1983', Urbana, University of Illinois Research Center, 1985.

Goodall, D., *Browsing in public libraries*, Loughborough, LISU, 1989.

Goodall, D., 'Use made of an adult fiction collection', undergraduate dissertation, Loughborough University of Technology, Department of Library and Information Studies, 1987.

Goodrich, C., 'Big numbers for innumeracy', *Publishers weekly*, 2 June, 1989, 46–7.

Grant, G. *et al.*, *On competence: a critical analysis of competency-based reform in higher education*, San Francisco, Jossey-Bass, 1979.

Greenfield, G., 'A tale of two novels', *The Bookseller*, 3 March 1989, 727–30.

Greenhalgh, M., 'The role of the library school', in Dixon, J. (ed.), *Fiction in libraries*, London, Library Association, 1986.

Griffiths, J., *Three tomorrows: American, British and Soviet science fiction*, London, Macmillan, 1980.

Griffiths, J.-M., 'A survey of competency requirements for library and information science professionals', in Armstrong, C. and Keenan, S. (eds.), *Information in the library/information school curriculum*, Aldershot, Gower, 1985.

Haffenden, J., *Novelists in interview*, London, Methuen, 1985.

Haigh, F., 'The subject classification of fiction: an actual experiment', *Library world*, 36, 1933, 78–82.

Hamilton, A., 'Mole triumphant over Archer', *The Guardian*, 11 January 1990, 24.

Hamilton, P. A. and Weech, T. L., 'The development and testing of an instrument to measure attitudes toward the quality vs. demand debate in collection management', *Collection management*, 10 (3/4), 1988, 27–42.

Hannabuss, S., *Managing children's literature*, Library Management Monograph, 10 (1), Bradford, MCB University Press, 1989.

Hanson, C., *Short stories and short fictions 1880–1980*, London, Macmillan, 1985.

Harrell, G., 'The classification and organization of adult fiction in large American public libraries', *Public libraries*, 24 (1), Spring 1985, 13–14.

Hasted, A. *et al.*, *PLR loans: a statistical exploration*, Stockton-on-Tees, Registrar of Public Lending Right, 1988.

Haycock, K., 'Research in teacher-librarianship: the implications for professional practice', *Emergency librarian*, 17 (1), 1989, 9–18.

Hayden, R., 'If it circulates, keep it', *Library journal*, 112 (10), 1987, 80–2.

Heather, P., *Young people's reading: a study of the leisure reading of 13–15 year-olds*, Sheffield, Centre for Research in User Studies, 1981.

Hennepin County Library, *Cataloguing bulletin*, 1 – 40, May 1973 to May/June 1979.

*Hennepin County Library materials selection policy*, Bloomington, Minnesota, Hennepin County Library, 1988.

Hermeneze, J., 'The "classics" will circulate', *Library journal*, **106** (20), 1981, 2191 – 5.

'The Hertfordshire fiction festival', *Library Association record*, **92** (4), 1990, 268 – 9.

Hicken, M. E., *Sequels: volume 1, adult books* (9th edn), London, Association of Assistant Librarians, 1989.

Hicken, M. E. (comp.), *Cumulated fiction index 1975 – 79*, Chesterfield, Association of Assistant Librarians, 1980.

Hicken, M. E. (comp.), *Cumulated fiction index 1980 – 84*, Chesterfield, Association of Assistant Librarians, 1985.

Hicken, M. E. (comp.), *Fiction index 1988: a guide to works of fiction available during the year and not previously indexed in the Fiction Index series*, Newcastle-under-Lyme, Association of Assistant Librarians, 1989.

Higdon, D. L., *Shadows of the past in contemporary British fiction*, London, Macmillan, 1984.

Hill, J., *Children are people: the librarian in the community*, London, Hamish Hamilton, 1973.

Hoggart, R., *Local habitation 1918 – 1940*, London, Chatto and Windus, 1988, 173.

Hutchinson, T. H., 'The mathematics of book publishing', *The Bookseller*, 11 November 1988, 1923 – 6.

Inglis, F., *The promise of happiness: value and meaning in children's fiction*, Cambridge, Cambridge University Press, 1981.

'International Booksellers Federation Economic Survey 1986', *The Bookseller*, 3 July 1987.

Johnson, D. W., 'Public library circulation holds steady in 1988', *American libraries*, **20** (7), 1989, 705.

Johnson, G., 'Silent pressures', *Library Association record*, **82** (10), 1980, 481.

Jones, N. and Jordan, P., *Staff management in library and information work* (2nd edn), Aldershot, Gower , 1987.

Katz, W. A., *Collection development: the selection of materials for libraries*, New York, Holt, Rinehart and Winston, 1980.

Kearns, C., 'Eccentric guide', *Library Association record*, **87** (10), 1985, 415.

Keating, H. R. F., *Crime and mystery: the 100 best books*, London, Xanadu, 1987.

Kempthorne, B., 'Well worth reading: an experiment in fiction promotion', *New library world*, February 1989, 25 – 6.

Kinnell, M., 'Children's literature and the role of libraries: delivering services', paper delivered at the Symposium on Children's Reading in Europe: the British – German experience, Goethe Institute, London, 14 March 1990.

Kipling, G., 'Only connect: libraries, fiction and the reading public – a report of the Branch and Mobiles Group one-day meeting, June, 1987', *Service point*, 37, 1987, 18–21.

Klause, A. C., 'Booktalking science fiction to young adults', *Journal of youth services in libraries*, 3 (2), Winter 1990, 102–16.

Kotler, P., *Marketing for non-profit organizations*, New Jersey, Prentice-Hall, 1975.

Larkin, P., *Required writing: miscellaneous pieces, 1955–1982*, London, Faber and Faber, 1983.

Lenz, M. and Mahood, R. (comps.), *Young adult literature: background and criticism*, Chicago, American Library Association, 1980.

Levin, M. P., 'The marketing of books: a national priority for the eighties', *Library trends*, 33, Fall 1984, 185–214.

Lewis, P., 'The future of the National Bibliography', *Library Association record*, **89** (10), 1987, 516, 519–20.

'Libraries agree to compensation', *Milwaukee journal*, 23 May 1985.

*Library and information news*, April 1990, 7.

*Library and information science abstracts*, abstract 88/1045.

*Literary market place* (50th edn), New York, Bowker, 1990.

Logasa, H., *Historical fiction: guide for junior and senior high schools and colleges, also for general readers* (9th edn), Brooklawn, New Jersey, McKinley, 1968.

Luccock, G., 'Induction training', in Prytherch, R. (ed.), *Handbook of library training practice*, Aldershot, Gower, 1986.

Lynch, M. J., 'Volumes held by public libraries, Fall '82', in *Libraries in an information society: a statistical summary*, Chicago, American Library Association, 1986.

McClellan, A. W., 'The reading dimension in effectiveness and service', *Library review*, 30, Summer 1981, 81.

McClung, P. A., 'Costs associated with preservation microfilming: results of the Research Libraries Group study', *Library resources and technical services*, **30** (4), 1986, 363–74.

McClure, C. R. *et al.*, *Planning and role setting for public libraries: a manual of options and procedures*, Chicago, American Library Association, 1987.

MacKay, S., *Redhill rococo*, London, Heinemann, 1986.

McLeish, K., *Bloomsbury good reading guide*, London, Bloomsbury, 1988.

McLelland, D., 'Education for school librarianship: the Scottish perspective', *International review of children's literature and librarianship*, 5, 1, 1990.

Magill, F. N., *Critical survey of short fiction*, 7 vols, Englewood Cliffs, New Jersey, Salem Press, 1981.

Mandel, E., *Delightful murder: a social history of the crime story*, London, Pluto Press, 1984.

Mann, P. H., 'Fiction and the reading public', in *Peebles '83: proceedings of the 69th Annual Conference of the Scottish Library Association, June 6–9, 1983*, Glasgow, Scottish Library Association, 1983.

Mann, P. H., 'Libraries and the reading habit', in *Proceedings of the Library Association Public Libraries Group weekend school, Sheffield, 1982*, Penzance, Library Association Public Libraries Group, 1982, 18.

Mann, P. H., *A new survey: the facts about romantic fiction*, London, Mills and Boon, 1974.

Mann, P. H., *A readers' guide to fiction authors*, Loughborough, CLAIM, 1985.

Mann, P. H., 'What price indexes?', *The Bookseller*, 6 October 1989, 1146–7.

Meade, C., 'Opening the book: putting libraries on the map', *British book news*, January 1990, 20–1.

Meadows, A. J., 'Educating the information professional', in Oppenheim, C., Citroen, C. L. and Griffiths, J.-M. (eds.), *Perspectives in information management I*, London, Butterworths, 1989, 169–86.

Milner, D., *Children and race, ten years on*, London, Ward Lock Education, 1983.

Moorbath, P., 'Why do publishers send out their catalogues?', *Aslib proceedings*, **41** (6), 1989, 213–16.

Moore, N., 'Employment market for information specialists in the UK', *Journal of information science*, 13, 1987, 327–33.

MORI, 'Books and libraries 1988', London, MORI, 1989 (unpublished).

Needham, C. D., *Organizing knowledge in libraries* (2nd edn), London, Deutsch, 1971.

Nixon, W., 'Agents and advances', *Publishers weekly*, 2 February 1990, 15–21.

Nottinghamshire County Council Leisure Services, 'Adult book selection: a policy document', Nottingham, Nottinghamshire County Council, 1988 (unpublished).

Office of Population Censuses and Surveys, Social Survey Division, *General household survey, 1987*, London, HMSO, 1989.

Olderr, S., *Olderr's fiction index 1987*, Chicago and London, St James' Press, 1988.

Pain, H., 'Professional education and children's and school librarianship', *Library Association record*, **89** (3), 1987, 131–5.

Pain-Lewins, H., 'The education and training of public librarians working with children and teenagers', *Training and education*, **6** (1), 1989, 3–14.

Palmer, J. W., 'Factors responsible for the acquisition of Canadian fiction by US public and academic libraries', *Library acquisitions: practice and theory*, **12** (3/4), 1988, 341–56.

Parker, A., 'New skills, new opportunities: the role of in-service training', *International review of children's literature and librarianship*, **1** (1), 1986, 1–21.

Pejtersen, A. M. and Austin, J., 'Fiction retrieval: an experimental design and evaluation of a search system based on users' value criteria', *Journal of documentation*, **39** (4), December 1983, 230–46 (Part One); **40** (1), March 1984, 25–35 (Part Two).

'Public libraries', *Which?*, February 1990, 108–10.

Public Library Data Service, *Statistical report '89*, Chicago, American Library Association, 1989.

*Publishers weekly*, 1989–90.

Pybus, R., 'The library case for the Net Book Agreement', *The Bookseller*, 26 February 1988, 744–50.

Radford, J. (ed.), *The progress of romance: the politics of popular romance*, London, Routledge and Kegan Paul, 1986.

Ranganathan, S. R., *The five laws of librarianship* (2nd edn), Bombay, Asia Publishing House, 1962.

Rath, B., 'Books in the leisure time squeeze', *The Bookseller*, 1 December 1989, 1760–2.

Rawlinson, N., 'The approach to collection management at Baltimore County Public Library', in Serebnick, J. (ed.), *Collection management in public libraries*, Chicago, American Library Association, 1986, 76–80.

Rawlinson, N., 'Give 'em what they want', *Library journal*, **106** (20), 1981, 2188–90.

Reavell, C., 'Joint promotions or burnt fingers', *The Bookseller*, 23 February 1990, 560–1.

Reginald, R., *Science fiction and fantasy literature: a checklist, 1770–1974*, 2 vols, Detroit, Gale, 1979.

Reichman, H., *Censorship and selection: issues and answers for schools*, Chicago, American Library Association and Arlington, Vermont, American Association of School Administrators, 1988.

Reynolds, A. L., Schrock, N. C. and Walsh, J., 'Preservation: the public library response', *Library journal*, **114** (3), 1989, 128–32.

Ritchie, S., *Training and management development in librarianship*, London, British Library, 1988 (Library and Information Research Report no. 34).

Rosen, E. M., 'Inquiring librarians want to know: today's research questions', *Journal of youth services in libraries*, **2** (4), Summer 1989, 369–71.

Rosenberg, B., *Genrereflecting: a guide to reading interests in genre fiction*, Littleton, Libraries Unlimited, 1982.

Ross, N., 'Getting the price right', *The Bookseller*, 16 September 1988, 1096–8.

Samways, A. J., 'The joint fiction reserve: an appraisal', *Journal of librarianship*, **12** (4), 1980, 267–79.

Sapp, G., 'The levels of access: subject approaches to fiction', *Reference quarterly*, **25** (4), Summer 1986, 488–97.

Sarchet, R., 'Epos at WHS: not so many black holes', *The Bookseller*, 18 August 1989, 487–90.

Savage, E. A. A., *A manual of book classification and display for public libraries*, London, Allen and Unwin, 1946.

Scherer, P., 'Paperbacks', in Owen, P. (ed.), *Publishing: the future*, London, Peter Owen, 1988, 63–73.

Schon, I., *A Hispanic heritage, series III: a guide to juvenile books about Hispanic people and cultures*, Metuchen, New Jersey, Scarecrow Press, 1988.

Schon, I., Hopkins, K. D. and Woodruff, M., 'Spanish language books for young readers in public libraries: national survey of practices and attitudes', *Journal of youth services in libraries*, **1** (4), Summer 1988, 444–50.

Sear, L. and Jennings, B., *How readers select fiction*, Maidstone, Kent County Library, 1986 (Research and Development Report no. 9).

Sear, L. and Jennings, B., 'Novel ideas: a browsing area for fiction', *Public library journal*, **4** (3), 1989, 41–4.

Sear, L. and Jennings, B., *Novel ideas: a browsing area for fiction*, Maidstone, Kent County Library, 1989 (Research and Development Report no. 10).

Segal, J. P., *Evaluating and weeding collections in small and medium-sized public libraries: the CREW method*, Chicago, American Library Association, 1980.

Shroder, E. J., 'The last copy center for fiction in Illinois', *Illinois libraries*, **71** (1), 1989, 57–8.

Smith, R. F., *Cumulated fiction index, 1960–69*, London, Association of Assistant Librarians, 1970.

Smith, R. F. and Gordon, A. J., *Cumulated fiction index 1970–74*, London, Association of Assistant Librarians, 1975.

Spenceley, N., 'Readership of literary fiction: a survey of library users in the Sheffield area', unpublished MA dissertation, University of Sheffield, Department of Information Studies, 1980.

Spiller, D., *Book selection: an introduction to principles and practice* (4th edn), London, Bingley, 1986.

Spiller, D., 'The provision of fiction for public libraries', MLS dissertation, Loughborough University of Technology, Department of Library and Information Studies, 1979.

Spink, J., *Children as readers: a study*, London, Bingley, 1989.

Stafford, D., *The silent game: the real world of imaginary spies*, Toronto, Lester and Orpen Dennys, 1988.

Stanley, S., 'Information sources', in Prytherch, R. (ed.), *Handbook of library training practice*, Aldershot, Gower, 1986.

Steiner, G., 'The end of bookishness', *The Times literary supplement*, 8 – 14 July 1988.

Stoakley, R., 'Publishers' pricing: the public librarian's dilemma', *The Bookseller*, 25 August 1989, 580 – 3.

Strachan, A., *Prizewinning literature: UK literary award winners*, London, Library Association, 1989.

Sumsion, J., *PLR in practice*, Stockton-on-Tees, Registrar of the Public Lending Right, 1988.

Sutherland, J., *Bestsellers: popular fiction of the 1970s*, London, Routledge and Kegan Paul, 1981.

Sutherland, J., *Fiction and the fiction industry*, London, University of London Press, 1978.

Taylor, J. N. and Johnson, I. M., *Public libraries and their use*, London, HMSO, 1973.

*The Times higher education supplement*, 897, 12 January 1990, 8.

Todd, J. (ed.), *Dictionary of British women writers*, London, Routledge, 1989.

Tongue, C., 'Opportunities to see: publishers' advertising in flux', *The Bookseller*, 6 January 1989, 20 – 4.

Totterdell, B. and Bird, J., *The effective library: report of the Hillingdon project on public library effectiveness*, London, Library Association, 1976.

Tucker, N., *The child and the book: a psychological and literary exploration*, Cambridge, Cambridge University Press, 1981.

'Tucson makes direct demand central to collection development', *Library journal*. **107** (6), 1982, 586.

Turner, S., 'A survey of borrowers' reactions to literary fiction in Beeston library', unpublished MA dissertation, Loughborough University of Technology, Department of Library and Information Studies, 1987.

UGC/NAB Transbinary Working Group on Librarianship and Information Studies, *Report of the Transbinary Group on Librarianship and Information Studies*, London, British Library, 1986, 63–4.

'UK double act has Hollywood taped', *The Independent on Sunday*, business news section, 18 March 1990, 6.

US Department of Education, Office of Educational Research and Improvement, *Services and resources for young adults in public libraries*, Washington, National Center for Education Statistics, 1988.

Usherwood, B., 'The elected member and the library: learning from the literature', *Public library journal*, **2** (5), 1987, 72–4.

Vinson, J. (ed.), *Contemporary novelists* (4th edn), London, Macmillan, 1986.

Vitale, A., 'Returns: how explosive growth makes a growing crisis', *The Bookseller*, 4 August 1989, 391–4.

Webb, T. D., 'A hierarchy of public library user types', *Library journal*, **111** (15), 1986, 47–50.

Whyte, H., *Glasgow crime fiction: a bibliographic guide*, Glasgow, Mitchell Library, 1977.

Williams, S., 'Agatha Christie and the mystery of the declining sales', *The Bookseller*, 24 March 1989, 1070–4.

Woodhead, M., 'Unit sales: have they passed their peak?', *The Bookseller*, 5 May 1989, 1553–5.

Woodhouse, R. G. and Neill, J., *The promotion of public library use*, Newcastle-on-Tyne, Newcastle-on-Tyne Polytechnic, Department of Librarianship, 1978 (British Library Research and Development Department Report no. 5470).

Working Party of the Literature Committee of the Scottish Arts Council, *Readership report*, Edinburgh, Scottish Arts Council, 1989.

Worpole, K., *Reading by numbers: contemporary publishing and popular fiction*, London, Commedia, 1984, 15–30.

*The writers' directory 1990–92* (9th edn), Chicago and London, St James' Press, 1990.

Yaakov, J. (ed.), *Short story index: an index to stories in collections and periodicals*, New York, H. W. Wilson, 1988.

Yates, J., *Teenager to young adult: recent paperback fiction for 13 to 19 years*, Swindon, School Library Association, 1986.

Yorke, D. A., *Marketing the library service*, London, Library Association, 1977.

Young, A., *Book retailing in the 1990s*, London, Booksellers Association, 1987.

'Young Adult Services Division', *ALA handbook of organization*, Chicago, American Library Association, 1989.

Zifcak, M., 'The NBA debate: a view from Australia', *The Bookseller*, 24 June 1988, 2459–60.

Zool, M. H., *Bloomsbury good reading guide to science fiction and fantasy*, Bloomsbury, 1989.

# Index